The Penobscot
Expedition

The Penobscot
Expedition

---

*Commodore Saltonstall
and the Massachusetts
Conspiracy of 1779*

George E. Buker

Naval Institute Press

Annapolis, Maryland

.

Naval Institute Press
291 Wood Road
Annapolis, MD 21402

Library of Congress Cataloging-in-Publication Data
Buker, George E., 1923–
    The Penobscot Expedition : Commodore Saltonstall and the Mas-
sachusetts Conspiracy of 1779 / George E. Buker.
        p. cm.
    Includes bibliographical references (p.) and index.
    ISBN 1-55750-212-9 (acid-free paper)
    1. Penobscot Expedition, 1779. 2. Saltonstall, Dudley, 1738–1796.
3. Revere, Paul, 1735–1818. I. Title.
E235.B85 2002
973.3'35—dc21

                                                            2001044697

Printed in the United States of America on acid-free paper ∞

09 08 07 06 05 04 03 02   9 8 7 6 5 4 3 2

First printing

Contents

Preface

THE BICENTENNIAL observance of the Penobscot Expedition in 1979 brought hundreds of reenactors to Penobscot Bay, Maine, to relive the event. The following year the Maine Public Broadcasting Network, using film of the reenacted battle, produced "Penobscot: The Battle No One Ever Heard Of."

In 1996 Sara Bradford, director for the Hersey Retreat Elderhostel, asked me to give a talk about the expedition. I was one of the many who had not heard of that battle. I spent the next four years researching and lecturing about this interesting, but little-known, event of the American Revolution. My conclusions are at odds with those of the 1779 Massachusetts General Court.

Acknowledgments

I THANK the following: Sara Bradford who introduced me to the Penobscot Expedition, Frank Sweet who provided me with my first basic readings of the expedition, Mike Nancarrow for his mathematical charts and calculations, and Robert C. Brooks who shared his historical research and knowledge of sailing on Penobscot Bay with me. Thanks also are due to the staffs of the Special Collections Section of the University of Maine Library, the Bangor Public Library, the Penobscot Marine Museum Library, and the Jacksonville University Library. I would have been lost without their help.

I alone am responsible for any errors of fact.

The Penobscot
Expedition

Chapter One

Bagaduce

THE FIRST TIME Paul Revere, of the midnight ride fame, and Dr. John Calef crossed paths was 1768. That year King George III of England demanded that the Massachusetts General Court rescind its circular letter to the other colonies supporting a boycott of the Townshend Acts. Seventeen members rescinded their actions, but ninety-two refused the king's request. Paul Revere publicized this event in his copperplate "A Warm Place—Hell." He depicted the seventeen rescinders driven by two devils into the maw of hell. Revere portrayed Dr. Calef with a calf's head, for that was the way the doctor pronounced his name.[1]

Eleven years later the two crossed paths again. The second event took place on Massachusetts's sparsely settled Majabigwaduce Peninsula (called Bagaduce, now Castine) on the eastern shore of Penobscot Bay in the province of Maine.[2] At that time, 1779, Lieutenant Colonel Paul Revere commanded Massachusetts's artillery train engaged in the United States' first major amphibious operation of the American Revolutionary War. Dr. John Calef, who may have taken up residence at Bagaduce the year before, volunteered his services as a surgeon to the recently arrived British occupying army.

Revere and Calef participated on opposite sides in Massachusetts's Penobscot Expedition to expel the British from their outpost in Maine. The expedition was a disastrous American naval loss. Some two score combatant and transport vessels were destroyed. The magnitude of the naval loss was not to be duplicated in American history until the Japanese attack upon Pearl Harbor on 7 December 1941.

Victory or defeat seldom hinges on one factor. Yet there was a component of the Penobscot Expedition that, while overlooked by most, loomed large in the expedition's disaster. It was the lack of knowledge of the technological limitations of square-rigged ships in restricted waters. Ships, not in the generic sense, but in the specific sense of large, three-masted, square-rigged, sailing ships, were limited in their ability to maneuver on the Bagaduce River. Some of the expedition's naval and militia officers displayed a lack of knowledge of these constraints in the inland waters of the enemy's harbor. Those who did not understand the technological limits wondered why ten armed, square-rigged, American ships could not sail into "that damned hole" and destroy three small British sloops of war defending the harbor.[3] Had the ground commander grasped the square-rigged ship's limitations and cooperated with the commodore's suggestion to either "Strike a bold Stroke, by storming the Enemys works, & going in with the Ships, or raise the Siege," the final result would have been different.[4]

This out-of-the-way confrontation was brought about primarily through the efforts of Britain's undersecretary of state, William Knox, and two Massachusetts Loyalists, Dr. John Calef of Ipswich and John Nutting of Cambridge. William Knox, born in Ireland, had been appointed undersecretary of state in the American Department in 1770. Before his appointment Knox had served as provost marshal of Georgia (1757–61), as agent in London for Georgia (1761–68), and as agent for East Florida (1763–70).[5]

Dr. Calef had served as a surgeon of a provincial ship of war during the reduction of Cape Breton in 1745. He was surgeon of the provincial hospital at Albany in the war of 1755 and later surgeon of a regiment at Louisbourg. For many years he served as a civil magistrate, field officer, and member of the Massachusetts General Assembly. He became interested in Maine's eastern region when Lieutenant Governor Thomas Hutchinson of Massachusetts sent him to England in 1772 to represent Penobscot settlers wanting a royal grant to confirm their land claims. Calef presented their case and returned to Boston. At the time nothing happened to further Calef's proposal.[6]

John Nutting, a commoner, was a successful housewright. In early life he served in the militia, participating in the unsuccessful 1758 campaign to reduce Canada. By 1768 he was a man of substance. Sailing in search of lumber sources, he became familiar with the Bay of Fundy and the coast of Maine. Nutting acquired considerable property around Bagaduce. He became prominent among the Loyalists in September 1774 when he moved his family to Boston to be under British protection. He helped build army barracks when the local tradesmen refused to work for the British, bringing in men and material from Maine for the task.[7]

In January 1775, just three months before Lexington and Concord, Calef wrote to influential friends in England that the people of Penobscot still awaited land confirmation. Further, they now requested their own government for the region. Calef was among the first to propose the separation of the Penobscot region from Massachusetts shortly before the Revolution.[8]

The shots fired at Lexington and Concord on 19 April 1775 began the Revolution. British troops, sent from Boston, were to collect colonial arms and ammunition gathered at Concord. The Massachusetts farmers, the famed minutemen, resisted the Redcoats and hostilities began. By the end of May, colonial militiamen surrounded Boston and Massachusetts General Artemas Ward took command of the American troops laying siege to Boston. General George Washington assumed command over the Continental Army on 3 July, less than a month after the Battle of Bunker Hill. Under the direction of Artemas Ward, who had been commissioned a major general and appointed by the Continental Congress as second in command, the Americans fortified Dorchester Heights and forced the British to evacuate Boston on 17 March 1776. (Boston has celebrated Evacuation Day as an official holiday ever since.) Several weeks before the British left Boston, John Nutting, along with his family and fourteen artificers, was sent to Halifax to build homes for the influx of refugees. Near the end of March General Ward, miffed that the Continental Congress had demoted him to second in command, resigned his commission.[9]

With the outbreak of hostilities, the British Cabinet was at loggerheads. Prime Minister Lord Frederick North wanted to employ reconciliation efforts even after hostilities began. Lord George Germain, American secretary, wanted to prosecute the war with quick, decisive blows. Viscount William Barringtion, secretary of war, felt the army alone was not sufficient to conquer the Americans. He wanted a naval war. Lord James Sandwich, head of the admiralty, fearing France's naval power, did not want to send many ships to the other side of the Atlantic.[10]

The first two years of the conflict were ambiguous endeavors for both sides. Beginning in August 1775 the American Northern Army engineered a two-pronged attack on Canada. One prong moved from Fort Ticonderoga to Montreal; the other went up the Kennebec River and through the Maine woods to Quebec. By July 1776 the repelled Northern Army was back where it started.

The British, after leaving Boston, moved to Halifax and regrouped. Believing there were more Loyalists in the southern colonies, the British navy attacked and was repelled from Charleston, South Carolina, on 28 June 1776; however, the next day, General William Howe arrived off Sandy Hook, New Jersey. By 15 September he landed on Manhattan Island, and for the remainder of the war New York City remained in British hands.

Lord Germain's strategy for 1777 was to sever New England from the rest of the colonies. It was an incredibly complex plan calling for three forces to leave Canada. One would follow the Richelieu River, Lake Champlain, and the Hudson River to Albany, New York. A second would march eastward from Fort Oswego on Lake Ontario along the Mohawk River to Albany. While from Halifax, Nova Scotia, a raiding party would sail along the coast of eastern Massachusetts to terrorize the populace and keep New England's minutemen from aiding New York. Finally, a force from New York City would go up the Hudson to Albany.

The plan went awry. The first group suffered a loss at Bennington, Vermont. The second was halted at Oriskany. Even the feeble effort from Halifax was a disaster. General Eyre Massey said he had good guides for the troops rendezvoused on the St. John's River ready for the coastal raid. Unfortunately for his plans, "Sir George Collier stole out of Halifax, made a futile Attack at Machias, was most shamefully drove from thence . . . which prevented the Eastern Coast of New England from being Alarm'd which was my orders . . . which if they had been executed might have prevented the Misfortunes that attend'd Lt. Genl. Burgoynes army, for it was at that critical time."[11] The force from New York City met opposition and returned to the city. By September 1777 General Burgoyne was surrounded at Saratoga. He capitulated on 17 October surrendering nearly six thousand men.

John Nutting, who piloted Commodore Sir George Collier on his ill-advised attack upon Machias, Maine, was later sent by Collier to England, but whether as a courier with the official report or as a witness is not clear. Nutting arrived in London when Lord Germain and William Knox were mapping out a strategy in the wake of the failure of the plan to sever New England from the rest of the colonies.[12] William Knox had always felt the southern colonies provided a better environment for British arms. The army could operate all year long, and the navy could provide vital support through the south's ice-free ports and rivers. He believed that once a major campaign began, the south's Loyalists and Indians would provide considerable support.[13]

As for the northern colonies, Knox proposed keeping bases in New York and Rhode Island. Philadelphia would remain under British control only if the Loyalists relieved regular troops for other operations. Yet another base was necessary in the north to protect Nova Scotia. Thus when Nutting reported to Knox, the two found a mutual interest in the role of Bagaduce for future British strategy. Knox, aided by Nutting, developed a plan to post a British force on the coast of Maine. From such a position the king's cruisers could cover the Bay of Fundy, protect Nova Scotia from harassment by New England privateers, and prevent a rebel land attack on that portion of Nova Scotia that later became New Brunswick. Finally, the region from the Penobscot River to the St. Croix River would provide a new province for the Loyalists driven from the rebelling colonies, which Knox suggested be called New Ireland.[14]

The British defeat at Saratoga brought France into the war as an American ally, drastically changing the British strategy. Lord Germain, searching for a new strategy, accepted the Knox-Nutting proposal to establish posts along the coast where Loyalists were located. In May 1778, when General Clinton replaced General Howe, Germain gave Clinton instructions: "If he could not bring Washington to a decisive battle, he was to confine himself to raids against the coastal towns and to the destruction of American shipping." Then in September Germain ordered Clinton to provide "for loyalists by erecting a province between the Penobscot and St. Croix rivers. Post to be taken on Penobscot River." Nutting, the messenger for these orders, carried further instructions "to be employed as overseer of carpenters who are to rebuild the Fort at Penobscot," meaning the former French Fort Pentagoet abandoned in 1704. Dr. Calef may have been among the early supporters wanting to separate eastern Maine from Massachusetts, but John Nutting brought Penobscot Bay to the direct attention of the British government.[15]

Nutting embarked for the colonies on the mail packet *Harriet*. After two weeks at sea the American privateer *Vengeance* crossed the *Harriet*'s course, and a six-hour chase followed. Nutting sank his dispatches just before the *Harriet* struck its colors. The *Vengeance* took its captives to the closest prize port of Corunna, Spain. Six weeks later Nutting returned to England. The Penobscot project was on hold until the following year.

Nutting's second crossing, in January 1779, was aboard HMS *Grampus* to New York.[16] Because Lord Germain sent his instructions by multiple messengers, General Clinton was aware of the plan and had already corresponded with General Francis McLean, then commander at Halifax. "Having received Orders of Governmt to Establish a Post on Penobscot River, I am therefore to desire you will make such a Detachment of Troops under your Command, as you shall judge proper and Sufficient to defend themselves."[17] All that was necessary was to send John Nutting with the home government's detailed orders to Halifax.

General McLean, a sixty-two-year-old bachelor, had spent his life in the military. Having served in a regiment of Scots hired by the Dutch in 1746, he later entered the Black Watch and participated in nineteen major battles in Europe, Canada, and the Caribbean. Then for fifteen years he had aided Portugal, England's longtime ally, as military governor of fortified cities on the border fighting Spain and France. When the American colonies rebelled, the British ministry considered that his military leadership and his administrative skill with civilian populations made him an ideal choice for governor of Nova Scotia.[18]

McLean's naval commander was Captain Henry Mowat. He joined the Royal Navy in 1752 and rose to lieutenant in 1758. Four years later he commanded HM *Canceaux*. Before the war he had spent several years patrolling for smugglers off New England and in the Gulf of St. Lawrence. Early in the revolution Mowat brought the *Canceaux* to Falmouth (Portland) to protect British interests. On 9 May 1775 the Sons of Liberty captured him while he walked along the shore outside the town. This act divided the town's citizens. The Sons of Liberty wanted to call out the minutemen to capture the *Canceaux*. The Tories wanted the town militia to free Mowat. Both sides agreed to release Mowat if he gave his word he would return the next day. Mowat, fearing an attack upon his vessel, reneged on his promise, and on 15 May he convoyed three British ships out of Falmouth. In retribution for Mowat's capture, the British sent him back on 18 October 1775 to bombard Falmouth. When gunfire did not destroy enough buildings, he sent ashore a party to torch the unscathed houses. Ultimately, two-thirds of Falmouth lay in ashes. Captain Mowat knew the locale well, and the people of Maine knew him.[19]

Since colonial times Maine has been known as Downeast because the prevailing winds are from the west. Thus ships sailing from Boston to Maine sailed downwind, or down east. At the time of the Revolution, Maine, larger than all the rest of New England combined, consisted of York, Cumberland, and Lincoln counties. The eastern boundary of Lincoln County was the St. Croix River, which divided Massachusetts from Nova

Scotia (New Brunswick). Historically the Penobscot River and Bay had been the dividing line between English settlement on the western shore and French settlement on the east. Only after the Treaty of Paris in 1763, which concluded the French and Indian War, did the English hold claim to the eastern shores of the river and bay. People termed the less-developed land between the Penobscot and St. Croix Rivers "to the Eastward."[20]

Penobscot Bay, midway down the Maine coast, reached inland forty miles from its outermost islands. Matinicus Rock on the west and the rugged Isle au Haut on the east were nearly thirty miles apart. Within the bay were more than two hundred islands ranging from the large Fox Islands (North Haven Island and Vinalhaven) to barren windswept off-shore rocks facing the broad Atlantic.[21] Old Man Ledge off Allen and Burnt Islands was the western boundary of Penobscot Bay. Roaring Bull Ledge offshore from Isle au Haut was the eastern boundary of the bay. There was also an eastern back door through Jerico Bay and the Egge-moggin Reach. Thus sailing Downeast the sailing marks were Monhegan Island then between Matinicus and the mainland up Two Bush Channel into West Penobscot Bay. When sailing for Bagaduce, one would take a course east of Long Island (Islesboro). The eastern entrance usually was by the back door via the Eggemoggin Reach. Yet getting to the Eggemoggin Reach generally required a pilot. Large vessels would pass between Isle au Haut and the Southern Fox Island (Vinalhaven) then hold Saddleback Ledge to port and head for Eagle Island. There were places on this route that could punch a hole in the bottom of a frigate.[22]

Brigadier General Francis McLean departed Halifax, Nova Scotia, on 30 May 1779, destined for Penobscot Bay. He commanded almost seven hundred troops. Escorting McLean's six transports was Captain Andrew Barkley's convoy, the frigate HMS *Blonde* (32 guns), the sloops *North* (20) Captain Gerard Selby, *Albany* (18) Captain Henry Mowat, and *Nautilus* (18) Captain Thomas Farnham, the brig *Hope* (16), and the armed schoon-er *Arbuthnot* (10). Reaching Penobscot Bay on 12 June, Captain Barkley anchored in the Bagaduce River. Several people came aboard the *Blonde* "and gave assurances of their peaceable disposition, on this the General, Capt. Barkeley [*sic*] and several officers landed on the neck without troops, and after conversing with several of the country people returned on board." On the thirteenth the general and captain boarded the *Nautilus* to examine Fort Point where they saw "a small neck of Land convenient for a Post of about 100 men, but not capable of extensive works."[23]

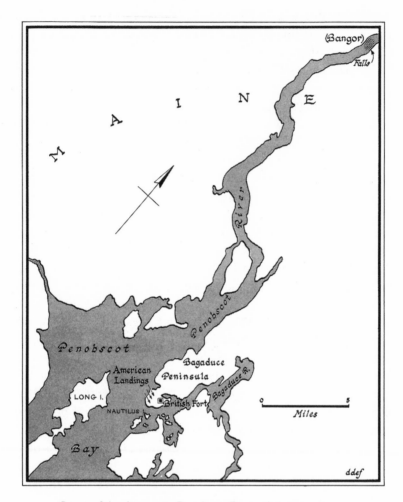

Scene of the disaster in Penobscot Bay and the retreat up
the Penobscot River, 25 July–14 August 1779.

On the fourteenth, while heavy rains prevented the troops from landing,
General McLean and Captain Barkley drew up a proclamation addressed
to the local citizenry. They said many inhabitants of the Penobscot area
were "well affected to his Majesty's person, and the ancient constitution
under which they formerly flourished, and from the restoration of which
they can alone expect relief, from the distressed situation they are now in."

Further, they acknowledged many had "seated themselves on lands, and cultivated them, without any grant or Title, by which their possessions can be secured to them or their posterity." Finally, they declared they had the power to promise that "whenever civil government takes place, they shall receive gratuitous grants from his Majesty . . . of all lands they may have actually cultivated and improved."[24]

On 15 June, at the head of the bay, Captain Henry Mowat of the *Albany* wrote to the American commander, Jonathan Buck Sr., as follows:

> Albany Penobscot River 15 June 1779
> Sir.
> Understanding that you are at the head of a Regiment of the King's deluded Subjects on this River and parts adjacent and that you hold Colonel's Commission under the influence of a body of men termed the General Congress of the United States of America, it therefore becomes my duty to require you to appear without loss of time before General McLean and the commanding Officer of the King's Ships now on board the Blonde off of Majorbigwaduce with a Muster Roll of the People under your direction.
> /s/ H. Mowat[25]

Meanwhile, at Bagaduce, General McLean landed fifty men to reconnoiter. They also marked out the camp for the troops. On 16 June 1779 the "Troops were landed and encamped & from thence to the 24th the time was imployed in landing Provisions, stores, &c. which was a most laborious work, there being a steep Hill to roll them up."[26]

The Bagaduce Peninsula, roughly triangular in shape, was a mile and three-quarters long on a northeast-southwest axis and about three-quarters of a mile wide at its widest. Much of the peninsula was heavily wooded. Its crest, a narrow plateau two hundred feet high, followed the same axis. The western side, facing Penobscot Bay, presented almost a mile of rugged broken bluffs rising precipitously from the rocky shore. The first one hundred feet of elevation was nearly perpendicular. After that, the slope lessened, requiring a three-hundred-yard climb to the summit. The northern side bordered a marsh. Access to the mainland was by a narrow isthmus through the marsh, which was sometimes submerged at high tide. The incline here was not as steep as the western side. The southeastern side, which bordered the Bagaduce River, had the most gradual incline, eight hundred yards from the shore to summit.

On the day the British troops debarked, Colonel Buck, by his actions, gave his answer to Captain Mowat. He loaded his family on his sloop *Hannah* and headed toward Pownalborough (Wiscasset) to report the events to his commander. While he could have selected a number of routes, the easiest sail would be to Townsend then by horseback to Brigadier General Charles Cushing's house. Buck arrived on 19 June and told his story. General Cushing immediately wrote to the Massachusetts Council. Using Buck's information, Cushing told the council that the British had arrived at Penobscot the previous Saturday. The force consisted of a frigate of 32 guns, two others of 20 and 18 guns, a brig of 16 or 18 guns, and a schooner of 10 guns escorting five or six transports carrying eight hundred troops. General McLean commanded, and he intended to build forts where the French Fort Pentagoet on Bagaduce and Fort Pownall on Fort Point once stood. Work began on the former before Colonel Buck left Penobscot Bay. General Cushing concluded: "If the General Court should think proper to send a suitable force of shiping which with other assistance by Land—It is thought they [the British] might easily be dislodged." Colonel Buck took Cushing's letter to Boston where he was reimbursed £157.10 for his "time & expense Penobscot to Boston on express."[27]

Several days after the British landed, the people up the Penobscot River gathered to discuss their options. The Redcoats "struck the inhabitants with terror—especially the women and children. . . . Provisions were very scarce, and the inhabitants almost destitute of arms and ammunition. A meeting was called of the principal officers, to determine on defence, or submission." Finally Captain John Brewer and a Captain Smith of Marsh Bay were chosen to inquire of General McLean his intentions. The general assured them that "if the inhabitants would mind their business, and be peaceable, they should not be disturbed in person or property."[28]

A British post to the Eastward would serve many uses. It would be a bulwark for New Ireland. Lying between the Penobscot and St. Croix Rivers, bordering New England and Nova Scotia (New Scotland), New Ireland would offer a haven for Loyalist refugees from the rebellious colonies. It reflected Lord George Germain's new strategy, begun in December 1778 with the occupation of Savannah, Georgia, to bring the American loyalists into an active role in Britain's war effort. While the major thrust was in the southern colonies, the occupation of Bagaduce was a similar, although smaller effort, in the northeast.[29] The plan would also protect Nova Scotia from an American invasion and would restrict Massachusetts and New Hampshire privateers from using the central Maine coast to harass British shipping between New York and Halifax. By fortifying on the eastern shore the British placed the waters of the river and the bay between themselves and American forces to the west. These same waters would force the rebels to use ships to repel them. Finally, General McLean knew that he had the additional security of the British navy's superiority, if needed, over these waters.

Nutting accompanied the general when McLean brought his detachment to Bagaduce. The 450 troops from the 74th Regiment of Foot (the Argyle Highlanders), 200 from the 82d Regiment of Foot (the Hamilton Regiment), and the 50 men from the artillery and engineers immediately began off-loading supplies.[30] The ship's boats plied between ship and shore carrying supplies. At the stony beach a line of soldiers passed the items up the human chain to the ground above. The provisions, artillery, and engineer and troop equipment mounted in organized mounds as the rowboats disgorged their cargo. Only a few small teams were locally available to help the men placing the material in the proper pile.

The general found the site of the former French Fort Pentagoet unsatisfactory. It was at the water's edge, too deep in the harbor entrance to bring guns to bear efficiently on the mouth of the Bagaduce River. McLean selected a site on the crest of the peninsula where his guns could reach both the entrance and the inner harbor. The site selected was several feet lower than the ground about six hundred yards farther to the west.[31]

General McLean also had the task of creating a rapprochement with the local citizens. Thus his joint proclamation with Captain Barkley offered amnesty for rebels "who shall, within eight days from the date hereof, take the oaths of allegiance and fidelity to His Majesty." Finally they promised "to alleviate the misery of the inhabitants of the villages and islands along the coast of New England, hereby declare that such of them as behave themselves in a peaceable and orderly manner, shall have full liberty to fish in their ordinary coast-fishing craft, without any molestation on our part; on the contrary, they shall be protected in it by all vessels and parties under our command."[32] Even as the troops were off-loading, General McLean broadcast copies of the proclamation throughout the area.

Reactions to the British offer varied. Some, like Colonel Buck, fled with their families westward. Major Will Eaton of Deer Isle loaded his family on his sloop and sailed west. Captain Will Reed of Naskeag, just east of

Deer Isle on the mainland, also sailed away. Yet many people, after reading the proclamation, simply returned to their chores. Six hundred fifty-one went to Bagaduce to sign an oath abjuring or denying "the authority of any sett of men calling themselves Congress, Committee, or by what other name they may be known, who have or may set up any government in opposition or in any manner repugnant to that of his Majesty King George the Third aforesaid."[33] Jane Goldthwait, daughter of Thomas Goldthwait a prominent Loyalist, wrote that when the British arrived her father gave the three boys living in their household their choice to stay or go. Nat took the oath without any hesitation. Jo and Ben ran off at the first opportunity to enlist with the Americans. Ben was shot in the first boatload to land at Bagaduce when the Americans returned to oust the British.[34]

Those people living beyond the immediate range of the British enclave wondered what was happening. Colonel Tristram Jordan of the militia set out from Falmouth to find out. He traveled east until he was within twenty miles of Bagaduce. The people he met told him they had seen General McLean's proclamation: "that they were invited by some of the principal Inhabitants of Majorbagaduce, Penobscot & Deer Island to come & take possession there, & requiring the Inhabitants to lay down their Arms & Swear Allegiance to the King of Great Britain or depart the place within 8 Days, in consequence of which many of the Inhabitants had complied & were at Work assisting them to Fortify." Eastward at Machias, Colonel John Allen said his spies reported that at "Union River, Naskeigh, & Deer Island, Most if not all the principal people, & Two or three from French-mans Bay & Gouldsborough have taken the Oath."[35]

These people, who lived far from the more-populated Massachusetts, suffered living under the rebel government. They made their livelihood carrying lumber, firewood, and fish to Boston, where they exchanged these products for the necessities they could not manufacture. When the British blockaded their coast, trade ceased. Money became scarce. The people neither trusted nor accepted the new American paper money. Now the British were promising trade, money, and the supplies they badly needed. Many people went home to await the new prosperity. Meanwhile, they tended their vegetable gardens, gathered hay for the winter, fished, and boiled saltwater for their preservative. General McLean evaluated the inhabitants. "The misery of the people to the eastward of Boston is hardly to be express'd, many during the winter having absolutely died of want, this and their having never been actively engag'd in the rebellion, gives us room to hope they are sincere in their professions, but the impossibility in our present circumstances of affording them protection from the threats of the opposite party obliges them to act with caution in shewing it."[36]

Ten days after landing, General McLean reported his situation to General Clinton. During his initial reconnaissance he examined Fort Point, the site of an earlier American fort. Fort Pownall, four miles up the bay from Bagaduce on the western shore, had been built in 1759 during the French and Indian War. McLean planned to detach part of his force and establish a small post at Fort Pownall at a later date. In a series of letters with Captain Barkley the two leaders agreed that upon the expiration of time for the local people to take the oath of allegiance the naval force would return to Halifax. Captain Barkley assigned Captain Mowat with the *Albany* to remain. General McLean, who wanted to explain to General Clinton why he had depleted Halifax's provisions, taken so many of its soldiers with him, and other information too difficult to write, sent Major James Henry Craig aboard HM *Hope* to New York to brief Clinton on his operations.[37]

But it took time for General McLean to secure his enclave. The centerpiece of his defense was the main fort on the peninsula's high wooded plateau. His engineers examined the ground and the approaches to the site. The troops cleared the land, stacked the logs, and guarded the supplies. When McLean learned the *Albany* would remain with his force, he did not neglect the harbor. Two batteries, one midway up the incline near Dice's Head, the other farther east on the shore, were placed to protect the *Albany*.[38] At this second battery, called Half Moon Battery, the general placed his four largest guns, 12-pounders. Mowat sent his marines to the island south of the entrance to build a third battery. In addition, McLean also "entrenched the border of the swamp," so the enemy could not gain a footing on the peninsula from the mainland. John Calef said that from the landing on 17 June to 17 July the focus was on preparing the defense. Yet it was 2 July before the first line staking out the fort was placed.[39]

Despite adverse conditions at Bagaduce, its inhabitants enjoyed some pleasant moments. Colonel Thomas Goldthwait, commander of Fort Pownall for some years and a Loyalist, fled with some of his family to Bagaduce for protection. His daughter Jane Goldthwait, twenty-four and single, wrote of some of those pleasant moments. The Goldthwaits boarded the armed schooner *Rachel* for the short trip across the bay from Fort

Pownall to Bagaduce. As there was no housing, they spent eight weeks living in the harbor aboard a prize snow, a two-masted, square-rigged, vessel similar to a brig. Though it provided cramped quarters for a family used to more gracious living, Jane wrote to her older sister that "We enjoy'd ourselves more than we ever have since we have been here; for our situation was a sufficient apology for everything that was wanting, . . . here we liv'd till the Siege began, . . . when it was thot most advisable for us to leave our watery habitation for one more secure on Terra firma."[40]

The family's new abode was the hospital. Some evenings a group gathered for a musical respite from the daily military trials. Jane described one such gathering: "There are also two Docrs which keep with us here, good cleaver Scots gentleman, one blows the german flute very prettily and the other the Clarinet—an exceeding fine instrument, there are 2 fiddles which two of the officers are practicing, and a third, a Mr. Stewart plays on most divinly so once in a while we make believe sing a song wch. they compliment us with a clap & upon the whole you see, we can't but spend some time pleasantly tho we are shockingly crowded for room."[41]

The *Blonde, Arbuthnot,* and *Hope* departed before the transports completed off-loading. Captain Barkley ordered the *North* and *Nautilus* to follow when possible. On 18 July the British received information that the Americans in Boston were raising an expedition to drive them out. Throughout the war rumors were rampant all along the coast; few ever materialized. Most people did not take the report of the expedition from Boston seriously. Captain Mowat was an exception. He had spent years on the American station and knew the importance of the Penobscot region to Boston's well-being. Captain Mowat prevailed upon General McLean to countermand Barkley's orders regarding the *North* and the *Nautilus*. He wanted those vessels to help defend the harbor. The general agreed and retained the two sloops of war. Mowat placed his three ships in line across the mouth of the harbor to defend against the expected attack.[42]

General McLean, relying on Mowat's advice, stopped work on the planned fort and concentrated on building a defense for the immediate future. McLean sent a call out to the settlements for volunteers. Captain John Perkins of Bagaduce gathered about a hundred men to work on the fort. They worked gratis for three days clearing the trees away from the front of the fort. The press to complete the fort caused the general to hire laborers to work along with his troops. This was the first time in months that the men had worked for hard currency. They felled trees, raised an abatis around the fort, and constructed platforms for the guns. Money was so scarce that the general had his dollars cut into five pieces for use as shillings. Yet troops and settlers together were not enough hands to raise the defenses, so Captain Mowat sent 180 sailors ashore to work on the fort. John Calef wrote that the general "shows the utmost vigilance and activity, giving everywhere the necessary directions, visiting incessantly, by night and day the different parts of the works."[43]

On 21 July General McLean received information that the American fleet of near forty sail had left Boston headed east. Work on the fort now continued day and night. Years later William Hutchings recalled those hectic days when he was only fourteen years old: "I helped to haul the first log into the south bastion. It was on the Sunday before the Americans arrived, and was the only Sunday on which I had to work in my life." McLean dispatched the armed schooner *Rachel* to New York requesting aid.[44] While waiting for reinforcements, McLean oversaw all aspects of defense within his limited resources.

Years later Captain Mowat summarized the British command's evaluation of their position. They firmly believed that the American army sent against them was greatly superior to their own force. Throughout the action on Penobscot Bay they thought the American land force numbered between two and three thousand men. Therefore, they believed everything depended upon keeping possession of Bagaduce Harbor. If the harbor was forced, the rebel's superiority could take the more convenient parts of the peninsula and cut communication between the British land and sea forces. Further, many supplies and stores were still on the beach at some distance from the nascent fort. Thus under Mowat's guidance, the three sloops of war anchored in line across the harbor entrance with springs attached to their anchors to present their broadsides to the approaching enemy.[45] The four transports were behind the war ships ready to ram and foul any enemy ships breaching the battle line of the sloops. Finally, on each side of the entrance were gun batteries to support the sloops of war. Mowat also planned his defense well, making full use of his meager resources.[46]

McLean's preparations on the fort were not as complete. According to Mowat the fort's site was several feet below the ground six hundred yards to the west. The parapet facing the higher ground was "scarcely four feet high." The remainder of the parapet, parallel to the harbor, and to the rear, was "not three feet high." The two bastions facing the harbor "were quite open." Many provisions, while shaded, were in the open. Gunpowder was in covered holes along the planned glacis. "There was but a Single Gun Mounted, & that a Six Pounder." Mowat concluded, "one may easier conceive than describe the anxiety & hopes of all concerned."[47]

Just before the Americans arrived in Penobscot Bay, Captains Brewer and Smith of Marsh Bay again called on General McLean to transact business for the people living upriver. Upon the completion of their transactions, they received their passes to leave Bagaduce. During their visit they had the opportunity to clearly examine the fortifications, and late in the afternoon Brewer noted some unusual activity among the troops. He told Smith it was time to leave. They went to their boat and had barely raised their sail before the *Albany*'s cannon boomed the signal to close the peninsula. They continued upriver ignoring the signal. Looking back down the bay they saw a large fleet standing up, which they suspected was the expedition from Boston. They continued upriver about six miles and camped for the night.[48]

The next morning they went back downriver three miles to see what would happen. Unfortunately, the fog was so thick that they could see nothing. They headed for Fort Point, landed, and moved inland a half mile. When the fog cleared, the American fleet was in full view. It had just gotten underway standing up the river under a small breeze. As the Americans passed the mouth of Bagaduce River the armed vessels fired at the three British ships. Captains Brewer and Smith watched the action intently until Brewer glanced westward and saw several whaleboats full of armed men under the bank. The two men hurried to their boat and were just unfurling their sails when the boats came alongside and orders were given for them to stand fast. It turned out that Captain Brewer's brother Colonel Josiah Brewer commanded the boats.

The colonel was part of an advance guard going to Buckstown (Bucksport) to stop communications between the British and the upriver settlers. Josiah Brewer ordered his brother John to accompany him. They arrived at Buckstown about 5:00 P.M. After stationing his guards, Colonel Brewer, learning that his brother and Captain Smith had recently been on the Bagaduce Peninsula, took them downriver to visit the American ships. The darkness and fog prevented them from arriving before sunrise on 26 July.[49]

Chapter Two

Massachusetts's Answer

GENERAL CHARLES CUSHING's letter of 19 June 1779 arrived in Boston on Wednesday 23 June 1779 while the General Court (the legislative body) was in session. The Massachusetts government received many other pleas from the Eastward for aid. Yet Cushing's was the first to tell of the occupation of the state's territory since the British evacuated Boston early in the war. A committee from both houses was given the task of considering the letter and recommending appropriate action. The next day the committee submitted its opinion. It was expedient to send a naval force to Penobscot to drive out the enemy before it became entrenched. The committee recommended that the Board of War gather all armed vessels fit for sea belonging to the state ready to cruise within six days. In addition, the committee wanted the Continental Navy Board Eastern Department and the owners of privately armed vessels in Boston, Salem, Marblehead, Beverly, and Newburyport to take measures to cooperate with the state vessels. The following day the General Court accepted the committee's recommendations.[1]

No sooner did the General Court accept the committee's decision, including its abbreviated six-day preparation, than it received a letter (dated 23 June) from Jonathan Jackson of Newburyport. Jackson and eight other owners of privately armed vessels in Newburyport offered their vessels for any proposed expedition. He further said the four vessels (owned jointly among the various men) could sail in a week's time. The ships were the *Vengeance*, twenty 6-pounders; the *Monmouth*, twenty-four 6-pounders; the *Sky Rocket*, sixteen 4-pounders, and the brig *Pallas*, sixteen 4-pounders. Jackson wrote that they had learned that the enemy had made, or attempted to make, a lodgment on Penobscot River. They sent a young man from that locale along with their letter to give more detailed information on the events to the Eastward.[2]

The General Court, pleased with this display of patriotism, answered the same day. It sent a copy of its resolve to launch an expedition to Penobscot and accepted the four vessels. According to the resolve, the state would reimburse expenses. The court urged them to man, water, and equip all the vessels for immediate sailing. Massachusetts would supply the provisions, which would be forwarded when obtained.[3] This was an auspicious beginning that boded well for a speedy reply to the British challenge. But as details for planning the expedition began to unfold, the possibility of leaving in six days diminished.

On 26 June the War Office in Boston wrote to Tristram Dalton, one of the Newburyport owners, asking for confirmation on the number of ships equipped and when they could be ready. The War Office sent its letter by express and asked Dalton to give his answer, for all of the owners, to the bearer of the letter. The letter reiterated the state's desire to fulfill its part, as stated in the original resolve. Dalton replied on 27 June.[4] Next day the General Court instructed the Board of War to immediately send provisions for a two-month cruise for the four vessels.[5]

On 30 June the Massachusetts government issued a series of requests and instructions. The House of Representatives sent fifteen thousand pounds from the public treasury to Captain Jonathan Parsons of Newburyport for the owners' use in fitting out their ships.[6] The War Office wrote Dalton that three state vessels would be ready for sea Saturday, 10 July. It also expected other ships from Boston and Salem to meet that deadline. It asked Dalton to pass the latest information he had concerning the enemy's actions on to its office. If he spent money for the information, the state would reimburse him. The government appointed Nantasket as the rendezvous.[7] The Massachusetts Council wrote the Navy Board Eastern Department in Boston asking for three armed Continental ships in the harbor. The 32-gun frigate *Warren* was most desired. The council assured the Continental Navy Board that the state would help in manning if need be.[8]

The Navy Board replied the same day. William Vernon, speaking for the board, said that the frigate *Warren,* the sloop *Providence,* and the brig *Diligent* were undergoing preparation for the expedition. The Continental ships should be ready in four or five days, provided they had enough men. The *Warren* needed at least one hundred men, most of them seamen. Vernon felt the sloop and brig might need some manning, but the frigate was the principal need. Vernon ended his letter saying that the board was "in full confidence that care will be taken to send a force Superior to the Enemy."[9]

On that same day, 30 June, the Massachusetts Council sent Joseph Simpson to seek the assistance of Governor Meshech Weare of New Hampshire. Weare received Simpson on 1 July and told him that the day before the New Hampshire Committee of Safety had resolved to join its sister state against the British threat in Penobscot Bay. Governor Weare offered New Hampshire's impressed privateer *Hampden*, a 22-gun ship, to the expedition. Weare thought the *Hampden* should be ready for sea in about five days, but it was 8 July before Titus Salter of Portsmouth received his appointment as captain of the *Hampden*. Captain Salter departed Portsmouth on 19 July to join the Penobscot Expedition.[10]

On 1 July the Massachusetts Council placed militia brigadier Solomon Lovell, a fellow politician, in command of the troops. The council ordered him to send three people to the Eastward immediately to hasten raising the troops. One went to Wells in York County; one, to Falmouth in Cumberland County; and the third, to Broad Bay in Lincoln County. General Lovell first served in the military in the French and Indian War. He was twenty-four when he volunteered for the Crown Point Campaign in 1756. As a first lieutenant under Colonel Richard Gridley, most of his nine-month service was on the shores of Lake George with little action. Upon the release of the New England contingent, he returned home, and between the French and Indian War and the Revolution, he remained in the militia and advanced to colonel. Lovell was a gentleman farmer, active in local politics, and represented his town, Weymouth, in the assembly for eight years. Although Colonel Lovell received his promotion to brigadier 24 June 1777, his principal command of troops in the field took place during the monthlong unsuccessful attempt to drive the British from Rhode Island in the summer of 1778. His years of political infighting greatly affected his modus operandi: Solomon Lovell was quick to note a competitor, and often resorted to scheming and maneuvering to enhance his public image at the expense of his competitor.[11]

General Lovell was to consult with the commander of the fleet before selecting the time of rendezvous. Two days later the council appointed Captain Dudley Saltonstall, the commander of the Continental frigate *Warren*, as commodore of the fleet destined for Penobscot.[12] Early in life

Commodore Saltonstall sailed on many mercantile voyages, gaining a reputation as a skillful commander. On 17 April 1762, during the French and Indian War, he took command of the letter of marque brigantine *Britannia,* making successful voyages to the West Indies and Europe.[13] In the first year of the Revolution, when Congress created a navy, Saltonstall was the senior of five captains appointed. He commanded the flagship *Alfred* under Commodore Esek Hopkins. He participated in the February 1776 attack on New Providence, the Bahamas. On the return voyage the squadron engaged the British frigate *Glasgow* off Long Island, but the *Alfred*'s steering gear was damaged and the *Glasgow* made good its escape.

By the spring of 1776 the Marine Committee and Congress had received many complaints from junior naval officers against their superiors. Any officer who had a friend with political clout among members of the committee or Congress wrote to them of their own abilities, embellished with lurid tales of the incompetence of their superiors. John Paul Jones wrote to Daniel Tillinghast, a naval agent at Providence, and to Joseph Hewes in Congress of his contempt for his captain, Dudley Saltonstall. This crescendo of complaints forced the Marine Committee to call several captains, including Saltonstall, to Philadelphia for an investigation. On 11 July 1776, the Marine Committee found the charge against Saltonstall was not well founded, and Congress ordered him returned to his command.[14]

Saltonstall next commanded the frigate *Trumbull.* On 4 April 1777 the Marine Committee in Philadelphia requested three of its frigate captains to put to sea immediately to intercept enemy transports reinforcing or supplying the British army in New York. Evidently the Marine Committee lacked up-to-date information on its frigates. Captains J. B. Hopkins of the *Warren* and Abraham Whipple of the *Providence* were sealed in Narragansett Bay by British ships blockading at the bay's mouth. Captain Saltonstall had dropped the *Trumbull* down the Connecticut River to Saybrook only to find his ship drew too much water to clear the sandbar at the river's mouth. Saltonstall too was trapped. Not one of the three was available to carry out the committee's orders.[15]

Yet Dudley Saltonstall did not give up that easily. He made arrangements to take command of a Connecticut privateer, a 10-gun sloop, also named the *Trumbull.* On 12 April 1777, off the Capes of Virginia, "I fell in with two transports from England, one of eight the other of ten guns. They engaged us three glasses [an hour and a half], when they struck their colours. They killed seven of our men and wounded eight more. We shattered them in a terrible manner and killed and wounded numbers of their crews." He sent in the two transports and added in a postscript: "I shall give you an account of the powder, military stores and arms on board them, and of my proceeding in general."[16]

Upon completion of his task, he returned to the Connecticut River and the Continental *Trumbull*. In spite of his efforts to get her over the bar that first summer, he was not successful. In the fall, he suspended operations. He wrote that he suggested to the Navy Board "the Building a couple of Camels to facilitate her removal and render the Navigation less uncertain" for the *Trumbull* the following summer. Camels were invented by the Dutch about 1688 to carry vessels into shallow harbors. They consisted of large watertight casks built to be placed under or alongside the ship's hull. When ready to use, the camels would be filled with water to submerge them to the required depth. Then they would be attached to the hull of the ship. When secured, the water would be pumped out. The camels and ship, becoming more buoyant, would lift and be able to float over the shallow water.[17]

By mid-November Captain Saltonstall had not received permission to build camels. Had he been privy to some of Navy Board member James Warren's letters he would have understood why. In a series of letters to John Adams, Warren pleaded for money. On 7 September 1777 he wrote, "We have wrote to the Marine Committee for money . . . and can do very little without [money]." On 12 October 1777 Warren said, "tho' we are ordered to do many expensive things are not supplied with a shilling to do it with. This is as bad as makeing bricks without straw." He continued the next year in the same vein. On 8 May 1778, "with the great Accumulation of Business which grows on us every Day, with six Sail of Ships and Brigantines on hand in this Port . . . we can't at this time Command 500 dollars." Obviously the Navy Board had no choice but to dismiss Saltonstall's expensive suggestion. The following summer was a repeat of 1777 with lots of work and no success. In November the Marine Committee ordered a stop to "attempts to get out the ship Trumbull." It was April 1779 before the board could proceed.[18] In May Saltonstall left the still-stranded Continental frigate *Trumbull* to become commanding officer of the frigate *Warren* in Boston.

Captain Saltonstall took command of the *Warren* sometime between 10 and 16 June. A seasoned seaman, he had trained in the merchant marine, fought as a privateer in the French and Indian War, and captained both the Continental frigate *Alfred* and the privateer *Trumbull* in combat. He was knowledgeable enough to recommend using camels to free the *Trumbull.* (Later, when the next commanding officer did free the *Trumbull,* it was by camels.) Yet Captain Saltonstall is a difficult man to understand. In an age when most leaders wrote voluminous letters, kept extensive diaries, and issued many public pronouncements, he seldom wrote. The result is that he is known largely through the comments of others. Samuel E. Morison offered some glimpses of the man in his *John Paul Jones.* Dudley Saltonstall was "a scion of the three first families of New England, [but] he seemed not to have resembled the Saltonstalls who for generations have been noted for their genial and democratic manners, but rather his mother's family, the Winthrops, who were notorious for their condescending attitude toward social inferiors." Captain Nicholas Biddle observed that Saltonstall was "a sensible indefatigable Morose man." John Paul Jones, who was his first lieutenant aboard the *Alfred* complained of his "Rude unhappy Temper." He appeared, in sum, to be a curt, gloomy, surly man who kept to himself.[19]

On 2 July 1779 the General Court ordered the naval officer for the Newburyport harbor to clear any ships applying for clearance for the Penobscot Expedition. Specifically it stated: "the ship Vengeance, Thomas Thomas, Commander, ship Monmouth, Alex Ross, ship Sky Rocket, Capt-Burke and Brigane Pallas, James Johnson [Johnston], Commander." The next day Samuel Horton wrote in his diary: "Ye Pallace, Sky Rocket and Capt. Gideons in a brig sailed for Boston to join ye fleet for Penobscot. Two more ships are going tomorrow."[20] In spite of the feverish activity, it took nearly a month to complete the gathering of vessels, crews, troops, and supplies for the expedition. Among the unforeseen difficulties of organizing the expedition were getting ship owners to release their vessels. The owner of the ship *General Putnam* in Boston was not available. The council ordered the sheriff of Suffolk County to impress the *General Putnam,* with all its tackle and appurtenances, and deliver her to the Board of War for fitting out for the expedition. In Essex County the owners and commanders of three ships needed by the council for the expedition refused to hire out their ships. Therefore, the council ordered the sheriff to take the ships *Hector, Black Prince,* and *Hunter* into service immediately. All ships were under state control for a "two-month cruise."[21]

Recruiting sailors proved to be another difficulty. Even before the British incursion, Commodore Saltonstall found recruiting sailors for the

Continental Navy difficult. In his account to the Navy Board Eastern Department he spent £146.13 to bring eleven men from New London to Boston and another £116.8 for sundry bounties for men enrolled on the *Warren* by 7 July 1779.[22] Few sailors were willing to sign on a Continental ship for wages. Also, as the Continental Navy did not recruit for single cruises, one might find oneself on an extended tour of duty. Yet the greatest detriment to enlisting in Continental service was the advantage of privateering. With twelve private property vessels signed for the expedition, the opportunity for profit was compelling.

Privateering flourished in Massachusetts. Often the owners of privateers were a syndicate of private citizens who were stockholders in the venture. The captain and crew earned a predetermined percentage of everything captured on the cruise and sold. Boston papers advertised auctions of captured items. Captured cannons brought particularly active bidding as even the Continental Navy bid for these items. Hurriedly the Continental Navy Board for the Eastern Department changed its policy and admitted enlistments just for the Penobscot Expedition. Yet it wrote that the demand for men for the armed vessels and transports thwarted its endeavors. Finally, the Massachusetts Council issued a warrant to impress seamen. Eventually this produced sixty men to complete the *Warren's* complement.[23] In spite of the support of the Navy Board and the General Court, it was three and a half weeks before the *Warren* was ready for sea.

In its quest for speed to outfit the expedition, the War Office in Boston even impressed provisions and supplies. The privateer *General Putnam's* prize the snow *Clinton* had its cargo impressed for 200 barrels of pork, 2,000 pounds of hard soup, 172 tierces of beef, 400 barrels of flour, and 2 tons of bread. The commissary general of the state added the impressed items to the provisions for the expedition. A judge appraised these items and that amount was paid to the owners. Massachusetts agents traveled the hinter regions for kitchen equipment such as kettles and bowls to prepare the food. Other agents scurried to buy small arms, cannons, powder, and shot.[24] As the armed and transport vessels gathered in Boston and other ports, and as the state's provisions and supplies built up, public confidence in the expedition increased. People wanted to share in the expected plunder. Individuals began to bid for a share of the wealth expected from the coming conquest. Many sailors, looking for immediate profit, began selling their shares to the eager speculators. By the time the Penobscot Expedition left Boston, public confidence was at its height.[25]

Massachusetts officials, equally confident of the success of the expedition, did not tell General Horatio Gates in nearby Rhode Island of the expedition or ask for Continental troops. Further, they did not inform General George Washington of their intentions. General Artemas Ward was foremost among the legislators desiring to keep this expedition out of the hands of the Continental Congress. General William Hazard wrote, the common belief was "If but ten Continental soldiers are concerned, the Continent will take all the honor." James Thacher said the Massachusetts General Court had such "zeal and confidence" that it neither desired nor consulted about using Continental troops. That body took upon itself "the undivided responsibility, and reserving for their heads, all the laurels to be derived from the anticipated conquest."[26]

Typical of that age, the Penobscot Expedition had no overall commander. General Lovell commanded the land forces. Commodore Saltonstall commanded the naval forces. And both leaders received instructions to cooperate with the other. The Massachusetts Council instructed Lovell to "promote the Greatest Harmony, peace and concord between the land and Sea Forces." He was to consult with the fleet commander so that cooperation with the troops under his command could "Captivate Kill or Destroy the whole force of the Enemy there both by Sea & Land."[27] Similarly, the Navy Board Eastern Department instructed Commodore Saltonstall to use his utmost "to Captivate Kill or destroy the Enemies whole Force both by Sea & Land." Toward that purpose he was to consult and preserve "the greatest harmony with the Commander of the Land Forces that the Navy & Army may cooperate & assist each other."[28] Yet after exhorting Saltonstall to "use your Utmost Endeavours," the Navy Board Eastern Department wrote to its superior in Philadelphia: "So much time has been taken up in preparing for this Expedition that we doubt the Success of it. The Enemy must be Stupid indeed if they do not reinforce that party with some additional ships."[29]

Meanwhile, recruiting the Maine militia was not going as expected. Major Jeremiah Hill, the adjutant general, arrived in Falmouth on 8 July. Earlier he had sent a letter to General Samuel Thompson telling of his orders. He also requested aid and assistance from Thompson. When Hill arrived, he met with the general and Colonel Jonathan Mitchell, who would command the Cumberland County troops. Hill discovered that there was reluctance on the part of many militiamen to muster. Hill suggested General Thompson use martial law to bring the men to muster.

Thompson agreed and sent parties out to various towns that were deficient in their quota. Major Hill said that martial law aided somewhat: "Some were taken & brought by force, some were frightened and joined Voluntarily, & some Sulk'd and kept themselves concealed." By 16 July, when Hill embarked his men for the rendezvous point at Townsend (Boothbay Harbor), he had 433 men. Again he sought out General Thompson to report the deficiencies. The general said that he sent orders to his colonels for the whole regiment. Thompson added that "if they would not go he would make the County too hot to hold them." Hill summed up the muster: "Some sent Boys, old Men, and Invalids, if they belonged to the train Band or Alarm List they were soldiers whether they could carry a Gun, walk a mile without crutches, or only Compos Mentis sufficient to keep themselves out of Fire & Water." When Hill got to Townsend, he found the York and Lincoln troops were "much like the Cumberland Troops, aforementioned." The troop returns for 20 July listed 893 total force. Hill awaited the arrival of General Lovell.[30]

General Lovell boarded the *Warren* in Boston Thursday, 15 July. The next day, all were ready for sea, but the fresh northeast wind parted the *Warren*'s cable and kept all ships at anchor. Saturday drizzly weather and the still fresh northeast wind kept the ships in place. Sunday, General Lovell went home to Weymouth to spend a few hours with his family. Finally, Monday, 19 July, ten armed vessels and ten transports sortied from Nantasket. The following night the group lay to off Portsmouth, New Hampshire. On 21 July the vessels arrived at Townsend where the *Hampden* and other transports waited. General Lovell moved ashore and made his headquarters at the Reverend Jonathan Murray's home. Here he met all the members of his staff, or as it was often called, family.[31] They were

Rank and Name	Title
Brig. Solomon Lovell	Commander, Land Forces
Brig. Peleg Wadsworth	Deputy Commander, Land Forces
Col. Samuel McCobb	Commander, Lincoln County Militia
Col. Jonathan Mitchell	Commander, Cumberland County Militia
Maj. Daniel Littlefield	Commander, York County Militia
Lt. Col. Paul Revere	Commander, Artillery Train
Maj. Jeremiah Hill	Adjutant General
Maj. William Todd	Brigade Major
Maj. Gawen Brown	Brigade Major

Col. John Tyler   Quartermaster-General
Capt. Gilbert Speakman   Commissary of Ordnance
Dr. Eliphalet Downer   Surgeon General

On 22 July Lovell examined the troop returns and found the quota deficient five hundred men, nearly a third missing. In spite of the poor turnout of troops, he ordered the men to draw their provisions, ammunition, and necessities for their mission. The next day he reviewed the troops. General Wadsworth said of the review that, "One fourth part of the Troops then appear'd to be Small Boys & old men, & unfit for the service." Immediately after the review the men embarked on the transports.[32]

Meanwhile, Lieutenant Colonel Paul Revere was checking his artillery. General Lovell had been on the committee to determine the number of cannons for the expedition. The committee recommended two 18-pounders, three 9-pounders, one 5.5-inch howitzer, and four 4-pounder brass fieldpieces. When Revere received his post as the artillery commander he asked for four more 18-pounders, with four hundred rounds for each gun. He reduced the 9-pounders to two, with 300 rounds each. He doubled the howitzers to two, with one hundred rounds each. Finally, he changed his four fieldpieces to two heavy French 4-pounders and two of the American light pieces. When Lovell reviewed the troops at Townsend, Revere found the militia had one 12-pounder on a field carriage with eighty-four rounds. He added that to his weapons. This 12-pounder was his only mounted field carriage heavier than his 4-pounders.[33]

When the *Charming Sally* and the *Defence* reached Townsend on 22 July, all vessels were together.[34] The thirty-nine vessels, eighteen armed and twenty-one transports, made an impressive gathering. In many ways the armed vessels were as ill prepared for their task as the militia was for its task. Often described by narrators of the expedition as a powerful fleet, the armed vessels of the Penobscot Expedition were more akin to a naval gathering than a fleet. There was no time for fleet training. The armed vessels were from three types of navies: the Continental Navy assigned three vessels to the mission; the Massachusetts state navy supplied three; the privateer navy provided twelve vessels. Essentially all three types of navies often acted as commerce raiders.

Congress established the Continental Navy on 30 October 1775. In December 1775 Congress authorized building thirteen frigates. The Continental Navy's most serious problem was recruiting seamen because it competed against the privateers. Privateer crews received a larger share of prize money. Often Continental ships sat in port waiting for seamen. Thus squadron operations were almost impossible to carry out, yet the Continental Navy, when it had the opportunity, sought to engage British men-of-war. But sailing alone meant that Continental ships, like privateers, often employed commerce raiding. Only New Jersey and Delaware failed to organize a state navy. Generally state navies consisted of shallow-draft vessels for coastal defense. Massachusetts and Pennsylvania included some small deep-water draft vessels to prey upon British merchantmen. As a maritime militia defending the state's coast, it also interdicted Loyalists supplying enemy ships lying offshore.

The privateers sailing with a commission or letter of marque primarily sought out enemy merchantmen with an eye toward profit. Their authorization for privateering was a license for piracy. The crew received a greater share of prize money, worked with less discipline, and most often engaged noncombat vessels. A privateer cruise provided the sailor with more profit and less danger. Thus the strategic mission to seek out and destroy enemy men-of-war was not a mission familiar to most of the personnel involved in the Penobscot Expedition.[35]

Commodore Saltonstall commanded ten ships, five brigs, one brigantine, one schooner, and one sloop. His major vessels in size and fire power were the ten large, three-masted, square-rigged ships. Of these ships the Continental Navy's 32-gun frigate was the largest and most powerful. The other nine were privateers. During the French and Indian War the American shipmakers built some large, sharp, and fast ship privateers similar to the British lines. These vessels also were known as frigates. Their deck plans were similar to the man-of-war frigates, having a raised quarterdeck and forecastle. This similar silhouette did not mean that the privateer "frigate" performed like the man-of-war frigate. Shipbuilders built the privateer for speed first and combat second. Yet having the same silhouette as the warship meant a merchant prey might surrender sooner, believing its attacker was a man-of-war. Whether Americans continued using this type of privateer during the Revolution, at least on the Penobscot Expedition, is questionable. In Maclay's description of the expedition's *Black Prince* he did not use the phrase "frigate." He wrote: "Perhaps one of the most formidable privateers that put to sea in the year 1778 was the *Black Prince,* of Massachusetts, Captain West. This vessel was built expressly for privateering, being among the first of this class of formidable war craft to get to sea."[36]

Saltonstall's lesser vessels included five brigs, one continental (*Diligent*), two state (*Tyrannicide* and *Hazard*), and two private (*Defence* and *Pallas*), a state brigantine (*Active*), a continental sloop (*Providence*), and a private schooner (*Rover*). The brigs and brigantine were square-rigged. The sloop and schooner were fore-and-aft sailors. All fore-and-aft vessels could lie nearer to the wind than the square-rigged vessels. Probably the schooner was the fastest laying closest to the wind.[37]

An aspect of Revolutionary vessels' propulsion, often overlooked by modern narrators, was the reliance upon rowing. Most of the smaller craft, the less-than-20-gun vessels, were fitted to row. Also, it was not uncommon to find oar ports on frigates, which were placed on the lower deck between the gun ports. Long sweeps, or oars, worked by several men to a sweep moved a vessel in a calm or aided its movement when in restricted waters. When under oars, the vessels were said to sail under a "white ash wind."[38]

Howard I. Chapelle, author of *The History of the American Sailing Navy,* gives the modern reader an appreciation of the classes of colonial sailing vessels. "Ships of the line, or in modern parlance, battleships, were the 70-, 80-, 90-, and 100-gun ships. The modern heavy cruiser or small battleship was represented in colonial times by the 40-, 50-, and 60-gun ships, while light cruisers were represented by 20- and 30-gun classes. Below the 20-gun ships were brigantines, snows, ketches, and other small craft, from 4 to 18 guns."[39]

The number of guns and their sizes differed greatly on each vessel from voyage to voyage. Contemporary and latter accounts are confusing. For example, the owner of the *Vengeance,* writing to the Massachusetts Council, said she had twenty 6-pounders; Sir George Collier, in his report, stated she had twenty-four guns without mentioning their size; later Admiral Chester felt she carried eighteen guns of 9- and 6-pounders. Thus while the name and type of vessel were not in dispute, the number and size of each vessel's guns were subject to interpretation. For this study Paul Revere's figures for the ship's guns were used. (See table 1.)

Saltonstall's captains ranged from the experienced Captains Daniel Waters and William Burke to Philip Brown who received his first command just before the expedition. Captain Daniel Waters served in George

Table 1. Armed Vessels of the Penobscot Expedition

Name (No. Guns)	Type	Pounders	Captain
Defence (14)	Brig	4	John Edmunds
Pallas (14)	Brig	4	James Johnston
Rover (10)	Schooner	4	Nathan Parker
Continental Navy			
Warren (32)	Ship	18, 12	Dudley Saltonstall
Providence (12)	Sloop	6, 4	Hoysteed Hacker
Diligent (12)	Brig	3	Philip Brown
State Navy			
Tyrannicide (14)	Brig	6	John Cathcart
Hazard (14)	Brig	6	John F. Williams
Active (14)	Brigantine	4	John Allan Hallet
Privateers			
Charming Sally (20)	Ship	9, 6	Alexander Holmes
Hampden (20)	Ship	9, 6	Titus Salter
General Putnam (20)	Ship	9	Daniel Waters
Black Prince (20)	Ship	6	Nathaniel West
Monmouth (20)	Ship	6	Alexander Ross
Vengeance (20)	Ship	6	Thomas Thomas
Hector (18)	Ship	6	John Carnes
Hunter (18)	Ship	4	Nathan Brown
Sky Rocket (16)	Ship	4	William Burke

Source: Paul Revere to General William Heath, 24 October 1779, Massachusetts Historical Society, *Collections* (Boston: Massachusetts Historical Society, 1904), ser. 7, pt. 2, 4:319.

Washington's fleet in the early days of the war. In January 1776 Waters commanded the schooner *Lee,* eight 6-pounders. He helped capture several British vessels. Congress appointed him a captain on 15 March 1777. Later in 1778 as a privateer he commanded the *Thorn* of sixteen guns. On the same cruise he captured the *Governor Tryon, Sir William Erskine,* and *Sparlin.* Owing to darkness the *Erskine* made good her escape. Captain Burke also served in Washington's fleet. Later he fell captive to the British.

After a prisoner of war exchange, he commanded the *Lynch*. Captain Philip Brown served as first lieutenant under Captain Hoysteed Hacker of the *Providence* when Hacker captured the brig *Diligent*. Hacker selected Brown to be the prize master to bring the *Diligent* in to Boston. He continued in command when the expedition fitted out although many senior Continental officers waited without pay for command assignment.[40]

Yet to be a competent captain one needed more than just experience as a commanding officer, one needed experience with one's particular vessel. For example, Captain Hector McNeill of the frigate *Boston* spent almost two months at sea without discovering how best to trim his ship. He said, "We have alter'd her trim frequently and find great difference in her going, but yet we never have been able to make her go as fast as some other Ships we have fallen in with, . . . I am Persuaded that She will One day Sail fast if her Trim can be discover'd. . . . To go best close haul'd she ought to be on an even keel That is 14 feet 3 inches, forw'r and aft. To go Large, or afore the wind, She must be 10 or 12 inches deeper aft than forward." This was the man Captain John Paul Jones said, "inherits more marine knowledge than any other Man, with whom I have had equal conversation, in the service."[41]

Of the ten ship captains on the Penobscot Expedition, five lacked experience with their vessel. Commodore Saltonstall assumed command of the *Warren* sometime between 10 and 16 June 1779. He made his first voyage on the *Warren* between Nantasket Roads and Bagaduce. The same for Captain Salter who assumed command of the *Hampden* on 9 July and departed on 19 July. Captains Ross, Thomas, and Waters received their ships on 28 June, 30 June, and 9 July, respectively, just weeks before departing for Bagaduce. Of the others Captains Holmes and West had command 6 and 9 months, respectively, before departing to the Eastward.[42]

The evening of 22 July the general had the senior land and naval officers meet for the first time. According to Paul Revere's diary, "There were some debates about the future operation of the Fleet, and Army; nothing material was determined; it was left to the General and Commodore, to settle." However, later Revere wrote to General William Heath that the proceeding "was an Epitome of the whole Campaigne, I shall be a little Particular. They met about 8 o'clock . . . there was nothing proposed, and of consequence nothing done; It was more like a meeting in the Coffee House, then a Council of War. There was no President appointed, nor any minutes taken: after Disputing about nothing two hours it was broke up."[43] The next morning the wind was unfavorable for their destination.

Finally, on 24 July, the expedition weighed anchor and set a course for Bagaduce. Table 2 lists transports for the expedition by name of vessel, the vessel's type, and its master.

Table 2. Transport Vessels of the Penobscot Expedition

Name	Type	Captain
Abigail	Sloop	McGlathery, William
Allen	Schooner	Tower, Levi
Bethaiah	Sloop	Freeman, Edward
Britannia	Sloop	Johnson, Robert
Centurion	Sloop	McLellan, William
Defiance	Sloop	Mitchell, Daniel
Dolphin	Sloop	Kent, Peleg
Fortune	Sloop	Drinkwater, David
Hannah	Sloop	Sampson, Mels
Industry	Sloop	Young, William
Job	Sloop	Sprague, Jonathan
Nancy	Schooner	Tarbox, Ez
Nancy	Sloop	Grafton, John
Pidgeon	Sloop	Little, Luther
Race-Horse	Sloop	Turner, Simeon
Rachel	Schooner	Wylie, John
Safety	Sloop	Kent, William
Sally	Sloop	Carver, Nathaniel
Samuel	Brig	Brown, James
Sparrow	Sloop	Drinkwater, Samuel
Unity	Schooner	Bubier, Joseph

Source: Ships' names from "List of Debts in the Naval Department on the Expedition to Penobscot, War Office, 23 September 1779," Massachusetts Archives Collection, 145:199; most of the captains will be found in *Massachusetts Soldiers and Sailors* and throughout Massachusetts Archives Collection, vol. 145.

The American expedition made an impressive sight. Yet looks were deceiving. The militia lacked a third of its scheduled numbers. The troops lacked training. The militiamen from Maine's three counties came together as a unit the day before departing. The expedition's armed vessels were equally ill prepared for the task at hand. Finally the two commanders and their staffs failed to arrive at a common strategy at their first meeting. It did not bode well for the expedition.

Chapter Three

Assault

THE DAILY WEATHER reports in this and the next two chapters came from the noon notation in HM *Albany*'s log, which used sea time for its log entries. The most important time for a vessel at sea was the meridian. At that time navigational observations determined the vessel's latitude position. Therefore, the vessel's day ran from noon to noon, while civil time began and ended at midnight. Table 3 defines the wind terms used in the log.

Saturday, 24 July 1779, northerly moderate breezes and fair weather—

The Penobscot Expedition sailed for Bagaduce. General Lovell, aboard the transport *Sally*, drew up orders for the landing. Upon arrival, Colonel Davis will man and prepare the flat bottomed boats for the troops. Major Littlefield's detachment will land first as an advance party to cover the flanks of the first line of the assault. General Wadsworth will command the first line. Colonel McCobb will bring the second line ashore. The train and artillery will stand by to act as ordered during the operations. General Lovell said he expected his officers and soldiers "not only to maintain, but to add new Lustre to the Fame of the Massachusetts Militia."[1]

In the early evening the commodore ordered the *Hazard* and *Tyrannicide* to sail ahead to Fox Islands to gather information on the enemy. By 10:00 P.M., abreast of the islands, the two vessels anchored. Each sent a boat of marines to gather intelligence. Lieutenant William Downs of the *Tyrannicide* pretended he and his men were British sailors. In this guise they visited several houses and talked to the people. They brought back three who seemed knowledgeable about Bagaduce. Captain Williams of the *Hazard* questioned them before sending them to the commodore. The

Table 3. Wind Terms Used in *Albany* Log

Term	Beaufort Scale	Wind Speed	Ship's Speed or Sails
Calm	0	0–1	
Light Air	1	1–3	just steerage
Light Breeze	2	3–5	1–2 knots
Gentle Breeze	3	5–10	3–4 knots
Moderate Breeze	4	10–15	5–6 knots
Fresh Breeze	5	15–20	close-hauled royals
Strong Breeze	6	20–25	single reefs top gallant
Moderate Gale	7	25–35	double reefs and jib
Fresh Gale	8	35–40	three reefs and courses

Note: The speeds are those a well-conditioned man-of-war would attain, sailing clean full in smooth water.

Source: Naval Encyclopaedia, 846, and Harland, *Seamanship in the Age of Sail,* 53.

information gleaned was that the British were still in the early stages of building their defenses.[2]

General Lovell also gathered information. When his transport anchored, he sent a boat to Camden to pick up Captain Mitchell. The general had arranged to meet Mitchell earlier, believing that the captain was well acquainted with the Bagaduce peninsula. While Lovell waited, some Penobscot Indians visited him in canoes determined to join his expedition. General McLean had earlier contacted them to enlist their aid, but they refused to join the British.[3] Lovell accepted their offer.

The British received updates on the Americans' approach. General McLean's troops worked on the ramparts with constant glances southward down the bay. Finally, late in the afternoon they sighted the Americans. To the British defenders the enemy fleet resembled "a floating island with innumerable trees." At 5:00 P.M. Captain Mowat fired a signal gun recalling his sailors from their work on the fort. That night British guard boats kept watch for the enemy fleet anchored off Fox Islands in the mouth of Penobscot Bay.[4]

Sunday, 25 July 1779, west moderate breezes and fair weather—

At 7:00 A.M. the American fleet assembled to stand up the bay. At 9:00 A.M. Commodore Saltonstall sent Captain Philip Brown of the Continental brig *Diligent* ahead to reconnoiter. Brown made all the sail he could set and cleared for action. From what the men from Fox Islands said the evening before, he expected the commodore to press an immediate attack. Abreast of Bagaduce, he saw the British fortifications. On the north side of the harbor, high on the eminence, a British flag flew over a fort. Below were two batteries guarding the harbor's mouth. South of the entrance, on a small island, was a third battery. Three anchored British sloops of war were in a close line-of-battle across the entrance. To the north, were the rocks of Bagaduce Point; to the south, an island flanked the vessels. What he may not have noticed was the three transports farther back. Captain Mowat had them ready to slip their anchors and run foul of the enemy if need be.[5] Captain Philip Brown wore around to return with his information. Heading back, he saw three men ashore waving their hats. Brown, concerned that the battery on Banks' Island might challenge his rescue operation, armed his crew sent to pick them up.

Back aboard the *Warren*, Philip Brown made his report. Then the three sympathizers told the commodore that the fort was under construction and far from complete. Saltonstall asked Brown for his opinion. Captain Philip Brown, eager to display his leadership ability, said there would never be a better time to attack. Saltonstall curtly replied, "None but madmen would go in before they had reconnoitered, & it would be the height of madness to attempt it."[6] The commodore's caution stemmed from sound seamanship. The tides of Penobscot Bay, ten or more feet, produced strong currents in the river as it ebbed and flowed. These currents in a narrow channel combined with the variableness of the winds in this landlocked bay made it difficult for large wind-propelled vessels to maneuver except during favorable wind and tide. A few miles northeast from the confluence of Penobscot Bay with the Bagaduce River, the river opened into a broad irregular-shaped basin that filled and emptied twice a day from the tide. Saltonstall's daylight opportunities to maneuver in Bagaduce Harbor occurred only under certain circumstances.

Besides these natural obstacles, the commodore had to contend with the three British sloops of war anchored athwart the entrance, which was less than six-hundred yards wide. Each of Captain Mowat's ships, with spring cables attached to their anchor chains, presented its broadside toward the approaching enemy. Mowat's defensive position employed the ideal offensive formation of crossing the T. He had the added benefit of not being underway or depending on the wind and seamanship to keep that position. First Saltonstall would have to wait for a favorable wind and tide. Then, while he could only engage his bow guns, he would have to advance directly in the broadside of all of Mowat's ships. If the lead ship became disabled, it endangered his remaining ships in the restricted sea room. Besides Mowat's ships, Saltonstall also had the fort on the eminence, two batteries below the fort, and a third on Banks' Island opposing him.[7] Finally, a sudden calm, not uncommon in the area, could place the commodore's vessels in crisis.

At 2:00 P.M. thirty-nine sail of both warships and transports arrived opposite Bagaduce. The transports continued up Penobscot Bay to an anchorage half a mile above the Bagaduce entrance. The ship *Sally* and the brigs *Hazard* and *Active* escorted the transports. Other armed ships stood off and on beyond gun range of the British. At 3:00 P.M. the commodore hailed the *Tyrannicide* to keep on his starboard quarter. Saltonstall wanted the brig to carry his orders to the ships when it was time to anchor, for he had no signal to come to anchor by day. Yet when the commodore hove to with his main topsail to the mast the other ships followed suit.[8]

About 4:00 P.M. Commodore Saltonstall boarded Captain Nathan Parker's small schooner *Rover* to sail around and issue instructions to his vessels. He ordered some of his attack ships to run in within gun shot of the enemy and fire their broadsides and run out again.[9] Shortly afterward five of the ships ran in to fire broadsides at the British ships. Mowat warmly returned the fire. The shore batteries joined the cannonading that continued until 7:00 P.M. The random firing produced little hull damage to either side.[10] Major Jeremiah Hill's observation was that some ships circling and saluting the enemy with their broadsides "were so far off that their shot never reached the shore." British lieutenant John Moore reached the same conclusion saying, "Though the firing was smart from both sides, yet the Y—s kept at such a distance that little or no damage was done."[11]

The American Loyalist Dr. John Calef's description, the one found in most historical narratives, differed. According to him, at 3:00 P.M. nine of the larger vessels formed in three divisions and stood toward the king's ships. At extreme range the first division hove to, presented its broadside, and began firing. Then the second and third divisions followed suit. The cannonade was brisk on both sides and the engagement lasted about four glasses (two hours). Calef had some disparaging remarks to make about the commodore's ships. He thought the fire was random and irregular. The maneuvers as the vessels backed and filled seemed to show confusion. Calef noted that the second and third divisions had the sole object of cutting the springs of the British men-of-war to swing them from their broadside. He was correct. The Americans were trying to destroy Mowat's broadside defense. Yet the king's ships suffered only in their rigging.[12]

The weakness of Calef's account hinged upon his timing, the number of American ships, and their maneuvering. He said the engagement took place from 3:00 to 5:00 P.M. (a period of four glasses). Downs, Mowat, the *Hunter* journal, and the journal in the *Nova-Scotia Gazette* mentioned that the action began at 3:30 and continued until 7:00 P.M. The American naval maneuvering related by Calef was missing in their accounts. To the contrary, these other reports lead one to believe that the attacking ships were milling about on their own. Neither Captain Mowat of the *Albany* nor Captain Farnham of the *Nautilus* mentioned any organized attack upon their vessels. Further, as the American armed vessels had sailed together only from Townsend to Bagaduce, the complicated maneuvering necessary to operate three divisions in a coordinated attack seems unlikely. Finally, Calef's nine attacking ships could not be, for the *Warren* and *Charming Sally* did not participate. The *Charming Sally* was guarding the transports. Commodore Saltonstall was on the schooner *Rover* assigning his smaller vessels to various support positions to help General Lovell's expected landing. By Calef's own account the *Warren* did not participate in firing until three days later.[13]

While the ships were cannonading, General Lovell's troops manned their boats for a landing against the high head of land, just north of Dice's Point, covered with trees and bushes. As Lovell watched his boats pull toward the beach, he became worried that the high wind might delay the second boat wave, stranding his first division on the enemy shore. Therefore, he recalled the attack before it made a landing. Yet Drummer William Moody said that "seven of our boats that went to land got almost ashore. The enemy lay in ambush and fired upon us and killed an indian."[14] As Lovell's men retreated, the British garrison manned their ramparts and gave three cheers for their men-of-war. The sailors returned the cheers. That night, as guard boats patrolled the harbor, the British sailors lay at quarters in case the enemy should return.[15]

Monday, 26 July 1779, southwesterly light breezes and clear weather—

At 4:00 A.M. Commodore Saltonstall came alongside the *Tyrannicide* and *Pallas*. He ordered Captains Cathcart and Johnston to run close to shore to cover the landing of troops. Later, at daybreak, General Lovell deployed his first division for a landing at the bluff point. After the wind of the previous day, Lovell wanted to use this calm period to safely put his troops on shore. Generally along the Maine coast during July and August, the early morning is calm. The sea breeze begins later, nearer 10:00 or 11:00 A.M. Captain Mowat reported that "at break of day the Enemy attempted to make good their Landing at the same place as before and were again repulsed."[16]

Later that morning Captain John Brewer, a militia officer who had been inside the British fort two days before, came aboard Lovell's ship to give the general his information. Lovell immediately called for Commodore Saltonstall to hear what Captain Brewer had to say. Years later Brewer recalled: "I then told the Commodore that being all the force he would have to meet, I thought that as the wind breezed up he might go in with his shipping, silence the two vessels and the 6-gun battery, and land the troops under cover of his own guns, and in half an hour made everything his own. In reply to which he hove up his long chin, and said 'You seem to be damn knowing about the whole matter! I am not going to risk my shipping in that damned hole!'"[17] Saltonstall ended that interview.

Captain Dudley Saltonstall's curt reply, "I am not going to risk my shipping in that damned hole," was typical of his terse, superior manner. Undoubtedly neither General Lovell nor Captain Brewer were acquainted with the limitations of large square-rigged ships. These ships were most efficient sailing with the wind. Thus winds blowing astern or off the quarter provided the best result; however, no sailing craft could sail directly into the wind, and square-rigged ships were the least efficient sailing close to the wind. They cannot sail closer than 75 to 80 degrees. To sail into Bagaduce River Saltonstall's ships needed a southwesterly wind to enter. But the crux of Saltonstall's concern was that once in the river his ships could not exit until the wind shifted to a northeasterly direction. Once he sent his ships in, he was in "that damned hole" until the wind made a con-siderable shift or until the ebb current was strong enough to allow his ships to drift out.

Failing twice in less than twenty-four hours caused Lovell and Salton-stall to hold a council of war aboard the *Warren* to assess their situation. At this meeting the officers concluded that the marines should first capture Banks' Island. Marine captain John Welsh, of the *Warren,* would com-mand the landing force. General Lovell had Lieutenant Colonel Revere send a fieldpiece and artillerymen with the marines. Three armed vessels supported the operation. To divert the British attention from the landing, the remaining ships would feint to enter the harbor. Lovell's first division would man their boats feigning to land with the marines. Then, when the marines possessed Banks' Island, his first division was "to fall up the river, and land the opposite side of the Peninsula."[18]

About half past two Commodore Saltonstall sent nine ships in a line across the harbor to begin firing, which the British returned.[19] The can-nonade continued while the tide was in their favor. Captain Williams, of the *Hazard,* which did not participate in the cannonading, went aboard the *Warren* where he found the commodore, General Lovell, and Captain Hallet. About five they watched the sloop *Providence* and the brigs *Pallas* and *Defence* get under way. It being calm, the vessels were under a "white ash wind." Williams thought the sailors rowed "in high spirits."[20] Under oars, the three vessels reached a narrow channel south of Banks' Island. On the way up the channel the *Pallas* encountered rock ledges in shallow water. Captain James Johnston had to anchor and wait for one-half flood tide to clear the rocks.[21] Marine Thomas Philbrook said, "At sunset, I landed with thirty marines from the *Providence,* with as many more from the brig, all under the command of Capt. R. Davis of the continental army [acting as a Marine officer]."[22] In all there were two hundred marines and artillerymen in the landing.

The island's gun battery faced westward covering the harbor's mouth. About forty British seamen from the Transport Service and Royal Marines manned this post. Only two of their four guns were in place. Yet they were facing away from the attacking Americans. Realizing the enemy greatly outnumbered them, the British rapidly fled to their ships. When Captain Mowat saw the retreat, he ordered his transports to move deeper into the harbor.[23]

Meanwhile, as the marines occupied the island, Saltonstall's ships, anchored across the harbor's mouth, feigned an attack to support the first division's landing on the southern tip of Bagaduce. "The Militia were to embark in their boats & make a feint towards the Harbor till the Marines had possession of the Island and then to make a push and land at Bagaduce." With three more hours of daylight and a calm wind, Major Littlefield's detachment foraged ahead of the first division as the advance party. Unfortunately for the operation, a shot from a British ship overturned Littlefield's boat "as they were landing some troops on the south point."[24] Major Littlefield and two privates drowned. Captain Cathcart said, "the plan of the Militia was put a stop to."[25] The first division abruptly returned to its transports. For the third time the militia failed to effect a landing. "These three or four days of Embarrassment on the part of the rebels," Captain Mowat commented, "gave our troops time to do something more to the Fort, to carry up the most necessary Stores, to mount several guns, and in short to devote every Endeavor to the present Exigency."[26]

Meanwhile the marines on Banks' Island quickly reached the summit, where they began building their own breastwork. Their works faced eastward toward the British ships. That evening General Lovell ordered Colonel Revere to send more officers and men with two 18-pounders, one 12-pounder, and a howitzer to the island. Soon sailors and militia joined the marines. All hands worked industriously through the night on their breastwork. Philbrook said they made as little noise as possible so the British ships would not hear them and guess their purpose. In spite of their attempt to be quiet, Mowat realized the Americans were changing the battery's orientation to engage his ships. He ordered the king's ships to slip their anchors and fall back to a second station and align as before. In the process, the *Nautilus* lost its small bower anchor and cable but took its new station. Captain Mowat's second position, while it still defended the harbor, no longer threatened American landings on Bagaduce bluff. By dawn the new American battery was ready.[27]

Tuesday, 27 July 1779, fresh breezes and clear weather—

Each day the general issued his orders, which were recorded in the adjutant's book. This morning the general thanked Captains Hacker, Johnson, and Edmunds for their assistance in the landing. He also singled out the marine officers and men "for their forcible charge on the Enemy . . . likewise to Brig. Genl Wadsworth & the Officers and men under his command for the seasonable Support he gave them."[28] Conspicuous by its absence was any mention of the support given by Commodore Saltonstall.

By daybreak the Americans had their ordnance mounted on the island's high point. Commodore Saltonstall assigned Captain Hacker to command the island. The sailors, protected by the *Providence* and *Pallas,* replaced the marines and militia on what the sailors called Hacker's Island. The marines returned to their vessels. At 9:00 A.M., Captain Johnston opened fire on Mowat's sloops of war. The cannonade continued for three hours. Marine Philbrook could see and hear the shots hulling the British ships. Two 18-pound shot slammed into the *Albany* halfway between her upper and lower decks. The impacts spewed splinters that wounded the surgeon and three men.[29]

That morning Lt. Peter Pollard of the brig *Active* presented a petition to Commodore Saltonstall. Thirty-two lieutenants and masters from the Massachusetts State Navy and the privateers signed it. None of the officers of the three Continental vessels signed. In essence the petitioners encouraged the commodore to descend immediately upon the enemy ships in the harbor. They feared that any undue delay would provide the British with the opportunity to strengthen their fortifications. While they did not offer the commodore any specific plans for the attack, leaving that to his better judgment, they urged action as soon as possible. There is no record of the commodore's response to the petition.[30]

In the afternoon a council of war took place on the *Warren* between the senior sea and land officers, including Captain Welsh of the marines. The subject was to decide the mode and time of attack. General Lovell said he had 850 officers and men for the task. Lieutenant Colonel Revere's artillery added 80 more men. Commodore Saltonstall said that he could supply 227 marines, officers and men. He further said that Captain Hacker had the *Defence* and *Pallas* to defend Banks' Island. All agreed the 1,157 men were sufficient force to bring against the British. When the topic of where to land came up, the naval officers felt it was out of their province and was an army-marine decision. Ultimately these officers scheduled the landing, under cover of the armed ships, for the base of Bagaduce bluff at midnight.[31]

Fog moved up the bay as the council ended. Some militia officers worried that the dampness might effect the powder, making it dangerous to land. But General Lovell, still aboard the *Warren,* insisted that the landings take place. The naval officers assigned to cover the landing received their orders. Captain Cathcart instructed his marine lieutenant to have his men ready at midnight. Then he went to the general's sloop to offer his help preparing boats for the assault. Lovell was confident that Colonel Davis would have everything ready, but he did ask Cathcart for his boat to carry Majors Brown and Lithgrow to see to the troops. Cathcart agreed and accompanied them. They visited most of the transports and found the troops in "great spirit." One colonel was not well, and other colonels complained they had not received their ammunition. When they returned to the general's sloop, Major Brown informed Lovell of the situation with the colonels. General Lovell then sent Major Hill and Lieutenant Downs back to "acquaint the Cols that it was his order to get ready to embark in their boats." Cathcart went with them for the first two or three transports before he left to return to his own brig. He wanted to insure that his marines were ready.[32]

Wednesday, 28 July 1779, West, Light Airs and Variable—

At midnight Major Jeremiah Hill, the adjutant general, received orders to embark the troops. All the marines and some of Colonel McCobb's regiment were on the right under the command of Captain Welsh. Brigadier General Wadsworth led his and Colonel McCobb's divisions in the center. The third division, under Colonel Mitchell, manned the left of the assault line.[33] It took much longer than expected to load the troops. At 1:00 A.M. marine lieutenant William Downs of the *Tyrannicide* loaded his men in the boats. An hour later sailors towed the *Hunter* and *Sky Rocket* through the fog to their stations off the beach. Colonel Joshua Davis, the agent for the transports, said it was 3:00 A.M. before most of the troops embarked. He did not have enough boats and so, at 4:30 A.M., he loaded the left wing on a large sloop.[34] According to Major Todd, the brigade major, the assault was to take place about 5:15 A.M., at sunrise. Due to the various loading times, the planned single assault wave became a piecemeal landing. Yet the heavy fog and the improbable landing site provided the Americans with the element of surprise.

About 3:00 A.M. Commodore Saltonstall again used Captain Parker's *Rover* to go alongside the *Tyrannicide* and ordered its captain "to fire into the Woods with the intent to scour them."[35] Saltonstall repeated his order to the *Hunter* and *Sky Rocket*. For the next half hour the three vessels fired solid and grapeshot into the wooded embankment. Then the marines made the first landing on the right.[36] When the boats scraped along the rocky beach, the marines leaped ashore. Captain Welsh quickly moved his men to the tree line. From above, the British discharged a musket volley. The marines answered from the beach then slung their muskets over their shoulders and began their climb up the precipice.

General McLean had his pickets out in all directions from the fort. He knew that from 25 to 27 July the rebels attempted to land along the western bluff. Yet his western picket, a captain with eighty men, threw back each threat. The general felt that the real assault would be elsewhere. He felt no fear of a landing on the west side because of "the natural strength of the ground." General McLean stated, "on the morning of the 28th, under cover of a very heavy cannonade, they, to my great surprise, effected their purpose."[37]

Lieutenant John Moore was on picket duty that morning just above the marines. Moore, with twenty soldiers, supported the 74th Regiment picket on the British left on the bluff. General McLean posted another picket on the British right. Another seventy soldiers manned a post closer to the fort, between the two pickets in the position of a fleche. This was the first active military engagement for most of the troops and officers. When the American boats first emerged from the fog, Captain Archibald Campbell of the 74th Regiment sent a sergeant back to report the attack. Unfortunately for the British, the sergeant got lost in the woods. The captain then ordered his men to hold their fire until the marines reached the beach. That saved the marines one, possibly two, volleys of musketry fire before they landed. The captain became apprehensive when his reinforcements failed to arrive.[38]

The marine ascent was difficult. Grabbing trees and shrubs to support themselves, they pulled their way up the steep slope. Often a sapling or shrub would pull loose from the ground. Then they would slide back until they grasped a firmer support. Gradually they inched upward, finally reaching the top of the precipice where the woods had a gentler slope. Now the marines advanced using their weapons. As the marines began to appear, almost rising from the ground before them, the British captain commanded one volley of musketry before ordering a retreat. Lieutenant William Downs, commanding the *Tyrannicide* marines, said, "We drove the Enemy from the ground which I think they might have kept till for ever, if they had chose to defend it."[39] It was probably at this time that Captain Welsh received his fatal bullet. William Reidhead of the 74th

Argyle Highlanders said the Americans had "one particular officer killed coming up the hill by one of the 82nd." Sergeant Lawrence's journal supplied a few more details. "One principal officer . . . was killed . . . as he was endeavoring to penetrate his way through a constant fire of small arms, and climbing a steep hill."[40]

Moore and his men were left behind near the 3-gun battery to hold off the attackers. Soon he saw some of his men retreating with the other Scots. He called for his Hamilton men to remain and act like soldiers. As the marines reached the terrace, after their initial climb, the musketry firing increased. Six of Moore's twenty men were killed. The young lieutenant, realizing that his post would be overwhelmed, also retreated to the main fort.[41] Meanwhile, the center section gained its beach shortly after the right wing began its climb. General Lovell, Paul Revere, and the artillerymen were with this group. Major Gawen Brown said, "the troops pushed for the shore and landed and formed as well as could be expected for a body of Militia." Brigade major Hill thought "the troops behaved with Spirit . . . but without any order of Regularity & it was with great difficulty we got them into any order or form of defense." Major Todd believed "the Success of that Assault was as much owing to the Generals Ordering off all the Boats as soon as the Troops disembarked as to the personal Bravery and Resolution of the Officers and Soldiers." An anonymous participant wrote, "Landed our troops under a shower of cannon and musket balls, some loss on both sides—never did men behave with so much courage—They jumped ashore, stood three fires from them, then drove them into their fort. . . . expect every moment to receive orders to make one more bold attack, which I am confident must prove favorable."[42]

General Wadsworth said the enemy opened fire on his group just as the boats touched shore. As each boat emptied, it immediately pushed off from shore. It was a harrowing time. The fleet was forced to fire overhead into the woods; the enemy's musketry rained down from the cliff. Paul Revere said that after forming on the beach they ascended the steep incline. At the top of the first incline, the men re-formed and marched into the woods. A little later General Lovell ordered a halt. While at rest the general received word that the marines had possession of the heights. Receiving this news, Lovell ordered Revere to bring a fieldpiece on shore immediately. The general thought it imprudent to storm the fort until he had a defense line formed. He ordered entrenching tools and armaments brought up. His troops began throwing up lines for defense.[43] Lieutenant

Colonel Paul Revere believed General Lovell should continue his assault and storm the fort. The British "not knowing our strength, and we being flushed with victory, I have no doubt they would have lain down their arms." Yet the Americans spent the remainder of the day digging in while the British waited for the final assault.[44]

As his soldiers on the left flank retreated to the fort, General McLean realized he must recall those on the right flank manning the entrenched border of the swamp before they were encircled.[45] Soon the assaulting Americans were in sight in the woods peering out at the British emplacement. McLean believed the rebels were more numerous than they really were. "I was in no situation to defend myself, I only meant to give them one or two guns, so as not to be called a coward, and then have struck my colors, which I stood for some time to do, as I did not wish to throw away the lives of my men for nothing."[46] After awhile, McLean realized the rebels were not preparing a final assault but were digging in for a siege. The general "considered that every day the Americans delayed the attack was as good to him as another thousand men."[47]

When Captain Cathcart saw a pinnace leave the beach carrying wounded men, he went ashore to look around. On the heights he met General Lovell and offered him two of his 6-pounders. Lovell accepted immediately. Captains Cathcart's and Williams's sailors brought the guns to the heights. When Revere returned from his first mission, Lovell ordered him to send to Banks' Island for the howitzer and fieldpiece. Then the general wanted two 18-pounders and a brass 12-pounder brought ashore. Lovell instructed Revere to call upon Colonel Davis for boats and men to help him. When Revere found a better place to land the cannons, the general told him to call on Captains Williams, Hallet, Holmes, and Cathcart for more support.[48]

Immediately upon taking the high ground, General Lovell scribbled off a letter to Jeremiah Powell, president of the Massachusetts Council. "This morning I have made my landing good on the S.W. head of the Peninsula." He explained the ascent was a hundred feet high and near perpendicular. Lovell told of the thickly wooded trees and brushes his men encountered. Then he said he was building a battery on commanding ground within a hundred rods of the British fort. He concluded, "hope soon to have the Satisfaction of informing you of the Capturing the whole Army, you will please excuse my not being more particular, as you may Judge my situation." General Lovell sent his express by a whaleboat to Falmouth where James Fosdick carried it by horse to Boston. The whaleboat, under sail and oars, traveled faster than a messenger could go inland through the woods. In 1764 a road was cut through from old Fort St. Georges (Thomaston) to Fort Parnall. That road connected to an earlier one from Falmouth to Fort St. Georges. The route was along the west side of the Camden Hills. But seldom-traveled forest trails quickly became overgrown with alders and underbrush; fallen trees blocked the path; crude bridges washed away; and trails soon reverted to almost trackless forests. Lovell sent a second express whaleboat to the Eastward to Colonel John Allen at Machias asking for troops.[49]

With General Lovell's first express, a precedent began for communicating between Bagaduce and Boston. After that, most dispatches traveled by small boat between Bagaduce and Falmouth, then to Boston by horse. For example, Stephen Hall and others of Falmouth received reimbursement for an express sent from Falmouth to Bagaduce by boat for six men and their provisions. John Colwell and Samuel Mason received payment for riding between Falmouth and Boston, or parts of the journey. Evidently this was similar to the later western Pony Express. Caleb Preble earned money by furnishing a horse for a post on his journey from York to Falmouth, a distance of fifty miles. When the message was particularly important, the council sent it to Falmouth by horse and further eastward by both land and sea. This last instance occurred when the council sent General Washington's warning of the British fleet leaving New York for Bagaduce.[50]

Again General Lovell issued his general orders. This time offering "heartily thanks the Brave Officers and Soldiers for their Execution this day in attacking and repelling the Enemies of their country & doubt not they will continue their Endeavour to new levels to the Standard of American Liberty."[51] The general completely ignored the actions of Commodore Saltonstall, his naval cannonade, and his marine's successful assault.

The small battery overrun by the marines allowed Commodore Saltonstall to move his ships closer to the harbor mouth. At 10:00 A.M. the commodore led three ships toward Mowat's battle line. This was Saltonstall's first encounter with the enemy. He received a basic lesson in combat tactics. On the way in he faced the broadside volleys of three ships plus the Half Moon battery's four 12-pounders. He could answer only with his bow guns until he turned broadside, although he also had support from the Banks' Island battery. Calef said the four ships "hauled by the wind at a long shot distance." The fire was brisk for half an hour. The ship's logs of the *Albany* and *Nautilus* recorded light west and northwest winds respectively. The wind may have been the deciding factor. Saltonstall dare not go too deeply into the harbor for fear he would not have the sea room under that wind to return to Penobscot Bay. The *Warren,* in the van, suffered considerably. Calef said, "Her main-mast shot through in two places, the gammoning of her bowsprit cut to pieces, and her fore-stay shot away. Their confusion appeared to be great, and very nearly occasioned her getting on shore; so that they were obliged to let go an anchor."[52] Saltonstall placed the *Warren* in a small inlet off Bagaduce Head where the enemy cannons could not reach her. It took two days to repair the damage. Mowat also learned a lesson during the engagement. He realized that his ships guns were not effective against Banks' Island battery. That night he moved his ships to their third location, deep in the harbor beyond reach of enemy guns.

Not all the action took place on Bagaduce peninsula; at sea off Penobscot Bay Captain Philip Brown, of the *Diligent,* patrolled for British reinforcements. At 6:00 A.M. he sighted a sail on the horizon. Brown gave orders for the chase. At sundown he came upon his prey, a schooner from Halifax with dispatches for General McLean. The schooner captain threw his dispatches over the side in a weighted bag just before being boarded. Brown immediately set out to report to the commodore of his capture, but "thick weather, & but small winds" delayed his return to Bagaduce twenty-four hours.[53]

At day's end Solomon Lovell was euphoric over his success. He confided in his diary, "When I returned to the Shore it struck me with admiration to see what a Precipice we had ascended, not being able to take so scrutinous a view of it in time of Battle, it is a[t] least where we landed three hundred feet high." By that time Lovell had added an extra hundred feet to the bluff's height. He continued, "I don't think such a landing has been made since Wolfe. as [*sic*] soon as we made good our landing I sent for the entrenching tools and we soon had a tolerable covering thrown up."[54]

Thursday, 29 July 1779, Southerly breezes and fair weather—

General Francis McLean reasoned the rebels must number at least 2,500 men. He based that on the number of transports the Americans employed. After all, he only needed six transports for 750 men, and the rebels brought a score of transports. He knew that his mission was to hold out until reinforcements arrived. To do this, he created a light infantry unit. He appointed Lieutenant Caffrae of the 82d Regiment to lead the unit and supplied him with 80 men, 40 from each regiment. With a couple of drummers and fifers to make noise, Lieutenant Caffrae moved against various enemy posts. His objective was not to overwhelm the enemy but to keep the rebels consistently on alert and off balance.

McLean hoped his light infantry would keep the Americans occupied, but he worried that the rebels might storm his fort. Recalling his service among the Dutch, he decided to employ the Chevaux-de-frise, the Friesland Cavalry. In the seventeenth century when the Spanish cavalry swept through Europe's lowlands, the Dutch of Friesland built a device to stop cavalry charges. In front of their emplacements, the Frieslanders placed long wooden beams with sharpened stakes attached as the first obstacle to take the cavalry charge. The device became known as Friesland Cavalry. McLean placed his Chevaux-de-frise behind his abatis as the second obstacle before the Americans reached the fort proper.[55]

Captain Mowat cleared the inner harbor and ordered the transports and other vessels hauled on shore and scuttled. Only the *St. Helena,* a former fourteen-gun letter of marque vessel, remained afloat. Mowat put six guns on her and added her to his battle line. Now Mowat's broadside consisted of four ships in the inner harbor. Captain Mowat sent all the offside guns of his ships ashore for General McLean's use. At 7:00 P.M. he sent all the sailors and marines ashore to work for the general, keeping only the captain, warrant officer, and ten sailors on each ship.[56]

Commodore Saltonstall called a council of war aboard the *Warren* to decide the fleet's actions. He told the captains that General Lovell thought it would not help the land force in its present situation to attack the enemy ships unless the British sailors could be kept from joining their soldiers.[57] He asked the captains their opinion about entering Bagaduce with the citadel upon the eminence and the waterside battery firing on them during their entry before they could engage Mowat's vessels. The captains rejected sailing into Bagaduce immediately. Upon the commodore's question about where to position the ships, they agreed to two lines from the bluffs to Banks' Island. The next question was: should they take possession of the battery captured yesterday, place guns there, and play upon the lower Half Moon Battery? The captains unanimously agreed. They decided that two captains should take charge of the battery and relieve each other. Captains Salter and Thomas were selected unanimously, and each ship would provide an officer and eight men for the undertaking. The naval council of war ended.[58] Evidently General Lovell would not accept the commodore's plan to place a naval force on land, for nothing was done to carry out the proposal.

With Mowat's ships in the inner harbor, Half Moon battery no longer protected the men-of-war. General McLean decided to bring its four 12-pounders up to the main fort and replace them with three navy 9-pounders. But during the day, while the 12-pounders were still at Half Moon battery, their shots forced Saltonstall's ships to move farther back.[59]

Friday, 30 July 1779, Do Fresh breezes and fair wea[the]r—

In the morning Commodore Saltonstall told General Lovell that he proposed attacking the enemy ships that day and he needed all of his marines. Lovell told him he could not spare the marines until he mounted his cannons, for "the enemy might land from yr Ships if they were attacked & attack me with their whole force in which case I would be in Danger of loosing my Cannon, or being totally defeated."[60] In the afternoon Lovell completed his battery. Its two 18-pounders, one 12-pounder, and one howitzer, just a quarter of a mile from the enemy, played upon the British. Both sides cannonaded through the remainder of the day. While little damage was done to the British walls, the storehouse roof within the fort received several shots. General McLean had the storehouse provisions moved outside the fort to a ditch in the rear.[61]

The row galley *Lincoln* arrived from Boston with dispatches. She was an excellent express vessel. Her breadth to length (1 to 7) bespoke speed. Her deck covered her hull from stem to stern. Steered by rudder and tiller, she used two masts with lateen sails and forty- to fifty-foot-long oars in her rowing banks. She was highly maneuverable and could maintain a course whatever the wind. Earlier, John Adams saw a row galley in a trial run advance four miles per hour against a four mile an hour current.[62]

Among the *Lincoln*'s dispatches was a letter from the Navy Board to Commodore Saltonstall. "We take the latest opportunity (by the express boat) to enclose you the deposition of Henry Potberry. . . . The Honble Council of this State & this Board have thought it necessary immediately to dispatch a messenger with Copys thereof to Maj. Genl Lovell & yourself with a view to convince you of the great importance & necessity there is of pushing the Expedition on with Vigour Conceiving no time is to be lost nor no prudent exertions of the land & naval force united to be delayed. Your own reflections upon the matter of the Deposition the possibility & even likelihood of the Enemys being reinforced will we hope Stimulate every officer & private in the Service with fortitude Courage & unswerved diligence in destroying the Cruel & wicked design of our Enemies at Penobscot." Amazingly neither the commodore nor the general referred to this letter in the councils of war nor did Lovell refer to it in his journal.[63]

Saltonstall had sent Philip Brown of the *Diligent* to reconnoiter the coast on 26 July. Brown captured a schooner from Halifax on the evening of 28 July, but weather kept him from returning until 30 July. Based on the Navy Board's letter, Saltonstall told Brown to prepare to leave the next day to watch for reinforcements.

**Saturday, 31 July 1779, Varble Light airs and fair wea[the]r
for the first part; middle and latter foggy—**

Heeding the Navy Board's warning, Commodore Saltonstall decided to augment Philip Brown's lookout mission, adding Captains Hallet of the *Active* and Parker of the *Rover*. When Brown requested permission to capture a ten-gun schooner laying in a harbor to the eastward, Saltonstall refused his request. The commodore said, "She is not worth going after, but it was of more consequence to look out for the Reinforcement and to give him the earliest notice possible."[64] The three vessels departed in company for the mouth of the bay.

With his cannons mounted, General Lovell agreed to release the marines. By now it was evident he felt the marines were his mainstays, and throughout the rest of the siege he always had some marines on shore. Meanwhile, Saltonstall held an informal conference with his captains. They were concerned about the danger the Half Moon Battery presented to their ships while entering the harbor. They decided to send marines and sailors on a night attack to destroy the battery. Their consensus was that Captain Burke of the *Sky Rocket* should command the naval attack force. The commodore asked General Lovell for land support for his endeavor. Lovell agreed, placing General Wadsworth in charge of the participating land unit. Lovell's objective was to destroy communications between the fort and ships. Saltonstall's objective was to destroy the gun emplacement threatening his ships entering Bagaduce.[65]

At sunset General Lovell sent some militia and marines to parade at the captured battery, halfway up the incline over Dice's Point. Marine Lieutenant Downs participated. He said the marines, under Captain Carnes, were on the left; the militia and Indians, under Colonel McCobb, were in the center; and the sailors, from different ships, landed and were on the right. While the land forces were gathering in the early evening, the sailors manned their boats to pull for shore, landing westward of Half Moon Battery. The night was foggy and the British failed to notice the American movements.[66]

Sunday, 1 August 1779, So[uth]erly Light Breezes and fair wea[the]r—

The Americans opened fire at 2:00 A.M., and the British sailors and marines responded with cannons and small arms. When the militia received the enemy fire they broke and ran. The marines on the left and the sailors on the right pressed on and forced the breastwork. Overwhelmed, the British retreated to the fort. With the coming of daylight, the fort's guns opened on the attackers. Augmented by fifty soldiers, the British counterattacked. It was the Americans' turn to be overwhelmed. After destroying a few hogsheads of rum and dismounting the battery's three 9-pounders, the Americans gave up their gains and returned to their lines with eighteen prisoners. Of all the sources cited, only Orderly Sergeant Lawrence of the Royal Artillery and Commissary Reidhead of the 74th Regiment mentioned the participation of the Penobscot Indians and their atrocities. Both said that the Indians scalped and stripped the fallen enemy. Lawrence and Reidhead's accounts were later confirmed by William Hutchings's report that he found "some bloody uniforms, tied up in a blanket, that had been stripped from the English soldiers killed that night."[67]

Captain Mowat viewed the American assault upon Half Moon Battery as a preliminary to sending ships into the harbor to attack his vessels. To strengthen his defenses, he recalled his seamen from the fort. He hoped his four vessels, with their broadsides facing an approaching enemy in the restricted water of the inner harbor of Bagaduce, presented the rebels with a challenge too formidable for them to accept.[68] Commodore Saltonstall reached a different conclusion from the failure to retain the captured battery. He knew the British could reestablish their battery any time they wanted. Thus when he sent his ships in, the enemy could run small cannons down the hill to the battery to harass his fleet as it entered and sortied. Therefore Saltonstall decided to adopt General Lovell's strategy of laying siege to the enemy. Before the day was out, he had his sailors searching for a site to attack the British. His men landed at Swet's Cove, traveled down the path to Westcot's place, and began constructing a battery to bring Mowat's ships under fire. Sergeant Lawrence said, "All last night the rebels were very hurried in making a battery at the back of Waistcoat's [*sic*] house, to damage our shipping." Reidhead added, "All yesternight they were making more batteries N.W. of the Neck and shipping, which is to annoy them."[69]

As was his custom, Lovell commented on the operations in his general orders. "The general returns his sincere and cordial thanks to the brave Officers and Soldiers both in the Land & Marine Department for their very spirited Behaviour in attacking and carrying the Enemy's Redoubt this morning at the same time Laments the loss of those brave few who had the misfortune to suffer in the attempt."[70] Again Lovell spoke vaguely about the actions of the "Marine Department" without mentioning Commodore Saltonstall's participation in the operation. General Lovell's diary entry that day ignored the efforts of the sailors and marines completely. He noted that Wadsworth's command "march'd with order till they receiv'd the fire of the Enemy when they broke, but notwithstanding this some brave fellows push'd into the Battery took 18 prisoners & kill'd 5 of the Enemy destroyed some stores and came off with the loss of 4 Men missing & twelve wound'd." His "brave fellows" who pushed into the battery were Saltonstall's sailors and marines, and one of the missing was marine lieutenant William Dennis.[71]

During that day General Lovell wrote two letters to Jeremiah Powell. His first elaborated on events since the successful landing on Bagaduce. He concluded that he had two choices: either continue a regular siege or risk the fate of a storm. He decided he must continue the siege. Later in the day he wrote again that with the advice of his officers it was "not practicable to gain a Conquest by a storm and not probable without length of time to reduce them by a regular Siege." Therefore, he reiterated that he needed a few regular, disciplined troops, grenades, and four 9-inch mortars with ample shells. He gave both letters to the Reverend Murray to carry to Powell aboard the *Lincoln*.[72]

Commodore Saltonstall also wrote to his superiors that day. His letter was more upbeat than the general's. He wrote of the harmony between the two forces sea and land. He told of the joint operations, dwelling on the landing on Bagaduce. He told of the attack that morning on Half Moon Battery and praised the spirit and vigor of the joint operations. He probably told of providing Colonel Revere with wads and ninety round shot for the artillery's 12- and 18-pounders. In return, the Navy Board wrote, "We acknowledge the Receipt of yours of the 1st Instant & are well pleased to see such a Spirit of Vigour & harmony prevailing in the operations of the Fleet & army."[73] Meanwhile, Colonel John Allan in Passamaquoddy received an express that day from General Lovell requesting immediate aid. The Indians with Colonel Allan were eager to go into battle, but the colonel had business to attend to in Machias before he could go to Penobscot.[74]

* * *

Thus the assault phase ended. The two land commanders had tested each other and were ready for the next phase. General Lovell failed to land his militia on the bluff three times. This reinforced General McLean's view that the real assault would be elsewhere. Thus Lovell's fourth attempt, at the same place screened by darkness and fog, surprised McLean. Based on the number of transports the rebels employed, General McLean assumed the invaders were two to three thousand strong. When the Americans reached the partially completed British fort, McLean was ready to surrender. However, General Lovell's earlier failures caused him to lose faith in his militia. He believed his 227 marines were too few to storm the British. Thus at the completion of a successful assault, General Lovell halted to dig in for a defensive position at a time when success was within his grasp. From then on the two land commanders operated under false assumptions. McLean thought the rebels too numerous for his force; therefore he relied on cannonading and probing the rebels with his light infantry to keep the Americans off balance. Lovell, fearing an attack by British regulars, dug in and was content to cannonade and engage the enemy in light skirmishes.

The two naval commanders had also sparred with each other. Captain Mowat prepared a sound defense for his three sloops of war. Using land batteries and a close line-of-battle formation across the Bagaduce River's mouth, Mowat was in a strong defensive position. Commodore Saltonstall countered by using his marines to capture Banks' Island, eliminating one of Mowat's defensive positions. When the Americans put large guns on

Banks' Island, it forced Mowat to move deeper into the river, preventing his vessels from opposing the American landing on Bagaduce Head. Thus the American assault faced only British musketry from above, for none of the enemy cannons could reach the shore at the bluff's head.

After the landing, the commodore led four ships into Bagaduce River. Saltonstall's *Warren,* in the van, suffered considerable damage from enemy broadsides and the Half Moon Battery. Captain Mowat, realizing the Banks' Island Battery was too powerful for his vessels, moved deeper into the harbor. He also added the *St. Helena* to his broadside defense. Meanwhile, the commodore decided he must neutralize Half Moon Battery before sailing in to challenge Mowat. While the Americans captured Half Moon Battery on 1 August, they could not hold the site. Thus Commodore Saltonstall ended his assault phase. He accepted General Lovell's strategy for his naval force. Saltonstall adopted a siege tactic by looking for battery sites to bring Mowat's sloops of war under fire.

Chapter Four

Siege

Monday, 2 August 1779, So[uth]erly Fair and pleasant wea[the]r—

General Lovell decided to join Commodore Saltonstall in searching for additional battery sites to harass the British men-of-war. To that end he sent General Wadsworth with Captain Daniel Waters of the *Putnam* to reconnoiter some islands east of Banks' Island. He also dispatched the *Lincoln* to Boston with Reverend Murray to deliver his letters to the council.[1] General Lovell also sent Captain Thomas of the *Vengeance* under a flag of truce to General McLean. Thomas asked about an exchange for a marine lieutenant William Dennis from his ship captured during the assault on Half Moon Battery. He learned that Lieutenant Dennis had died of his wounds the day before.[2]

Tuesday, 3 August 1779, Varble Cloudy wea[the]r with Rain—

This day an anonymous letter writer in the *Pennsylvania Gazette* wrote, "Tis said their force is about 900 Highlanders, besides tories and sailors from their ships. We about 1200, besides sailors, and a fine fort within point blank shot of them, and expect every moment to receive orders to make one more bold attack, which I am confident must prove favorable."[3]

At Commodore Saltonstall's request, General Lovell sent a detachment under Brigadier Wadsworth with one 18-pounder, one 9-pounder, and a fieldpiece to the fleet's battery emplacement at Westcot's place. Seamen from the *Hazard* and *Tyrannicide* helped move the artillery from the transports to shore. They landed in Swet's Cove and hauled their guns one and a quarter miles to the intended site. As he had done with the battery captured by the marines, Lovell had his militia man the Westcot Battery.[4]

Both Orderly Sergeant William Lawrence of the Royal Artillery and Commissary William Reidhead of the 74th Regiment had followed the building of the Westcot Battery since 1 August. Lawrence noted that the rebels worked on their battery positioned to play on the British ships. Reidhead also said the battery was to annoy their shipping. Calef first mentioned this battery on 3 August saying that the enemy was busy building a battery to the northward, on the mainland, just above the king's ships. Surprisingly the *Albany* and *Nautilus,* the intended objects of the Westcot Battery, first noted the battery construction in their ship's logs on 4 August.[5]

Wednesday, 4 August 1779, Varble Pleasant wea[the]r—

The Westcot Battery began firing at the British ships. General Lovell thought the distance was too great to be effective, yet Calef said the fire was brisk and the men-of-war suffered damage in their rigging and hulls. The distance was too great for the ships' lighter guns to return fire; therefore Captain Mowat kept his ships' company below deck for safety. His official report stated that some shots hulled the ships but did not cause any material damage. The *Nautilus* received a shot in its hull. The captain also said that the distance was so great he did not return the fire.[6]

As a diversion to the cannonade, Lieutenant Caffrae of the 82d Regiment took a party of light infantry out in front of the American battery opposite the British fort. His musicians played Yankee Doodle in defiance of the rebels. General Lovell feared this was a prelude to a British attack upon the new battery on the main. He ordered a hundred men to reinforce General Wadsworth, fifty men held in readiness, and his whole army under arms. Lovell concluded that "the Men are much fatigu'd being continually on some service or other, either Picket or throwing up works, and are begining to [be] sickly." Calef reported some skirmishing between the pickets with a few losses on both sides. Among the enemy's casualties were several Indians.[7]

Thursday, 5 August 1779, Varble Do weather—

Captain Mowat decided that the Westcot Battery, commanding the opposite shore from Bagaduce, would allow the rebels to make a lodgement similar to their attack upon Half Moon Battery. If that took place, the enemy forces would separate the fort and men-of-war. He felt it necessary to build a redoubt, manned by fifty seamen, equipped with eight ship's guns, to keep his communications with the fort open. He had a square redoubt marked off and began construction.[8]

General Lovell also planned a defensive work. The British had yet to build the canal across the Bagaduce Isthmus when the expedition arrived. Thus from 2 to 5 August, Lovell cleared a road across the isthmus, built a covered way leading to the isthmus, and placed a small battery on the mainland just northeast of it. This was his escape route to the mainland in case he was unable to board his transports. Brigade Major William Todd felt the soldiers' fear that the privateer ships might leave the expedition unexpectedly diminished after the construction of the escape route to the mainland.[9] Yet Wadsworth felt that was not enough. He asked General Lovell if he should go upriver to find ground "Convenient for Covering the Shiping" should enemy reinforcements arrive. Lovell replied, "We had no Forces to spare" in case they found such ground to do anything.[10]

Colonel Davis, as the agent for the transports, grew uneasy at the inactivity of Saltonstall and the fact that Lovell completed a secure land retreat for his men. He worried for the safety of his transports. He asked the general what he planned for the transports in case of a retreat. General Lovell replied that he had no "power to secure a retreat for them while the Enemy Shiping kept possession of the Harbor of Bagaduce."[11] Then General Lovell sent a letter to Commodore Saltonstall saying, "I have proceded as far as I Can on the present plan and find it inafectual for the purpose of disloging or destroying the Shiping I must therefore request an ansure [*sic*] from you wether you will venter your Shiping up the River in order to demolish them or not that I may conduct my Selfe accordingly /s/ S Lovell BG."[12] This was the first request Lovell made to Saltonstall to enter Bagaduce Harbor.

Friday, 6 August 1779, SW Pleasant wea[the]r—

Upon receiving General Lovell's letter, Saltonstall held a council of war aboard the *Warren*. The commodore asked whether the ships should go in as the general requested. The assault captains, Thomas, Holmes, Nathan Brown, Burke, Salter, Carnes, and Waters, said nay. Among the auxiliary ship captains, Hacker, Williams, and Cathcart said yea, and Philip Brown, and Hallet said nay. The captains then decided that, if the general stormed the citadel, they would go and destroy the enemy shipping. What if the general took position on the lower ground behind the fort and held it? The auxiliary captains Hacker, Cathcart, Williams, and two assault captains Waters and Burke said they would go in. The final question was, what if the general stormed the citadel at the time the ships moved in? Seven assault captains agreed to go in, Saltonstall, Carnes, West, Holmes, Salter, Thomas, and Brown. Apparently Waters and Burke, having agreed to go in if the general held the low ground, felt they had expressed their yes on the earlier question. Thus nine of the ten assault captains would attack if the general stormed the fort simultaneously. Alexander Ross, the tenth assault captain, may have been absent, for there was no record of his casting a vote. This was the first council of war to name the participants voting. Commodore Saltonstall sent the proceedings immediately to General Lovell.[13]

Lovell held his council of war that same day. He read the fleet's proceedings to his officers. Then he asked them if, in their present condition, they would support the fleet by storming the fort. Their answer was a unanimous no.[14] Lovell immediately entrusted the proceedings of the two councils of war to Major David Braddish and sent him to Boston. The general told Braddish that "in our present situation it was impracticable" to support the fleet. Braddish and six men rowed and sailed a small boat to Falmouth. Then Braddish hired horses to ride to Boston. He arrived on the morning of 12 August.[15]

Saltonstall's council of war provided the questions the captains grappled with and their individual vote. Unfortunately for posterity, the reasons behind the participants' votes were missing. Yet at other times some captains revealed their rationale. The *Hunter* journal for 9 August stated, "after much debate and vote passed for the ships to go into the harbour, and attack the British ships, though it was judged by the Commodore and many others, that the attack would be attended with great risque and danger of having our ships much injured, as we should be exposed to the fort, which we could not in the least annoy." Three days later the writer recorded that "unless the General could possess himself of the point near the British ships, it would not be advisable for our ships to go in, as they would be exposed to the fort and artillery rundown from the point, which would annoy us to a very great degree; as the harbour is so narrow that we cannot readily get out again,—therefore the plan for the ships going in has proved abortive."[16]

Captain Nathan Brown of the *Hunter* answered questions as follows:

Q. What obsticles had your shiping to encounter provided you made the attack excepting the firing of shiping?

A. The guns from their main Fort, which I suppose was half a mile distant from the shore. The weight of their metal we supposed twelve pounders. The hulls of our shiping would not have been exposed to the fire of the Fort at the time we should be actually engaged with the ships.

Q. Whether the Enemys Shiping could not have been destroyed, provided the general had not taken as aforesaid?

A. In my opinion they could.

Q. Why was the attack not made?

A. My opinion was that the Shiping could receive more damage in the Attack than we could benefit by the destruction of the enemy shiping. The damage we should have received would have been mostly from the fort, as it is possible the Enemys Shiping would not have fired more than once or twice.[17]

Captain John Carnes of the *Hector* said, "It is my opinion that our Navy might have destroyed the Enemy's fleet . . . but this would have been at a great risk from the fire of the main Fort, for we should have been exposed to it going up, in lying there, & in our return."[18] Captain Titus Salter of the *Hampden* thought that the attack upon the Half Moon Battery "removed every Difficulty out of the Way that might Endanger our Shipping in going into Bagaduce harbour to attack . . . [and] if it was thought not safe in lying in the Harbor after taking the Enemys Ships which might be Doon with Ease when ever Orders were given for that Purpose. We should not [have] been obliged to lay exposed to the Fire of the Enemy's Fort as there was a large Bay that we might gone out of Reach of the Enemy's Shott."[19]

Captain Jonathan Parsons, who was with the expedition, presented an articulate explanation of the captains' views. He noted that the advantages gained versus the damages received was an important consideration. "If we had gone in we must have [torn out except the last four letters . . . *erly* (properly?)] moored and our broad Sides to bare in which time we must doubtless meet with considerable loss, and damage, and the probability was that they would then set fire to their Ships, retreat to the Citadel, and leave us to stand the blast of their Ships and the fire of their main Fort, till we could get out again, . . . what advantage have we gained, . . . it would not have facilitated the reduction of the Enemy's Fort[.] Genl Lovell could not at any time have fought them in open ground, . . . by this line of

Conduct we should have subjected our Fleet to loss, and damage, for that which upon the Reduction of their main Fort would naturally fall to us without either: Genl Lovell had sent for Men, & Means sufficient for that purpose, and from the importance of the object, and their interest of those to whom he applied, he had an undoubted right to expect their speedy arrival, therefore the proposed plan of going in under these circumstances was unjustifiable."[20]

* * *

Why did the ship captains fear entering the harbor? At this juncture of the expedition most historical narrators blamed the failure to attack on either the commodore's cowardliness, the privateer captains' self-interest, or both. Except for Admiral Colby Chester's study, no narrative discussed the technical limitations of square-rigged vessels. By design, these vessels were most efficient when pushed by the wind; therefore, they sailed best when running free with the wind astern or off the quarter. No sailboat could sail directly into the wind. Yet by sailing at an angle to the wind (tacking) it could zigzag a course toward the wind. A square-rigger, the least efficient sailing vessel for getting back to windward, sailed no closer than 75 to 85 degrees to the wind (close-hauling). At the end of each tack the ship must come about to the opposite tack. According to Jack Coggins, a square-rigger of this period "meant much pulling and hauling—slackening and tautening of innumerable lines—and might take as much as fifteen minutes before all was sheeted home and belayed and the vessel on her new course." Thus tacking in a square-rigger was a laboriously slow task, taking considerable minutes on each turn of the zigzag.

Captain Richard Bailey of HMS Rose Foundation sailed HMS *Rose* as captain for sixteen years; three of those years were before the ship had engines installed. When asked to comment on Coggins's statement of fifteen or more minutes, he replied, "well, that is not really true. It depends on how hard the wind is blowing. How competent the people are, what kind of current there is. We can tack this ship in five to seven minutes if there is a nice brisk wind of say fifteen knots, not much in the way of seas, and competence among the crew. If we can do something in five to seven minutes, they [the eighteenth-century crews] could probably do it in less." Then Captain Bailey began to cite exceptions such as sailing in a river. He noted the ship's stern generally tending down current, and the head rig generally tending down wind and sitting sideways in a light breeze: "So there are a lot of idiosyncrasies to ships like this and it's difficult to say how long [tacking would take]." Captain Bailey continued, "We tend to time everything by push button today—you know push the button and it happens immediately. It just does not work that way."[21]

A rule of thumb says that under the best conditions a square-rigger could make one-half the wind speed. Yet in combat, dry, tarred wooden hulls and dry canvas presented a fire hazard, especially when the crew deployed their guns and gunpowder on deck. Thus when engaged, square-riggers normally clewed up or raised their courses, the lower sails, creating fighting sails. These technical limitations could result in Saltonstall's assault vessels crawling into combat.

The Bagaduce River was a tidal fairway, so it was possible for a vessel to use the tidal current to enter or sortie without waiting for a wind. Yet wind and tide are sometimes complicated matters. If the current was favorable to the vessel's destination and the wind opposed, the ship could move with the tide and use the wind to move back and forth across the current for control. This would be a windward tide. If the current was favorable to the vessel's destination and the wind was in the same direction, it was a leeward tide. This combination seemed to favor a more rapid movement. Yet under certain circumstances the vessel was under less control. For example, a ship moving downwind near the rate of the current, within a knot or so, would not be moving through the water and thus would have no steerageway. Without steerageway, there was no directional control over the ship to avoid a fixed obstruction.[22]

Overlooked by most narrators was the fact that the square-riggers had little sea room in the harbor to maneuver to expose their broadsides. Both Captains Parsons and Hacker said the ships needed to moor to bring their broadsides to bear.[23] Yet mooring a square-rigger with a spring hawser to bring the batteries to bear was a complicated time-consuming evolution. This evolution done in the face of four broadside vessels and the enemy fort, later the fort and redoubt, invited heavy causalities.

Gunnery was an important factor in the captains' reluctance to enter Bagaduce Harbor. This was the era of smoothbore cannons firing spherical projectiles. The propellant was black powder. Aiming and firing were particularly difficult aboard ship. The gunner had to predict the pitch and roll of his vessel to hit his target. Generally gunners aimed along the gun barrel then stepped away before firing, to escape the gun's recoil. Of course the pitch and roll in the harbor were at a minimum. Still, cannon fire was inaccurate at long ranges. When attacking fortress walls, ships' gunners preferred "a range of 60 to 80 yards, a range of 100 to 150 yards was acceptable, but 300 yards or more was considered excessive." From the harbor combat area to the fort on the heights was between 1,000 and 1,200 yards. In addition, the fort was at a 200-foot elevation. With the flat trajectory of Saltonstall's guns, the commodore and many other fleet officers believed it was impossible to harm the fort. On the other hand, the fort, from its elevation and with its larger guns, could keep the rebel fleet in range throughout an assault operation. That was why the assault captains demanded cooperation from the land force. A militia attack could divert some of the fort's guns from the fleet. Further, it would keep the enemy from running smaller guns down the declivity to challenge the assaulting Americans.[24]

Operating under these limitations, what would be the best condition for an attack? The participating seamen left no answer to this question, probably because it was common knowledge; however, other officers experienced in sailing gave their opinions of how Saltonstall should have attacked Captain Mowat's vessels. Rear Admiral Colby M. Chester, U.S. Navy, served on sailing ships during the Civil War, surveyed the coast of Maine, and worked in the Hydrographic Office in Washington. In retirement he made a critical analysis of the Penobscot Expedition. He considered that the currents, the narrow channel, and the variableness of the winds made "it almost impossible for wind-propelled vessels of any considerable size to manoeuvre in the [Bagaduce] river except at slack water, and then only when the wind is favorable. . . . The idea of the American Ships entering the harbor of Bagaduce under the circumstances [of the land batteries and British ships would] be foolhardy in the extreme, except as a last resort."[25]

Captain Elliot Rappaport of the Maine Maritime Academy's schooner *Bowdoin* sailed out of Castine for eight years. He said if he planned an attack on Castine in a square-rigged ship he would wait for a flood tide in the afternoon with a southwest wind to sail in as quickly as possible. After destroying the sloops of war, he knew he could go beyond the British guns to wait for darkness to leave on the ebb when the wind was calm. The current averaged two or three knots, sometimes as strong as four or five knots depending on a full moon tide, a spring or neap tide.[26] Captain Robin Walbridge of the Tall Ship Bounty Foundation sailed HMS *Bounty* for fourteen years. After looking at the Penobscot River chart, he said that winds from 150 through 330 degrees would be good for entering Castine, but a square-rigged vessel could not leave under those winds. When sailing to windward, he figured that he sailed seven miles tacking for every mile made into the wind. Under fighting sails, his speed would be less than half normal speed. Further, he said that a more important reason to clew up lower sails in combat was to allow the captain to see well enough to conn his ship during the action. If he had to enter under Saltonstall's conditions, he wanted either a strong breeze on the ebb so that if his vessel received damage he could drift out of the harbor or, preferably, to ride the flood in and have the wind to push him out.[27]

Captain Bailey looked at the Penobscot River navigation chart and a copy of Calef's chart and said, "It would be very easy to get there in a Southwesterly breeze, but it might be another matter to get out. . . . You would be committed to staying for a while." He did not want to speculate on Saltonstall's options for there were too many unknown intangibles for him to venture an answer.[28] Captain Austin Becker, of the Providence Maritime Heritage Foundation, sailed the Continental Sloop *Providence* for two years. He felt that entering Bagaduce harbor with a southwesterly breeze would be easy, but leaving would be difficult even for a sloop. His sloop, without engine power, could get no closer to windward than 60 degrees, or 70 degrees if he carried his square-rigged topsail. The narrowness of the harbor entrance would also necessitate a slow passage while tacking to exit. After examining John Calef's map of Bagaduce and his navigation chart, he exclaimed, "Oh! *That* was Commodore Saltonstall's 'damned hole.'"[29]

Michael Nancarrow, professor of mathematics at Jacksonville University, has enabled us to visualize Saltonstall's problem mathematically. To simplify the problem, he assumed that the Americans needed to sail one nautical mile to get out of the harbor after engaging the enemy ships. He also assumed they would be sailing into the wind with negligible current and tacking at an angle of 80 degrees in a channel 600-yards wide. He came to the following conclusions: To proceed one mile sailing directly into the wind under the assumed conditions, a ship would have had to travel a total distance of 5.76 nautical miles; it would have had to tack 19.14 times; and assuming that it was traveling at two nautical miles per hour, it would have taken 2.88 hours to travel one mile. (For Professor Nancarrow's charts and calculations, see the appendix.) Of course, judging from maps it is apparent that the American ships would have had to sail farther than one mile after engaging the enemy sloops. Throughout their departure from Bagaduce Harbor they would have been subjected to fire from the Citadel, which was above and beyond their gun range. It would have been a harrowing several hours of defenseless travel.

* * *

Meanwhile, minor skirmishes and occasional cannon firing continued that day. The Westcot Battery cut some rigging and dismounted a 6-pounder on the *North*. Captain Mowat sent seventy seamen from his ships ashore to build his sailors' redoubt. Mowat also sent a quantity of musket cartridges for soldiers in the fort. That night guard boats from both sides exchanged a few shots during their patrols.[30]

Saturday, 7 August 1779, Varble Calm & Clear wea[the]r—

That morning General Lovell called a council of war on board the *Hazard*. Both land and sea officers attended. Lovell wanted to know, in light of the two councils the day before, what further measures should be taken. Commodore Saltonstall suggested either "Strike a bold Stroke, by storming the Enemys works, & going in with the Ships, or raise the Siege." General Lovell replied that he was "not in a Situation with his present force to Storm."[31] Lovell then asked Saltonstall the status of his sailors, were they "easy in their Situation & whether a sufficient number of them to defend the Ships can be held to carry on any further Operations." Saltonstall replied that due to desertions among his impressed seamen it was improbable. He then asked his captains their views. Captains Holmes, Carnes, N. Brown, West, and Edmunds felt it was improbable. Captains Salter, Waters, Thomas, Williams, Burke, Hacker, and Cathcart felt there was no difficulty with their crews. Among the ten assault captains five did not feel they could carry operations much further. Four assault captains felt they could continue, and Captain Ross, of the *Monmouth*, was either absent or failed to voice his opinion.

General Lovell then said he thought he could take possession of the land to the rear of the fort. He believed 400 men could hold the present line while he took 750 men to operate between the fort and the enemy ships. Colonel Revere answered that there were not that many soldiers available. Lovell replied that he expected that number soon. Captain Burke then asked the field officers if they thought they could lead their men in the open field against the British. Lieutenant Colonel Jordan felt he could. Colonels McCobb, Howard, Mitchell, Revere, and Major Hunter felt they could not. Lovell then asked his field officers if it would be expedient to divide the army and take possession in the rear of the fort. Lieutenant Colonel Howard felt it was possible; Colonels McCobb, Mitchell, Revere, Jordan, and Major Hunter did not believe it possible. Commodore Saltonstall asked General Lovell if he could reduce the enemy without a reinforcement of men and stores. Lovell said he could not.

Then General Lovell asked the council whether the siege should continue or not. Thirteen voted to continue: Colonels McCobb, Mitchell, Lieutenant Colonels Howard, Jordan, Major Hunter, General Wadsworth, General Lovell, Captains Salter, Waters, Cathcart, Williams, Thomas, and Hacker. Three of the assault captains, Salter, Thomas, and Waters, voted to stay. Eight voted to end the siege: Lieutenant Colonel Revere, Captains Carnes, Holmes, West, Brown, Burke, Edmunds, and Commodore Saltonstall. Thus six of the assault captains and one auxiliary captain voted to end the siege. Colonel Revere voted to raise the siege because "if we could not Dislodge the Enemy in seven days, we ought to Quit the ground; for w[h]ere the Enemy has command of the Sea, and the fate of the Expedition, depends on the movements, on that Element, we ought not to risqued so much as we did." The council closed without making a final decision, concluding to continue the siege until information from Boston respecting reinforcement arrived.[32]

Paul Revere later amplified the council of war's discussion: "The Genl said he could not subdue the Enemy without a Reinforcement of men and Stores. The Field Officers of the Militia said their men would not face the Enemy in the open ground. . . . Six capts of the Armed Vessels, said, their men were so uneasy and deserted so fast that if we staid 3 days longer, they should not have enough men left to work their Vessels, that they had been there, 8 days longer than they had expected, their was danger of a Reinforcement to the Enemy; and should a Superiour Fleet to theirs arrive we should lose the whole Fleet."[33]

This council of war presented Commodore Saltonstall with a choice of equally unsatisfactory alternatives. General Lovell and his officers turned down supporting the commodore's assault ships in an all-out attack on the British forces. The majority of officers overrode the assault captains' desire to raise the siege if the land force could not support their attack. The assault ship captains believed their losses would be unacceptable without the assistance of the land force. Every day's delay brought the probability of British reinforcement. Yet Commodore Saltonstall could not raise the siege and sail off leaving the land force to its fate. Saltonstall's dilemma seemed to have no satisfactory solution.

At the end of the inconclusive council both commanders renewed their own strategies. General Lovell detached a small party on his right into the fields as a decoy to draw out a British party. He had one hundred men concealed in the woods to aid his decoys. The British sent out about eighty men to rush the Americans and cut them off from their lines. Lovell's hundred soldiers rushed the enemy and a skirmish followed. It was a minor affair with two Americans hit; one was wounded, the other died. The British had two wounded, Lieutenant McNeil of the 82d, and a private. Commodore Saltonstall continued his plan of building batteries nearer to Mowat's vessels. He set out with Captains Waters, Williams, Salter, Holmes, and Burke in two or three small boats to reconnoiter the point north of Haney's Point (Henry Point) where the Americans already had a picket. Captain Farnham of the *Nautilus* saw the enemy boats cross the lower part of the harbor for the mainland. He sent Lieutenant Congalton with several boats to chase the rebels. The Americans landed, fired on the British sailors, then fled into the woods to escape capture. Meanwhile, Captain Mowat organized a larger party to capture the rebels. Lieutenant Caffrae of the Light Infantry Company with fifty soldiers manned Mowat's boats. When this second wave arrived on shore the soldiers and sailors went into the woods searching for the Americans. When Saltonstall's remaining captains saw the British force land to hunt for the commodore and his party, they sent a hundred sailors to the rescue. The British forces, outnumbered, returned to their ships towing their prizes, the original boats abandoned by the Americans. The Americans rescued the initial reconnoitering party, except Commodore Saltonstall. The only casualty was Captain Ross, who broke his leg during the flight. Later Lieutenant Story acted as captain of the *Monmouth*.[34]

Sunday, 8 August 1779, SW Light airs and Foggy weather—

Early in the morning American sailors sighted Commodore Saltonstall on the shore and returned him to his ship. He said that he ran deep in the woods eluding his pursuers. He could not find his way back to the shore until early morning. General Lovell decided that the fleet's new battery site was sound. He sent Brigadier Wadsworth with volunteers to the point north of Haney's Point to start construction.[35]

Captain Hoysteed Hacker of the Continental armed sloop *Providence* penned a letter to General Lovell and Commodore Saltonstall. "Seeing we are Come to this period of time without any Determined Resolution, I think it my Duty to make my Sentiments known, Which the Subsequent lines are my full Oppinion."

1. The *Warren*, *Putnam*, and *Hampden* would enter the harbor, anchor abreast of, and engage the enemy ships. [It appeared that Captain Hacker was not aware that the British line held four ships.]

2. The *Sally, Vengeance, Black Prince, Hector, Monmouth, Sky Rocket,* and *Hunter* were "to form a Line against their works on the Hill, and to keep up a Moderate but Continual Fireing in order to Annoy them, so as to take their Attention" from the first three ships.

3. Simultaneously, the battery on Nautilus Island would cannonade the enemy.

4. The ships would land one hundred marines to join three hundred militia to assault the "Lately Errected Battery on the Low Ground," to intercept British seamen and marines in case they should try to reinforce their fort.

5. "At the Same time for our Capital Fort to keep up a fireing of Cannister & Grape to heave Shels or any Other war like Combustables they mey think Necessary to Confuse & Annoy them whilst we continue our Attack on the Shipping and Lower Works, takeing Care at the Same time that they don't fire from our Foart Any Shot that may Damage our Troops between the Enemies upper and Lower Forts."

6. General Lovell with the rest of his army in his fort could then decide what to do next.

Captain Hacker also solved the objection of the last council concerning possessing the lower battery, which the Americans could not hold. He suggested that the men go under the bank, which would be free from the enemy and covered by the assault ships. Finally, in a nota bene he wanted the general and commodore to call a council immediately.[36]

Captain Hacker was not the only one thinking of the future. After General Lovell failed to provide a plan for retreat, Colonel Davis decided he needed to make a set of signals for his transports, just in case. When he showed his signals to Lovell, the general ordered that only a general officer or Colonel Davis could authorize employing the signals. Davis then distributed them to his captains.[37]

One of Captain Mowat's plans for the future came to fruition this day.

At 10:00 A.M. the Westcot Battery brought the fieldpiece to bear on the British sailors working on the seaman's redoubt. Yet the redoubt's northern facing, built first, protected the laboring seamen. Also General McLean provided soldiers daily to stop any American landing from destroying the work in progress. By evening McLean and his engineer approved the completion of the redoubt. Although the seaman's redoubt had smaller guns and a less advantageous location than the earlier Half Moon Battery, it gave Mowat one more battery of eight ship's guns to bear on rebel assault vessels.[38]

Monday, 9 August 1779, Variable Light airs & foggy weather—

It was about this date that Saltonstall learned he could sail up the Bagaduce River out of reach of the fort's guns. Captain Waterman Thomas, a volunteer officer, said that a few days after the Westcot Battery opened he heard Westcot tell Saltonstall "that he could carry the Warren & all the Ships up the Majabagduce River about two miles above the Enemies Ships, & Also told him there was pleanty of water up the South Bay four miles for his ship."[39] Captain Carnes of the *Hector* said, "After this discovery it was determined in council to attack the Enemys Shiping provided Gen Lovell would take a post so as to cut off the communication between the Enemy's Shiping & fort."[40] The commodore displayed a signal for his captains to come aboard the *Warren*. Although not calling a formal council of war, he wanted to consult on future actions.

The captains spent much time debating their options. Throughout the discussion the captains were uneasy because the siege had taken so much time. They also worried about the number of desertions from their ships. Finally, they voted to attack the British ships, contingent upon the army attacking the fort simultaneously, "though it was judged by the Commodore and many others, that the attack would be attended with great risque and danger of having our ships much injured, as we should be exposed to the fort, which we could not in the least annoy." They sent their decision to General Lovell for his concurrence.[41]

Tuesday, 10 August 1779, SW Light breezes & variable—

Commodore Saltonstall called a council of war for his captains. He wanted to discuss the most advisable measure to follow. One was Captain

Hacker's letter; evidently he had not seen it the day before while consulting with his captains. The other was the plan already begun to build a battery on the eastern shore opposite the shipping. Should they "pursue Captain Hacker's plan or the Plan and Battery in conjunction?"[42] Before the naval officers had an opportunity to voice their opinions General Lovell and his field officers arrived. Saltonstall suspended his questions and deferred to the general. After some discussion of the army's taking possession of the grounds, the general asked his officers if they could hold the ground eastward of the enemy's citadel. The land officers decided unanimously that they could hold the ground. Then the fleet captains all agreed to go in and destroy the enemy's shipping. The council concluded to hold a coordinated land and sea attack the next day.[43]

James Morris, master of the *Hazard,* had served as master under the commodore when Saltonstall was captain of the frigate *Trumbull.* As the *Hazard* would not be in action during the attack, Morris received permission to board the *Warren* to help his commodore. He found the crew building barricades on the bow in anticipation of receiving the concentrated fire from the British ships during the *Warren's* approach.[44]

Wednesday, 11 August 1779, SW Light airs & cloudy weather—

Commodore Saltonstall deployed his marines between his assault ships and ashore for the storming. He sent a first lieutenant and 24 men to the *Hampden,* and a second lieutenant and 15 men to the *Putnam.* Lieutenant Downs of the *Tyrannicide* went ashore "with 25 as good Marines as ever walked a Vessells deck every Officer & man on board of our Vessell seemed animated with a fresh flow of Spirits on thinking that we [were] to make a general attack." In all, Saltonstall supplied Lovell with 120 marines under Captain Davis.[45]

General Lovell ordered Major Jeremiah Hill, his adjutant general, to parade 600 good men by detachments or volunteers if possible. Major Hill called on Colonels Mitchell and McCobb for 200 each. He asked Major Cousins for 73 and the remainder from the new levies of men from the surrounding area. Mitchell raised 200 with difficulty, and his good men included boys, old men, and invalids. Colonel McCobb could find only 146 soldiers. Of Major Cousins's men, 20 deserted the night before, and in the morning he sent 30 soldiers out to find them. Cousins did the best he could, and with the levies from the new men, Major Hill mustered 400 instead of the 600 requested. Among the new men were two companies of the 5th Militia Regiment, Deer Isle and Naskeag, from the mainland southeast of Bagaduce. These 143 men arrived sometime between 8 and 11 August. They were assigned to Colonel McCobb's regiment. The officers and men thought they were going to storm the fort, which Hill gave as the reason for not filling the quotas: "Numbers of men Skulking in the Woods to prevent the suppose[d] impending Danger. Col. Mitchell's officers were so terrified at the idea of Storming, that they found fault with the Colonels nomination & absolutely drew Lots on the parade who should go to take the command of their men."[46]

With 200 fewer men than he expected, Lovell did not believe his forces were ready to storm the enemy or to hold the ground between the fort and the fleet. General Lovell sent word he "was not ready with his troops."[47] Also he sent a letter to Commodore Saltonstall stating the time had come for his department to act. "The destruction of the Enemy's ships must be effected at any rate, although it might cost us half our own"; however, Lovell did not think that would be the case. He heard from an enemy deserter that "the moment you enter the harbor they [the British] will destroy them [their vessels]; which will effectually answer our purpose." As for building more batteries against the enemy, it was out of the question; they had run out of time. "The information of the British ships at the Hook (probably sailed before this time) is not to be despised; not a moment is to be lost."[48]

Rather than carry out the plan for the land and sea forces to cooperate, he decided to "try my own men after so much Skirmishing how they wou'd act in a Body." He sent 200 men, out of the enemy's sight, to the deserted Half Moon emplacement. From there small parties attempted to decoy the British out into the field for an engagement. General McLean sent a hundred men, out of rebel sight, to hide in a cornfield close by the battery. Nothing happened all afternoon as both sides waited for the other to act. Finally, as it grew dark, Lovell gave the signal to retreat. As the Americans withdrew, the British "sallied from their concealment & gave them a fire which put them in such confusion that notwithstanding the superior behavior of the three Commanders it was impossible to form them but retreated in the greatest hurry."[49] According to the British, 50 light infantrymen gave the rebels a "volley of small arms and a tap of the Grenadier's march, accompanied with Yankey Doodle, which so daunted these poor devils that they hove some of their arms away and ran to the woods."[50]

Later that evening General Lovell held a council of war at his headquarters. Officers present were Brigadier Wadsworth, Colonels McCobb and Mitchell, Lieutenant Colonels Revere and Howard, and Majors Hunter and Larabee. The question discussed was, in view of the day's performance, could they hold the enemy's fort and the ground to the rear? They were unanimous in agreeing that they could not. Besides citing their lack of numbers, the council concluded "the great want of Discipline & Subordination many of the Officers being so exceedingly slack in their Duty, the Soldiers so averse to the Service & the wood in which we are encamped so very thick that on an alarm or any special occasion nearly one fourth part of the Army are skulked out of the way and conceal'd. The Council then broke up."[51] The minutes of the council seemed inconclusive. However, the *Hunter* journal for 11 August was quite conclusive. "A Council was convened this night by the General in camp, the result of which was, That he judging his army was not sufficient to oppose the British on account of their inexpertness and want of courage, and not being in expectation of any reinforcement, thought it highly advisable, with the advice of his officers to raise the siege."[52] Another influencing factor was dwindling ordnance supplies: shells used up, only a few 12-pound cartridges left, and three-quarters of small arm cartridges expended. They agreed to tell Commodore Saltonstall of their decision the next day.[53]

Thursday, 12 August 1779, SW Pleasant weather—

General Lovell and Colonel Revere boarded the *Warren* to relay the army's decision to the commodore. Lovell asserted that he lacked an adequate number of men to stand with the enemy in the field and he was going to take off his heavy cannons. Saltonstall appeared surprised, saying he was ready to go into the harbor. The two leaders decided to hold another council to decide what to do. Saltonstall called a naval council of war to inform his officers of the decision reached by the army's council of war held the night before. His question to his officers was, "whether under our present Circumstances there is a propriety in the Ships going in." The council responded no and agreed to wait on the general to know what other measures he might propose. The vote was twelve nays to two yeas, Captains Waters and Salter casting the yeas.[54]

In spite of the army officers' decision the previous evening, General Lovell pleaded with his militia to stand firm. "My Soldiers, By the blessing of Providence we have arrived to this height, toward the Reduction of the Enemy, we have faced them with every resolution, and have forced them from Sundry Posts: . . . and let after Ages say pointing to the Heights of Majabigwaduce, there landed the American Troops, forced the Enemy from their out Posts, . . . there did they fight, and fighting some few fell, the rest still victorious, firm, inflexible still fighting conquer'd." Further, Lovell brought Wadsworth and his volunteers back to camp, ending the construction of a battery above Haney's Point.[55] Yet the general gave orders to Revere to begin preparation to remove the heavy cannons, and for Gilbert Speakman, his commissary of ordnance, to collect all the loose ordnance stores at the various emplacements at a convenient place. Revere reported getting on board the transport the brass 12-pounder and howitzer that day, and one 18-pounder to the beach that evening. Later that night Lovell ordered Colonel Davis to embark the 18-pounder. Speakman carried out his orders except for the battery at Hacker's Island.[56]

The British also were making plans. On this day a deserter came in and informed them that the Americans intended to coordinate an attack by land and sea the following day. General McLean felt that the American numerical superiority, both at sea and land, were such that the rebels would do just that. He decided to throw up a small work, about 150 yards outside the fort, armed with five 6-pounders to play on the enemy ships as they entered the harbor. One hundred men manned the battery.[57]

Meanwhile, unknown to either the Americans or the British on Bagaduce, settlers and fishermen on the west side by the mouth of the bay were sighting vessels offshore in the sea fog. As people saw more sightings, they decided the vessels' destination was Penobscot Bay. Inhabitants began firing their guns to warn people farther up the bay of the sightings. When the signaling reached Belfast the people knew a fleet was approaching, but whose fleet was it? They did not know if it was "an English fleet, or our fleet returning from Penobscot with success or miscarriage, or whether it is a fleet of Jamaica ships," rumored bringing supplies to the British. In fact, Admiral Sir George Collier was approaching.[58]

Friday, 13 August 1779, SW Light airs & pleasant weather—

Captain Mowat received a deserter this day reporting that a "council held this morning on board the Warren, it was determined to force the harbour next tide, and take or destroy the men of war; that five ships were destined for this service, one of which was the Warren; but that the Putnam, of twenty guns, was to lead; and that each ship was doubly manned with picked men." When, at noon, five rebel ships got under way and moved into line at the harbor entrance with the *Putnam* in the lead, Mowat called his marines back to their ships; ships' guns were double-shotted; and transport crews manned the *St. Helena*.[59]

Actually the discussion of the council of war at the American headquarters was not as specific as Captain Mowat's deserter implied. First, the officers unanimously agreed that there were things that could be done to reduce the enemy. The army officers felt they should reconsider and take possession of the ground in the rear of the fort. But they could not agree on how to take possession of that ground. Finally, after a debate the general asked if the council favored evacuating. The vote was fourteen to stay and ten to evacuate. Those for remaining were Generals Lovell and Wadsworth, Colonel Mitchell, Lieutenant Colonels Jordan, Howard, Majors Hunter, Brown, and Larabee, and from the fleet Captains Hacker, Cathcart, Story (who was acting captain for the *Monmouth*), Williams, Waters, and Salter. Those for evacuating were Colonel McCobb, Lieutenant Colonel Revere, and from the fleet Commodore Saltonstall, Captains Holmes, West, Edmonds, Burke, Thomas, Carnes, and Nathan Brown. With that vote the council disbanded.[60]

Despite the council's vote, at noon Lovell ordered Captain Perez Cushing, the artillery officer at Westcot's Battery, to take off the 18- and 9-pounders. The battery had only a fieldpiece left. The captain of HM *Nautilus* said that in the morning the northeast redoubt [Westcot Battery] fired until noon. Then he saw the rebels take the guns away from the emplacement. On the beach Colonel Davis spent the whole day loading ordnance stores.[61]

In the afternoon General Lovell brought four hundred men to the rear of the enemy's fort. He escaped detection by using the bank to shield his movement. Then he sent word, through Captain Burke, to Commodore Saltonstall to bring his ships into the harbor. At 5:00 P.M. the commodore signaled his ships to weigh anchor. There are no extant American plans for the assault on the harbor. Yet Captain Mowat learned from a deserter that the rebels planned to use five ships. The *Putnam* was in the van, followed by the *Warren*, and as the *Hampden* received extra marines, it probably participated. The other two ships are not known. Evidently Saltonstall anticipated having a ship for each of Mowat's four plus the seaman's redoubt. The wind was light from the southwest, with a slack tide. Flood tide began at 5:49 P.M. and continued until 12:04 A.M., which allowed the commodore to use the wind and tide to attack the British ships. Then he could continue up the Bagaduce River out of gun range of the citadel to await a calm and ebb tide for his exit.[62]

Captain Salter was on Banks' Island watching the land force work its way around the enemy's emplacements. When the commodore signaled for his ships to weigh anchor, Salter made his way back to his boat and returned to his ship. At 6:00 P.M., while they were maneuvering to enter the harbor, the *Diligent* came into view flying four flags at her main topgallant. The signal flags meant Saltonstall's lookout patrol had sighted enemy ships approaching the bay. The assault ships hauled to their wind and anchored. Less than an hour later strange ships appeared down by the Fox Islands at the mouth of the bay. Until Saltonstall knew more about the strangers, he would keep his ships in the bay. He sent word to General Lovell to return to his lines. Lovell returned immediately without engaging the enemy. The commodore ordered Captain Carnes of the *Hector* to beat down to investigate. When the wind died away and the flood tide began, the current carried Carnes back up the bay. He anchored and lay till morning.[63]

Captain Mowat, ever-watchful of the rebel ships, saw the five ships cast off their springs at 5:00 P.M. They appeared to get under way preparing to enter the harbor. At 6:00 P.M. he saw an armed brig appear with four flags flying from her main topgallant masthead. The rebel ships reversed and held their wind out in the bay. Just at sunset "Three Strange Sail were seen in the offing which we supposed to be King's Ships."[64]

For more than a week the *Putnam* and the *Hampden* were the closest ships to the mouth of the harbor. About the same time that the *Diligent* came into view, Salter saw the strange ships to windward. He immediately hove up and began wearing around. To the British it appeared he was entering the harbor and shots began dropping near his ship. When he cleared the enemy's guns, he stood off during the flood tide. He only anchored after the calm set in.[65]

Earlier in the day Saltonstall's three lookout ships at the mouth of the bay had joined to exchange information. At two in the afternoon, Captain Hallet of the *Active* thought he saw five sail standing in through the haze. Hallet hailed Captains Parker of the *Rover* and Brown of the *Diligent* for their opinions. Parker said he heard them three days earlier in the heavy fog, but the thick weather and light wind kept him from reaching this point any earlier. Brown confirmed that there were five ship-rigged vessels. Hallet asked Brown to report this to the commodore immediately. Meanwhile he would keep to the wind of them until he learned how many ships there were.[66]

Captain Parker, of the *Rover*, decided that his 10-gun armed schooner should move away from the two combatant fleets. He headed southwestward into the sea haze for safety. Unfortunately for Parker, in the fog he came upon HMS *Galatea* and became the first Penobscot Expedition vessel captured. The *Galatea* captain thought he had captured a small American coastal cruiser not realizing it was one of the vessels besieging General McLean.[67]

What the three captains saw was Sir George Collier's reinforcement. The British squadron consisted of the 64-gun ship *Raisonable*, two 32-gun frigates *Blonde* and *Virginia*, the 28-gun frigate *Greyhound*, and two 20-gun frigates *Camille* and *Galatea*. The 14-gun sloop *Otter* departed New York with the squadron 3 August. All headed for the rendezvous point, Monhegan Island, just west of Penobscot Bay, but during the voyage fog separated the vessels. The *Otter* failed to arrive at the rendezvous. Sir George Collier had no contact with the *Otter* during his rescue operations.[68]

Meanwhile, Captain Brown bent on all sails he could as he headed up the bay. At 6:00 P.M., when within view, he placed signal flags reporting incoming ships on his mainmast. It was about 10:00 P.M. before he anchored and gave Saltonstall his information. The commodore passed this on to the general and told Lovell he expected a complete report when the *Active* arrived. It was midnight before Hallet anchored and gave his assessment that there were seven square-rigged enemy ships standing in. Saltonstall immediately notified Lovell and recommended ordering the transports upriver when possible.[69]

* * *

Fortune had at first shone on the Americans. If Commodore Saltonstall had sailed into Bagaduce Harbor, he would have braved the guns of the citadel and General McLean's most recent emplacement of five 6-pounders specifically placed to fire upon his ships during their entry. At his destination he would have faced Captain Mowat's four ships' broadsides plus the guns of the sailors redoubt. Finally, the British reinforcements would have trapped his five assault vessels in the harbor.

The siege phase began with Saltonstall and Lovell looking for battery sites to harass the British men-of-war. The commodore's sailors built a site on the main north of Mowat's anchorage. Lovell sent General Wadsworth to look at some islands east of Banks' Island. The fleet site, Westcot Battery, came into being first. Mowat countered Westcot Battery by building a seaman's redoubt to check a landing similar to Half Moon Battery's assault. The redoubt also provided a shore battery to support his four vessels.

General Lovell shifted his emphasis to getting the fleet to sail into Bagaduce Harbor. Saltonstall agreed, if the general would cooperate by storming the fort to divert its attention away from his fleet's entrance. Truly the American commanders had a dilemma. Lovell felt his militia could not face the enemy troops and it was up to the fleet to break the impasse. Saltonstall believed he would suffer too much damage sailing into the harbor without aid from the land force. Finally, 7 August, at a council of war, Saltonstall suggested either "Strike a bold Stroke, by storming the Enemys works, and go in with the Ships, or raise the Siege."[70] It took from that meeting until 13 August for the two commanders to realize their interdependence and plan to execute a joint strike. But time ran out. British reinforcements were in Penobscot Bay.

Chapter Five

Retreat and
Rout

At midnight General Lovell received Commodore Saltonstall's rec-ommendation to retreat. Lovell began his second major action of the cam-paign. As on the initial landing, he benefited from darkness and a heavy fog. Minutes after midnight Major Jeremiah Hill, his adjutant general, broke out a hundred fatigue troops to carry off entrenching tools and other important articles. By 1:00 A.M. the regimental commanders roused their troops. Word of the retreat swept the American camp. There were no skulkers on this operation. As silently as possible, wrapped in darkness and fog, the troops formed, ready to march.

Colonel McCobb had his regiment ready by 2:00 A.M. and at the water's edge an hour later. At 5:00 his men were aboard their transports. Colonel Mitchell roused his regiment. About daybreak, 4:00 A.M., Mitchell's regi-ment marched out of camp. Just after sunrise they began loading. It was calm, foggy, and nearing the end of the ebb tide. As the transports filled they were towed offshore.[1]

General McLean rose early that day. He walked outside his fort before sunrise, surveying the situation. The rebel camp seemed too quiet. Going back inside, he ordered a party to check the enemy emplacements. Soon word came back that the rebels were no longer there. McLean sent Lieu-tenant Caffrae's light infantry unit out to establish contact with the enemy. He also sent another unit to the isthmus hoping to prevent the Americans on the mainland from returning to their ships.[2]

Artillery Captain Perez Cushing and volunteer Captain Waterman Thomas, posted at Westcot Battery, received their evacuation orders sometime after 1:00 A.M. Fortunately their two largest cannons had gone to the shore the day before. Still, they had their equipment and a fieldpiece to haul down the rocky trail to the isthmus. They crossed over to Bagaduce before the British troops arrived and charged them. The Americans made it to the safety of the woods, but the enemy captured one militiaman. The British dared not go into the underbrush for fear of running into the main rebel army. About 5:00 A.M. the battery loaded aboard. Their boat to the transport could not carry the men, equipment, gun, and carriage. The carriage remained on the rocky shore.[3] When Captain Mowat learned the enemy had broken camp, he sent Lieutenant Robertson with a list of the rebel fleet to the reinforcements. At 6:00 A.M. the British sailors, helped by the troops, began bringing their cannons back from the fort. It took all morning to rearm the sloops of war and prepare for sea.[4]

By daylight most of the American fleet captains were up assessing the situation. Captains Waters, Holmes, and Thomas boarded the *Warren* to talk with Saltonstall. The three requested the commodore's barge to go down to look at the enemy ships. On their way they passed the *Active* and learned that its first lieutenant had just returned from a similar trip. In the fog the lieutenant got near enough to hear the British sailors talking on deck. A little closer and he saw the enemy. There were three ships of 32-, 24-, and 20-guns. Farther away he saw three others, but could not decide their size or the number of guns. The British saw him also and rushed to hoist out boats to capture him. The lieutenant returned immediately to the *Active*. The three captains decided that information was enough. They returned to the *Warren*.[5]

Well before 8:00 A.M. the commodore called his captains for a council of war. Those attending were the privateer Captains N. Brown, Burke, Carnes, Holmes, Thomas, Waters, and West. The Massachusetts state navy Captains Cathcart, Hallet, and Williams also participated. Those absent were the Continental Captain Hacker, privateer Captains Ross and Salter, and auxiliary Captain Edmunds. Cathcart said some captains wanted to go around the west side of Long Island and flee. Others wanted to go upriver and make a stand. Hallet said the commodore and a number of commanders felt the risk of engaging the British was too great. "A motion was made to move up Penobscott River where we might with the help of the Militia, make a Stand and Protect our Shipping, or at least burn them and save our Crews from being captives." They discussed the three options. Unfortunately for posterity, no detailed minutes of these discussions were kept. The official council of war record stated only that Salton-stall posed two questions. Shall the fleet engage the enemy? The answer was a unanimous negative. Shall the fleet go up the Penobscot River? That question brought a unanimous affirmative.[6]

Captain Titus Salter saw the commodore's signal about eight. When Salter reached the *Warren* the captains were leaving. He asked Saltonstall if he had any orders. According to Salter the commodore replied, none, he believed "we must all shift for ourselves."[7] Expecting a fight, Salter went to General Lovell's sloop to ask for some troops. With Lovell's permission twenty militiamen volunteered to join the *Hampden*.

The bay was still foggy, and Lovell could see only three enemy ships. The general ordered Thomas Berry to take a boat from the transport *Sally* and observe the upcoming operations. Berry had orders to inform the Massachusetts Council "of any thing material which I should discover of the Enemies strength after I left him [Lovell]." When the fog cleared, Berry saw three more British ships. Berry sent the pilot upriver. The last he saw of the American vessels they were "about two gun shot a Head of the Enemy just above the old fort point."[8]

Salter's visit to General Lovell took place just as the flood tide began to influence the transports. Colonel Joshua Davis, agent for the transports, received Lovell's orders to go up the bay at eight. Twenty-one vessels began towing and drifting up the bay in spite of the calm wind. Half an hour later Davis noticed the vessels were standing a course for Belfast on the western shore of the upper bay. Davis immediately rowed over to the general to find out why the change in direction. Lovell replied some people had told him "Belfast was the safest retreat." Davis explained to the general that under the present flood tide it would not be possible to reach Belfast. He recommended changing course to go upriver suggesting the Narrows as a safe retreat. Lovell agreed and Davis sent the signal for the transports to change course.[9]

The Narrows was a striking reach of the river with a narrow section at each end. Between the two was a reach of 3.7 miles. Odam's Ledge (Odom Ledge), in midriver where the banks closed from a bay to a river, was just above Mill Cove. Beyond the ledge the western bank was steep rising from water's edge to two hundred feet, but not as steep as Dice's Head. Orphan Island (Verona Island) was the eastern bank. At the northern end of the reach the river took an almost ninety-degree turn to the west. The two ends of the Narrows presented difficulties for sailing vessels. Odam's

Ledge divided the river current. At the northern turn, the current made a dramatic change in direction that demanded challenging work managing the sails. The high western bank funneled the winds "either directly up or directly down the river. When the wind was from the north and the tide was ebbing, no 18th century sailing vessel was capable of going upriver. With the wind from the south, it was a simple downwind run upriver irrespective of the tide, particularly for the taller ships grabbing the air above the ground effect layer."[10] The journey from Bagaduce Head to Fort Point covered 7 miles. Fort Point to Odam's Ledge another 3.2 miles. The Narrows Reach added 3.7 miles. The Americans felt the Narrows would delay the enemy for a day; the British would need river pilots or daylight to breach the Narrows.

The morning continued with three groups of vessels becalmed in Penobscot Bay. General Lovell's northern transport group towed and drifted on the flood tide. Commodore Saltonstall's armed vessels strung out in line across the bay off Bagaduce Head. Sir George Collier's squadron, the southernmost, waited for a breeze. As the transports neared Fort Pownall, General Lovell scribbled a brief note to Powell telling the Massachusetts Council that British reinforcements were in the bay. He told of his retreat "without loss, & is now on his way up Penobscot River to to [*sic*] take Post at Fort Pownal." He had great anxiety as "the two Fleets were closing together." Captain Salter told him earlier that the commodore "was very much dejected." Then General Lovell, bringing up the rear, passed the care of the transports to Brigadier Wadsworth. He also asked Wadsworth to go ashore to see if Fort Pownall was a suitable place to fortify. Lovell was under no apprehension of danger to his transports, for they were six or seven miles above the armed vessels. He felt the matter would "be disputed off Magadigwaduce." General Lovell left the *Sally,* and accompanied by Major Todd took his barge for the *Warren* to encourage Saltonstall.[11]

Throughout the morning, as the transports departed, the sailors at Bank's Island kept firing at the enemy. Finally, at 10:00 A.M. the *Nautilus* captain sent armed boats to the island to capture the rebel battery. When the British approached, the sailors spiked their guns and fled to their ships. The *Nautilus* crew captured two 18-pounders and one 12-pounder. The first and last vestiges of the Penobscot Expedition's assault and siege were silent.[12]

Upon boarding the *Warren,* Lovell found that a fresh breeze from the southward was springing up. The British first division, only two miles below the Americans, was under full sail. Even more surprisingly, Lovell learned that the armed vessels, while waiting for the sea breeze to reach them, were preparing to weigh anchor and flee upriver. The general immediately set out for his transports, still becalmed, to give further directions.[13]

Commodore Saltonstall, unaware that the transports at Fort Point were awaiting General Wadsworth's assessment of defending Fort Point, could not understand why they remained at anchor. Why were they not moving, however slowly, upriver? He was waiting for the southerly breeze to reach his vessels so that he could weigh anchor. It was nerve-racking to watch the enemy ships approach and not have enough wind to flee. As his future actions would show, Saltonstall had his plan well in mind: gain time and distance over the enemy so he could safely land his crew and destroy his ship.

At 1:00 P.M. Captain Mowat's sloops of war were ready to join battle against the rebels. General McLean sent his light infantry unit with the vessels, just in case the rebels tried to make a stand somewhere up the Penobscot. Mowat faced a sail against a headwind from the southwest with light airs (one to three knots), and the slack tide between flood and ebb. His vessels warped down the Bagaduce River. Warping meant that rowboats carried kedge anchors forward alternately to the extremity of the warp, or anchor cable; then the sailors on the vessel would winch her up the anchor cable. It was a slow process. An hour later, the sloops of war reached the bay, unfurled their sails, and set out for the *Blonde, Virginia,* and *Camilla.* Some distance astern Mowat saw Collier's second division. Now, all nine British ships were in the chase after the rebels.[14]

Half an hour after Mowat began warping, Saltonstall signaled his ships to shift for themselves. As his armed vessels began weighing anchors, unfurling sails, some breaking out oars, all headed up the bay. The commodore's intention soon became clear. By 1:00 P.M. Colonel Revere noticed the armed ships under sail standing upriver. He went aboard the general's sloop to let Wadsworth know this, for his vessel lay out of sight of the armed vessels. Simultaneously Colonel Davis signaled for his transports to make for the Narrows.[15]

An hour later while checking the western channel of Penobscot Bay, Captain Philip Brown of the *Diligent* saw the armed vessels already underway. He left the American fleet before the morning's council of war. He had to judge the fleet's actions by its movements. He saw some vessels heading for the north end of Long Island as if they might escape the enemy. Most of the vessels were heading upriver. "I got underway, determined to share with my Commander & obey such orders as might be given me by my superiors. I saw that every vessel was making the best of a bad bargain & endeavoring to get up the River as fast as possible. Took pattern by them & for fear of being runover (being a small vessel) turn as fast as my neighbors."[16]

The British ships saw the rebel fleet under way and fleeing upriver. The *Blonde*, in company with the *Virginia* and *Galatea*, drove the enemy before them. Not one American vessel returned a shot to the British fire. At 3:00 P.M. the *Blonde*'s captain saw two ships and a brig haul round to the southwest to escape down the western channel. The *Blonde* and *Galatea* "hauld close to the North End & cut off their Retrait. They then wore & stood after the Body of the fleet; the Galatea Pursued the Brigg & Drove her on shore."[17] The squadron's remaining ships, and Mowat's three sloops, continued to chase the main force headed for the Narrows.

Captain John Edmunds of the brig *Defence*, being pursued by the *Galatea*, was not driven ashore. His two pilots, brothers Elisha and Eben Griffin, lived on the shore of Cape Jellison Harbor (Stockton Springs Harbor), an inlet between Brigadier's Island (Sear's Island) and Cape Jellison. The brothers probably convinced Captain Edmunds that they might be able to hide in the harbor and slip out after dark. But Commodore Sir George Collier directed Captain Collins of "the Camilla to proceed into the inlet & take the Defence, but she prevented that measure being carried into execution, by blowing herself up. She was a new brig, & carried 16 six pounders."[18]

Then the *Blonde* and *Galatea* stood after the two rebel ships, firing several shots at them. At 4:00 P.M. the *Hunter* ran ashore and her crew scrambled for the bank. Two boats from the *Galatea* tried to board the *Hunter*, but rebel musketry from shore drove them off. The boats returned to the *Galatea*. Then Sir George Collier sent Lieutenant Mackey of the *Raisonable* and "50 men to board the Hunter, which he succeeded in without loss, tho' many popping shots were fired at him by her crew in the woods; she is a very fine ship of 18 guns, and said to be the fastest sailing vessel in America."[19]

Meanwhile, Captain Titus Salter, the only American captain to trade shots with the British, wore his ship around and tried to rejoin the fleet. The two British ships turned upon the *Hampden*. At 4:30 they fired at her, hulling her several times. The *Virginia* joined them. Captain Salter said,

"my Ship Saileing heavey the Enemy Soon Came up With me three fri-
getes and fiered upon one after the outher and Cutt away my rigen &
Stayes &c and huld me Sundrey times and wounded Sum of my men. I
found et Emposable to Joyane our flet agin was abliged to Strik all thow
Contrary to my [will]." At 5:00 Captain Salter struck his colors. The log of
the *Blonde* recorded the event: "At ½ past 4 fired several shot at the other
ship and Huld Her, as did the *Virginia*. At 5 she struck to us; sent a Boat
with an Officer to board Her, which she did, and made sail after us. . . . At
9 the Boats returned from the prize *Hamdon* of 22 Guns."[20]

While the American captains opting to run down the western channel
were challenging the British, the remaining captains were closing in on
the Narrows. It was a pell-mell race. Transports, nearest to the Narrows,
were the tortoises moving slowly with wide ungainly hulls, the last to
receive the sea breeze. Small men-of-war were the hares using oars, sails,
and trim hulls to leap forward toward the prize. Larger ships, using stud-
ding sails, were faster than the tortoises, but slower than the hares.[21] All
headed toward the Narrows. At 4:00 P.M. Captain Williams, of the *Hazard*, came upon Lovell's barge below the Narrows. Williams took the general and his crew aboard his vessel as he continued upriver. When the
Hazard came abreast of the transports, General Lovell ordered Major
Todd to take a boat to carry instructions to his staff on the transport *Sally*.
Lovell did not want his officers to destroy their vessels while out of pistol
shot of the enemy. If they had to go ashore, all hands should go upriver to
where the *Hazard* was. Lieutenant George Little of the *Hazard* accompanied Todd. When Todd arrived at the *Sally*, the troops and staff were on
shore at Mill Cove. Todd was unable to pass the general's instructions to
his staff.

Both Major Todd and Lieutenant Little gave depositions about that
evening's efforts. Todd said he left the *Hazard* when abreast of the transports, visited the *Sally*, and returned to the *Hazard*. Lovell sent them back
a second time, and they returned to the *Hazard* at 8:00 P.M. Little gave
essentially the same information, except he said they left two miles above
Odam's Ledge and made only one trip. Bald Head, ten miles above the
ledge, required a trip of fifteen miles in two hours. The river was at flood
tide, with the current aiding the rowers. Todd made much faster progress
than previous speeds that day.[22]

In spite of the minor conflicts in testimony, both men reported the same
events. When they boarded the transport *Sally*, the troops and staff were

ashore hiding. Todd decided to take some of the general's necessary baggage and his own for the trip upriver. Returning after sunset, they saw Captain Burke alone on the *Sky Rocket* anchored above the Narrows. They hailed him and asked why he was at anchor. Burke replied that his men had deserted, he was aground, and he planned to burn his ship. They entreated him not to, saying they would send help. Burke agreed to wait, but half an hour later they saw the flames of the *Sky Rocket* shooting skyward.[23]

The *Hazard* was among the first vessels to reach Odam's Ledge. Other hares were close behind. A few transports were near the ledge when the Massachusetts state navy and the Continental sloop *Providence* arrived. Colonel Davis, the agent for the transports, was farther back among the transports, striving to get above the Narrows. He expected the armed vessels would make a stand below Odam's Ledge. "To my great mortification they all passed the transports without any notice or assistance which put the troops on board in the utmost confusion." The enemy ships were approaching rapidly. Many transport captains panicked, and Colonel Davis lost command over them. Some transports ran ashore at Mill Cove in disorder.[24]

The first of the large assault ships to reach the Narrows was probably the *Charming Sally*. Early in the morning before the transports departed Bagaduce, Saltonstall requested troops for some ships. Adjutant General Jeremiah Hill, Captain White of the Continental Army, an artillery lieutenant, and twenty-nine militiamen boarded the *Charming Sally*. When Captain Holmes came aboard, he ordered the sailing master to make all possible sail upriver. The *Sally* passed most of the transports before reaching Odam's Ledge. As the enemy ships approached, the transports began landing troops. Hill noticed the confusion on shore. It was obvious no engagement was in the offing. He asked Captain Holmes, when convenient, to put the military personnel ashore. The first person Hill met on the beach was Colonel Mitchell. Hill suggested the colonel should collect his men and keep them together if possible; then Hill went downriver to the transport area at Mill Cove.

The transports grounded on the western shore, and the troops scrambled over the side. The British ships, intent on pursuing the rebel armed vessels, paid slight attention to the transports disgorging troops onto the beach. Around 6:00 P.M. the first transport captain set fire to his vessel.

With more transports struggling to beach and disembark troops, burning transports became part of the panic. Probably unknown to the Americans, the act of burning vessels stopped the British ships from moving closer. HMS *Blonde*'s log recorded "At 6 upewards of 20 sail of small Vessels run on shore, the most of them they set fire to, which Oblig'd us to anchor." British captains had no desire to bring their ships close to burning transports that might explode at any time. The *Albany*'s log said by sunset most transports were on shore, with many burning, but the American assault ships continued up the river.[25]

The *Putnam* entered the Narrows at 7:00 P.M. Four transports succeeded in passing through the obstacle. The *Warren* was the last ship to pass Odam's Ledge. As the wind subsided, the flood tide took over and the *Warren* drifted upriver as far as Marsh Cove before grounding. Through a series of fortuitous events (burning transports, calm winds, flood tide, darkness, and the treacherous Narrows), the commodore's ships made good their escape.[26]

Captain James Brown of the brig *Samuel* was astern of the *Warren* when he first entered the Narrows. Brown carried Colonel Davis, fifty artillerymen, and artillery supplies. Davis had Brown follow the *Warren* hoping to receive assistance, but the *Warren* offered none. When the *Samuel* had difficulty going upriver, the artillerymen became most anxious to go ashore. Finally, Brown landed the troops and some provisions. When Colonel Davis brought the artillerymen and provisions ashore, the men jumped out and fled into the woods. Colonel Revere and Captain Cushing tried to collect them, to little avail. A few of the men remained to help Davis, who decided to row upriver with his supplies. Upon reaching the *Hazard,* he told General Lovell what he carried. Lovell asked him to return and bring up more provisions. By the time Davis reached the transports that were on shore, it was dark. He found it impossible to gather more supplies. On his return, he found four transports above the Narrows. He filled his boat with some of their provisions, and ordered the four to go to the head of navigation (Bangor).[27]

Meanwhile, Captain James Brown hoped to continue. He towed a small boat for his four-man crew in case he must abandon the *Samuel.* About the time that his rowboat broke free, he knew he could not sail the *Samuel* any farther up the river. He picked a spot on the western side of the Narrows between two burning transports. Brown left his sails in position, dropped the anchor, and fearing the explosion when his ship caught fire, fled. Later during the flood tide the crewless *Samuel* floated free and began drifting upstream.[28]

Meanwhile, at Mill Cove Major Hill found Captain Carver, master of the *Sally,* the general's transport, some crewmen, and some of Lovell's staff milling around. He joined Captain Carver and the few others who would agree to gather provisions from the beached transports. General Wadsworth arrived at nightfall and they moved inland to a nearby house. Hill found that there were several officers camped in the woods close to the house. He tracked them down and tried in vain to get them to join General Wadsworth. The officers refused. They meant to leave the next day for the Kennebec River. Colonel Tyler said that Lovell's orders were to take care of themselves, which was the prevailing mood of the officers and men that evening. Hill gave up. Returning to the house, he finally bribed six or seven men with three quarts of wine taken from the transports to post guard around the house.[29]

From the time the armed fleet weighed anchor, General Wadsworth at Fort Point had little opportunity to rest. The general gave orders to Colonel Davis to send two flat-bottomed boats to the point to take off the hospital. Then he had the cattle driven off and the buildings burned. Wadsworth left just as the armed vessels passed the point, with the British not far behind. By the time he reached Mill Cove the transports were "in a Cluster in the Eddy on the westerly Side the River. One Sloop had run on Shore & more seem'd to be inclined that way."[30] While the larger vessels were at the mercy of the current and wind, the rowboats and canoes could pass at ease whether with or against the current. If with the current, the crew could row or paddle in the channel; if against the current, they moved closer to shore where the current was not as strong.

At the Narrows General Wadsworth left Doctor Downer in charge of the flat-bottomed boats with the hospital patients. He joined two Indians in their canoe and moved up through the Narrows to look for a suitable site to defend.[31] As he passed the transports he told the captains not to run on shore as long as they could keep afloat without drifting down on the enemy. He recalled earlier urging General Lovell to build a redoubt at the Narrows for just such a retreat. But Lovell refused saying "it would dishearten our Army & shew them that we do not expect to succed—& forgetting the good old Maximum 'to keep open a good retreat.' . . . O, then how we wished for a place of rendezvous, the transports might have been saved."[32]

When he passed the ordnance brig *Samuel* he ordered a brass 12-pounder readied in a flatboat while he found a place to mount it in the Narrows. General Wadsworth in his canoe outdistanced all the other American vessels and reached the northern end of the Narrows where the river turns westward almost ninety degrees. This was the ideal place to defend against the enemy. As he prepared to return downriver, he noted "the Hazard which was then the headmost Vessell" reaching the turn. At the time he was not aware that General Lovell was aboard the lead vessel.[33]

Upon returning to Mill Cove, Wadsworth found the transports "chiefly on Shore in a Cluster & on fire." The smaller armed vessels had passed Odam's Ledge. He thought that if the heavier ships formed a line below the ledge they could stop the enemy advance, allowing the transports to escape; however, one by one the ships passed through, heading upriver. General Wadsworth saw a small schooner drifting down toward the enemy with its crew on board and no small boat to escape to shore. At this time Colonel Paul Revere's Castle Island barge rowed up the shore toward Revere. Wadsworth went over to order the barge to rescue the crew. "In this I was directly oppos'd by Lieutenant Colonel Revere who said that I had no right to command either him or the Boat & gave orders to the contrary." Shortly after this Revere changed his mind and sent his barge to the schooner; Wadsworth promised him "An Arrest as soon as the Army should be collected."[34]

Then Wadsworth tried to collect troops to save stores from transports not burning. The enemy, anchored a safe distance from the burning vessels, sent boats to pull off the unburnt transports. The general found there was little he could do. "The Troops were cheefly dispers'd or gone back into the Woods & the rest not to be commanded. By the help of a few Individuals, chiefly Officers, a small Quantity of Provisions & Amunition was got on Shore." By 10:00 P.M. there was nothing more to accomplish. He retired with his band to a house on high ground just inland from the river. Here he met twenty other officers and men who bedded down for the night.[35]

At midnight HM *Albany* anchored above Sandy Point in nine fathoms of water. She was with the *Blonde, Greyhound, Virginia, Galatea, North,* and *Nautilus.* Just a short distance west and a little earlier, sailors of the brig *Defence* completed their task. They cut into the main timbers of the aft section, spread gunpowder in the section, and ignited the fuse. At midnight the explosion blew out the aft section and the brig went to the bottom. On the Penobscot River, the fleeing American vessels were strung out from the grounded *Warren* at Marsh Bay to the anchored *Hazard* at Bald Hill Cove, 3.5 and 10 miles respectively above the Narrows.[36]

Sunday, 15 August 1779, SW, First and latter parts Calm Middle light breezes—

Doctor Downer continued upriver all night. In the morning he was at the head of navigation, abreast of Captain Brewer's house on the east bank. He told Brewer that the siege was ended and that the American fleet and army were coming up the river with the British fleet chasing them. Downer stopped, dressed his patients, and fed both crew and patients. He asked Brewer where was a safe place for his patients. Brewer suggested Major Treat's place about two miles above the falls. The doctor brought his patients there and left them in the care of Doctor Herberd. Downer left his medical chest with Doctor Herberd before heading downriver.[37]

At 4:00 A.M. Captain Waters anchored after a night of towing the *Putnam* upstream. When he anchored, all the armed vessels except the *Warren* and *Vengeance* were ahead of him. Half an hour later, at daylight, General Lovell left the *Hazard* in his barge and hastened downriver. He told Major Todd to stay with the brig to collect any troops that might come up the river. Todd saw no troops that day. Colonel Davis passed the general, who asked him to secure his provisions; so when the colonel reached the head of navigation he crossed over the falls to protect his supplies. He also found settlers above the fall who could supply him with fifty head of cattle and a quantity of potatoes. Having made those arrangements, Davis sought a place to sleep for he had not slept in three days and nights. Colonel Davis fully expected that when he awoke the general would make his stand at the head of navigation and his supplies would be needed.[38]

General Lovell took Captain Waterman Thomas, a volunteer officer, Lieutenant George Little of the *Hazard,* and seven sailors, to man his barge on the way downriver to assess what had happened. On the way they came upon the sloop *Pidgeon,* Captain Luther Little, and Paul Revere. Lovell wanted Revere to gather his corps and whatever artillery he could and go to the head of the river to prepare fortifications. Revere replied that the ordnance brig and the transport carrying the artillery were burnt. He also said that he had sent his barge downriver to find his troops. The general replied that he would get guns from the ships.

Continuing, they found the *Warren* aground by Marsh Bay. Commodore Saltonstall told Lovell that the ordnance brig had drifted upriver during the night and was three miles below the *Warren*. The general sent Thomas, Little, and his boat crew to try to bring the brig upriver. Flood tide began at 7:30 A.M. and continued until 1:30 P.M. that day. As the water rose both the *Samuel* and *Warren* floated free and drifted up the river. Lieutenant Little noticed two enemy boats in pursuit. As the ebb tide began, the vessels anchored to keep from drifting downstream. When a breeze sprang up, all craft weighed anchor and the chase continued. In midafternoon the breeze died and the ebb current took over. Lieutenant Little, realizing he could not overtake the commodore, decided it was prudent to burn the brig. The enemy, seeing the fire, anchored immediately. Little and crew rowed up to the *Warren* now at Oak Point.[39]

When they came aboard, they found the commodore and the general discussing what should be done. Obviously Saltonstall had decided to carry out his plan to put the crew ashore, burn his ship, and return to Boston. Lovell begged him not to set the ship afire. The commodore knew the general had been low on ammunition before they left Bagaduce and the troops were miles below them. No troops had passed them on land during the voyage upriver. There was nothing at the head of the river except the fleeing ships. What was to be gained in using sailors to fortify a wilderness with no means for obtaining supplies, armament, or reinforcements—and when confronted with a superior force of ships and troops downriver chasing them?

Saltonstall turned to Lieutenant Little and asked what more could he do? Little replied that as far as he could see, he had done nothing. Little asked the commodore why he had not fired his stern chasers coming up the river to cover the transports? Saltonstall replied it would have done no good, they would have fired again. The commodore's desire was not to engage the enemy and suffer personnel casualties, but to gain separation enough to allow the crew to disembark and destroy his ship. Obviously Lieutenant Little did not grasp Saltonstall's plan for he continued giving examples of engagements. "I advised him to get springs on his cables & get his eighteen pounders on one side & defend the ships as long as possible, as it's impossible for more than one ship to engage you at a time, & I would stay on board & assist him. His reply was this would be means for the Enemy to get his ship."[40]

Little replied that before the enemy got the ship, he would set fire to the magazine. At that, the *Warren*'s second lieutenant said there were better men than Little aboard. He also said he had orders to burn her. Lieutenant Little replied that neither he nor his commander had shown themselves to be better. When asked if he knew what ship he was on, Little replied the *Warren*. The second lieutenant then reminded Little to take care what he said aboard the ship. Little belligerently replied, "I should see him on shore where I should be as good a man as he was."[41]

At this time General Lovell offered to stay on board and assist the commodore with all that lay in his power. Commodore Saltonstall replied, "It would be best for him to go up the river." The general told Saltonstall that he would leave and order a boat from every ship to come to his assistance. In parting Lovell said, "It would be worth while to cut a road through Kennebec if we never saved the Ships to save the guns, Sails, & Rigging."[42]

First Lovell boarded the *Putnam*. He asked Captain Waters to send assistance to the commodore. Shortly after, Captain Holmes of the *Charming Sally* boarded the *Putnam*. Both captains decided to go to the *Warren*. Waters and Holmes found the *Warren* aground. When they learned the enemy was below the ordnance brig they asked the commodore if he could get under way. He replied that he needed the flood tide, which would begin in a few hours. Meanwhile, Saltonstall had his sailors prepare the ship for burning. As Waters and Holmes left to return to their ships, they clearly saw the flames shoot up from the ordnance brig.[43]

Lovell's next stop was the *Vengeance*. When he asked Captain Thomas to aid the commodore, Thomas replied he had all his men ashore, and he would burn his ship. General Lovell tried many arguments to change Captain Thomas's mind. Finally, Thomas told the general he could have the ship. Lovell replied he would accept her rather than have her burned. Of course Lovell had no personnel to accept or to handle the *Vengeance*, and so he moved on up the river.

Captains Carnes of the *Hector* and West of the *Black Prince* repeated Captain Thomas's plan. They intended to land their people and burn their ships. General Lovell offered many reasons not to destroy their ships. He said that if they got their ships up to the head of the river they could put the ships' cannons on shore and fortify the site. They could hold out "until they [the state] could send to France for shipping to get them out of the river and I make no doubt but, that they could." He also said "he would call in the Militia & cut a road [through] to Kennebec River and get provisions that way, and if the Ships Could never be got out it would be worth while to Get Guns, Sails, Rigging across to Kennebec." The general insisted they could keep the enemy at bay with five hundred men until the French shipping arrived. General Lovell's arguments meant nothing to the privateer captains. They knew there were no soldiers at the head of the river, no provisions, and little ammunition. More important they knew they could expect the British ships and troops the next day. Further, they were privateers, not militiamen or Continental soldiers. They refused to change their plans.[44]

* * *

Early in the morning at Bagaduce, Sir George Collier requested that General McLean send some of his men upriver to aid his sailors in case the rebels fortified some site. McLean told of his light infantry being on board Mowat's sloops. Collier said his vessels also had soldiers, but he wanted to make sure he had every advantage. McLean prepared to embark two hundred more soldiers on the *St. Helena* to go upriver.[45]

Even earlier in the morning, at 5:00 A.M., the *Blonde* signaled for all lieutenants to man and arm boats to attack the transports around Mill Cove. At 10:00 the *Albany* weighed anchor and came to sail moving closer to the *Blonde* also at sail. An hour later, the two came to anchor at the Narrows of the Penobscot River. By 1:00 P.M., although the tide was at ebb, the wind picked up and the seven British vessels took up the pursuit of the rebel fleet. It was a slow procession with the breeze barely compensating for the ebb current. By the time the tide shifted to flood at 7:30 P.M., the wind was calm. The British drifted upstream until 9:00 before anchoring in three and a half fathoms. No rebel vessels were in sight. At 11:00 P.M. Captain Mowat led a group of two armed boats from each vessel to continue upriver. He believed the *Warren* was at anchor four or five miles ahead. The group continued until the tide changed at 2:00 A.M., then they headed back.[46]

Meanwhile, when General Lovell left the *Hazard*, Captain Williams continued upriver to the head of navigation. When he arrived below the falls, he anchored next to the *Providence*, *Tyrannicide*, and *Diligent*. Major Todd and Captains Williams, Cathcart, Hacker, and Philip Brown went ashore to find a place to fortify. Then the four captains decided to look farther downriver. Major Todd, following the general's orders, remained to gather the troops coming up the river. The captains found several places suitable for fortification and continued downstream to tell the commodore. Farther down they boarded the *Vengeance* where they learned that the captain planned to burn his ship. Captain Brown asked them if they would not stay and help defend the vessels. The privateersmen answered that they came for eighteen days and their time was over. A short distance farther they met Captains Waters and Holmes who informed them that the commodore was landing men and preparing to burn his ship. They turned and headed for the falls. Upon returning, they saw the *Hector, Black Prince, Monmouth,* and *Charming Sally* coming up to their anchorage. Some ships were landing men.[47]

When Captain Williams returned aboard the *Hazard,* his sailors crowded around telling him that the private sailors told them that the small public vessels were to remain but the private ships would be burnt. They worried that, if that were so, they would become prisoners. Williams assured his crew that if he had to burn the vessel he would care for them and get a pilot to take them through the woods. Later Captain Cathcart came aboard and told Williams that his sailors had the same worries. Some of Cathcart's crew manned a boat to leave, and he had to have others fire upon them to bring them back. He had the mutinous sailors placed in irons belowdecks.[48]

Captain Philip Brown boarded his vessel just after dark and immediately ordered his master to give the sailors cloth to make knapsacks for their provisions and clothes. About 11:00 P.M. Captain Hacker called to Brown that the general had arrived and wanted to send boats down to tow the commodore. He and the other auxiliary officers sent their boats as soon as possible. Brown said the "news of the commodore being like to get up put new life in my officers & men & wished nothing more than to Fortify & defend our vessels."[49]

Monday, 16 August 1779, Varble, Light Airs and Calm wea[the]r—

At 8:00 A.M. the Continental and Massachusetts naval officers discovered that the private ships around them were burning. The burning ships were close to the naval vessels, and there was every reason to expect the conflagration would sweep the anchorage. Captain Philip Brown came on deck of his brig *Diligent* just in time to see one of the transports burst into flames. Soon after, the ship *Black Prince* blazed up. Fire from the *Black Prince* quickly spread to the *Monmouth*. Philip Brown knew that no one in authority had ordered the burnings. He was concerned with the number of vessels nearby that still had crews on board and was aware that the *Providence*, closer to the inferno than his ship, had no boats alongside. Further, he knew that the armed ships had their guns loaded. "I thought myself in as much danger as if I had an enemy to engage." Brown went ashore in his small boat to get a more suitable craft to take off the *Providence*'s sailors. Captain Brown got a lighter alongside the *Providence*. Then Brown heard the sailors of the *Hazard* screaming for God's sake come and take us off. The *Hazard* was close to both burning ships. Again Brown went to the shore for a craft. It was just after low tide and the craft on shore were high and dry. Brown yelled for someone to help him budge the boat. He yelled and tugged for what seemed to him a lifetime before one person grabbed the gunwale opposite him. Then another person began pushing on the bow and gradually the boat slid over the rocks and mud into the river. When Brown had time to look, he saw his ship's carpenter opposite him and General Lovell pushing on the bow. As he pulled alongside the *Hazard* the sailors said they had put out the fire. Captain Brown returned to his own ship, which was a safe distance away, and began off-loading his crew. It was then that some sailors from the *Warren* came up to him. They told him that they had off-loaded the day before. Brown supplied them with provisions and clothing for the trek through the woods.[50]

Meanwhile volunteer Captain Waterman Thomas set off in a flat-bottomed boat loaded with provisions, hoping to clear the area and save supplies for the march home. Lieutenant Little accompanied him. As they passed two of the ships, Little hailed someone on shore to ask if they had their guns armed. The person called back that they were armed with langrage, pound shot, and grape. Langrage was a projectile used for destroying the sails and rigging of an enemy vessel. It consisted of various pieces of iron bound together to fit in the bore of the gun. As the langrage left the gun the binding would break and iron pieces would spread similar to shotgun pellets. Obviously the guns still carried the projectiles placed in them on 14 August when the fleet first saw the enemy ships.[51]

As the captains of the remaining vessels gathered, they realized it was the end. One by one they burned their vessels. Captain Holmes did not destroy the *Charming Sally* until all the other crews were ashore. Captain

Williams ordered his sailing master, James Morris, to set fire to the *Hazard*. When the arrangements were complete, the officers and sailors set off through the wood for the Kennebec River. Sailing Master Morris set aside a boat and supplies for himself. Morris was too much of a sailor to tramp through unknown woods. He planned to take his chances skirting along the shore and work his way back to an American settlement and eventually to Boston.[52]

General Lovell was devastated. His successful assault against overwhelming odds had been negated. Then his successful withdrawal from Bagaduce, again against overwhelming odds, had been negated by the panic-stricken militiamen fleeing into the woods. He did not know what to do. He could not return to Boston without some tangible success to bring back to the General Council. He needed time to think and plan. Then it came to him. He would go up the river to the Penobscot Indians and make a treaty to keep them from turning to the British. General Lovell took Colonel Joshua Davis, Major William Todd, Doctor Eliphalet Downer, and five others with him to forge a peace treaty with the Indians.

Downriver at 8:00 A.M. the British ships heard several discharges of cannons and some larger explosions. They assumed the rebels were destroying their vessels. The *Blonde, Camilla, Albany,* and *Nautilus* weighed anchor to sail upriver. At 2:00 P.M. they anchored near the entrance of Marsh Bay. The captain of the *Blonde* sent an officer under a flag of truce up the Penobscot. At the head of navigation the British officer saw his first rebel, Sailing Master James Morris. He informed Morris he was from the *Blonde* with a message from Sir George Collier to the commodore: Sir George Collier would allow Commodore Saltonstall to keep a ship to carry his men to Boston, if the commodore delivered up and did not destroy his other vessels. After looking around at the scene of destruction and delivering his message, the British officer turned downriver. At 6:00 P.M. the officer arrived at the *Blonde* reporting all the rebel vessels destroyed.[53]

Early that Monday morning General Wadsworth arose and gave orders to collect the troops. Few could be found. Those that were, when they heard of the general's orders to gather, disappeared quickly into the woods. Some fled with their officers and some without their officers. By 8:00 A.M. Wadsworth had a collection of officers gathered at his headquarters. Colonels Samuel McCobb and John Tyler, Lieutenant Colonel William Howard, Majors Gawen Brown and Jeremiah Hill, and several captains and junior officers milled about waiting for Wadsworth's decision. Of the enlisted men only forty, from Colonel McCobb's regiment, remained. After discussing their situation and later learning of the burning of the fleet, General Wadsworth decided that detaining officers without men served no purpose. The general set off with Captain Burke, his seamen, and some militiamen for Camden. Others took different routes.[54]

Tuesday, 17 August 1779, Varble, Light Airs and Calm—

At 2:00 P.M. the British ships weighed anchor and dropped down the Penobscot. They met the transport *St. Helena* carrying troops to help destroy the rebel forces. While dropping down the Narrows, the *Albany* scraped ground but did not stop. At 7:00 P.M. the British ships anchored and set fire to two sloops dismantled by the rebels. That night the *Nautilus's* sailors cleared the decks and the tars got their hammocks down for their first night's rest off the ship's decks in twenty-four days.[55]

Years later colonel, formerly captain, John Brewer wrote about the Penobscot Expedition against Castine. In listing the American ships taken and destroyed, he included several that were not mentioned in the Massachusetts Archives. His armament differed from Paul Revere's list. He also noted where each vessel met its end.

> The Warren 32 guns, Monmouth and Vengeance, 24 each; Putnam and Sally, 22 each; Hampden and Hector, 20 each, Hunter and Black-Prince, 18 each; Sky-Rocket, 16; brigs Native, Defiance, Hazard and Nancy, 16 guns each; Delaware, Tyrannicide and Providence, sloops, 14 each; Spring-Bird 12, and Rover 10, together with 24 sail of transports. The Warren, Commodore Saltonstall was burnt at Oak-Point Cove; the Putnam and Vengeance burnt opposite Hampden; the Hunter and Hampden were taken; the Sky-Rocket was blown up near Fort-Point Ledge; the Spring Bird was burnt; the Nancy and Rover were taken; one brig was burnt near Brigadier Island. The following vessels were destroyed at the head of navigation, opposite Bangor, viz: - Ships Monmouth, Sally, Hector and Black-Prince, were burnt and blown up. Brigs Hazard, Tyrannicide and Delaware burnt, the sloop Providence blown up. Total, 4 ships, 3 brigs, 1 sloop and 3 transports. Of the whole fleet taken and destroyed were 10 ships, 10 brigs, 1 sloop and 24 transport and store-ships, making 46 vessels in the whole.[56]

The *Sky Rocket* must have played the role of a ghost ship, as did the *Samuel,* for the depositions of Major Todd and Lieutenant Little clearly stated that the *Sky Rocket* was aground just above the Narrows. If the *Sky Rocket* was at Fort Point Ledge, it would have been impossible for Todd and

Little to converse with Captain Burke; therefore, the remains of the *Sky Rocket*, must have drifted south during an ebb tide to end up at the Fort Point Ledge. The brig *Pallas* was on detached duty to the east of Penobscot Bay at the time the British reinforcements arrived, so it escaped capture or destruction.

* * *

Saturday through Monday, 14–16 August 1779, revealed eighteenth-century naval warfare's restrictions imposed by nature itself. These limitations included wind, tide, current, day, night, and clear or foggy weather. The Penobscot Expedition's retreat and rout encountered all these limitations.

General Lovell's retreat was his second successful major operation of the campaign. Just after midnight on 14 August the troops received orders to evacuate. This was an order no one challenged or skulked. The Americans had darkness and fog to cloak their movements, and by dawn most were aboard the transports. That morning the bay was calm and flood tide just beginning. Silently the transports drifted and towed up the Penobscot. They left the armed vessels in line across the bay waiting for the British.

Before eight that morning the commodore held his last council of war. The captains discussed three courses of action, sail around Long Island and flee; sail upriver and with the militia make a stand; or go upriver, disembark the crews, and destroy the vessels. The British stopped the three captains who tried to go around Long Island. The armed auxiliary captains selected the second alternative. In their haste they passed their transports, causing the panic that sent the transports ashore. Many transports burned; the militia scattered into the woods; and the rout began. Commodore Saltonstall and the remaining assault captains succeeded in gaining separation from the enemy, disembarking their crews, and burning their ships.

Meanwhile, General Lovell turned command of the transports over to General Wadsworth and returned to check on the commodore's actions. When he found out Saltonstall's plan, he tried to return to his command. Before he reached the transports, Captain Williams of the *Hazard* picked him up. The *Hazard*, as the first armed vessel to pass by the transports, was one of the vessels that created the panic and rout. Later Lovell spent a day trying to get the assault ship captains to go to the head of navigation and fortify, even though he had no troops to aid in the fortification. The commodore and assault captains continued their goal of disembarking crews and burning ships. In the end General Lovell realized there was nothing left to do and set off upriver to keep the Penobscot Indians allied with the Americans.

Neither the land nor the naval commander planned for the contingency of British reinforcements. Yet in spite of the rout, or because of it, the Americans avoided a confrontation with the enemy, thus saving many lives. Ships and supplies were lost, but most men made it home.

Chapter Six

Homeward Bound and
the Accounting

ONCE THE MILITIA, marines, and sailors landed, their homeward journey varied. For some, it was every man for himself. Others, like Drummer William Moody of Colonel Jonathan Mitchell's Cumberland County Regiment, stayed with their military unit during their travels home. Moody was on shore when the armed vessels passed the transports. He took a boat to board the transport *Centurion* for provisions. He landed supplies and returned to take off others. The company guarded four prisoners during this period. At daybreak Sunday, 15 August, the company took to the woods and soon became lost. While wandering aimlessly, they came upon General Wadsworth with others from their regiment and some sailors and marines. After crossing a large meadow, they struck a road in the woods and followed it until 7:00 A.M. when they stopped for breakfast. They crossed the Passagassawaukeag River in canoes and arrived in Belfast at noon. Captain Warren bought two sheep for eighteen dollars. Then they "arrived at a fine plantation and had a good dish of tea. Gen. Wadsworth and Capt. Buck supped with us. Had a fine barn to sleep in and rested comfortably."[1]

Monday, 16 August, they began at dawn and marched through marshes, beaches, and woods to Ducktrap (Northport). That morning one prisoner escaped. The men continued traveling along the shore and encamped at night. Tuesday they again followed the shore and at 1:00 P.M. reached Camden. Moody's company stopped at Clam Cove (Glen Cove), where they drew some fresh beef then took over a large barn for their barracks. Over the next few days the men began leaving the company headed for home. By Sunday, 22 August, the company broke up because it had no provisions. Moody, Company Commander Captain Warren, and five others headed home to St. George, arriving on Thursday, 26 August.[2]

Marine Sergeant Thomas Philbrook of the continental sloop *Providence* had a different experience. He claimed the journey home was as badly managed as the rest of the expedition. When the captains set fire to their ships, everyone was adrift in the wilderness. There was no order, no command structure, no plan of action. He claimed there were many hunters and Maine natives who knew the woods and knew where to go. Yet they left without helping the sailors and marines, who were novices to the woods. All the sailors and marines knew was that the Kennebec River lay to the west. Philbrook believed the military leaders should have sought out the experienced woodsmen and employed them as pilots to guide others homeward. "Some got to their homes in two days while most of us were six or seven days before we came to an inhabited country. I got through on the seventh day, after keeping a fast for three days. From Portland, I took passage in the frigate *Boston,* Capt. [Samuel] Tucker, was treated with much politeness by him and his officers."[3]

Seaman Thomas Hiller also of the *Providence* gave a noncommittal account of the final journey, saying they marched through the woods as far as Falmouth, where they rested and received provisions. "Then we that belonged to the Continental service were transported to Boston by water." His statement came from his pension application where there was no need to embellish his trials.[4]

Israel Trask, crewman of the *Black Prince,* told of his adventures after his ship blew up at the head of navigation on the Penobscot River. "With many others, I escaped to the dense forests and traveled through the wilderness about three hundred miles." He carried a pack with a light blanket, a small piece of pork, a few biscuits, a bottle of wine, and one shirt. As he made his way across streams and through underbrush his shoes gave way on the second day of his march. The rest of the way he walked barefoot. Between Beverly and Ipswich, he met a company of farmers returning from the salt marshes. When they learned his story, they "spread before me the payments of their luck." He lost track of time, but he believed it was September when he arrived home because farmers cut and cured salt fodder in the low tides of September.[5]

Lieutenant Colonel Paul Revere wrote in his journal that on the evening of 15 August he boarded the *Vengeance* for news. Captain Thomas told him he had landed some men and delivered provisions to some soldiers who had none. He planned to burn his ship in the morning. Revere went ashore and with two officers and eight men encamped a mile from the river. Next morning he set off with his group for the Kennebec River. He arrived at Fort Western (Winslow), on the Kennebec, where he found most of his officers and men. "After supplying them with what money I could spare, I ordered them to Boston by the nearest route." According to two of his officers, he told them that he was so lame he could walk no farther. He and three other officers bought a boat to go back to Boston. He turned his command over to Captain Lieutenant Thomas Newcomb. By sundown, Newcomb and Lieutenant Nicholas Phillips overtook Captain Cushing and the remainder of the Artillery Corps and continued home in their company.[6]

Micajah Lund, a sailor on the *Vengeance,* said that after destroying the ships "their crews took to the woods, and on foot found their way back to the province of Massachusetts." When they reached Newburyport, they told of the disaster. The townsmen sent the schooner *Shark* with provisions for the relief of the soldiers and sailors gathered along the Kennebec River.[7]

Not all the men rushed westward. The two companies of the 5th Militia Regiment, Deer Isle and Naskeag, broke away and in small groups headed east. For days the men skirted the British positions to get home. The island men took longer, for they had to cross Eggemoggin Reach. In the end the families were together, but now under British control.[8]

The previous statements convey some of the hardships inflicted upon the fleeing survivors. What about the wounded Americans that Doctor Downer carried above the falls and left in the care of Doctor Herberd? Captain Brewer's friends prevailed upon him to go to Bagaduce to find out about their own status. At the Narrows, Brewer went aboard the *Blonde* to ask the captain for a pass to the fort. Receiving his pass, Brewer continued to the fort and met with General McLean. The general asked him his mission. Brewer told him the people upriver wanted to know their status. If it was favorable, many planned to remain. If not, many would leave. McLean replied, "Go home and tell them if they will stay in their houses and live peaceably and mind their business, they shall not be hurt; but if not, all the houses that are left shall be burnt."[9] Brewer then asked what would be done about the sick and wounded from the expedition. He wanted to send them home as soon as possible. McLean asked Brewer if he had transportation for them. Captain Brewer said he knew of a vessel he could fix up. McLean agreed to the project and even offered to provide supplies if necessary. On his return upriver, Brewer charted the schooner *Hannah*, employed a master and crew, and brought all to the head of navigation. Here the schooner underwent a conversion fitting platforms and bunks for the invalids.

A few days later Captain Mowat arrived and anchored off the cove where Brewer lived. Mowat took great interest in the schooner's conversion. Almost daily Mowat called Brewer aboard the *Albany* to check on its progress. Often Mowat shared wine or brandy with Brewer. When the day arrived to load the invalids and head downriver, Mowat gave Brewer a pass to carry him through to Bagaduce.

At Marsh Bay Brewer learned that Captain Alexander Ross of the *Monmouth* and his cabin boy were ashore. Brewer brought the two aboard and entered Captain Ross's name as George Ross. Brewer may have used "George" to throw the British off as to his identity. Brewer omitted the fact that Ross captained one of the ships during the expedition. At Bagaduce Brewer presented his list to the general. McLean supplied provisions and a pass for the master direct to Boston or any other more convenient port. When the *Hannah* departed for sea, Brewer began his trip home. He arrived late at night tired from his exertions caring for the invalids. Later the Massachusetts Council allowed Brewer £103.4 "for fitting Schooner Hannah to receive sick & wounded Seamen & Soldiers & transporting them to Majorbigwaduce 30 miles."[10]

The same night that Brewer returned home, Ichabod Colson of Marsh Bay told Captain Mowat that Brewer had taken Captain Ross aboard the schooner. Early the next morning Mowat sent his boat to bring Brewer aboard the *Albany*. Brewer sent back a message that he had traveled all night and was tired. He said he would come aboard in the afternoon. As Brewer made ready to go to the *Albany*, he saw Mowat land his boat on the point of land below his house. Brewer got in his canoe and paddled over to meet him. The two met and for a while it was a stormy scene. When Brewer admitted doing something that Mowat had not ordered, Mowat became angry. "You d—d rebel! I have a good mind to run you through." Brewer opened his coat and said, "There is your mark, do it if you dare! I am in your power." Captain Mowat stalked off. The next day both men's tempers had cooled and they began a more cordial relationship.[11]

Another boatload of sick or injured Americans and their prisoners was sent to Boston from Camden. General Wadsworth ordered Captain Burke to impress a boat or small vessel to carry these people to safety. The general knew he could not provide the proper care on the coast of Maine with British reinforcements and an upsurge of Tory activity anticipated.[12]

General Wadsworth arrived in Camden on 17 August. Here he learned that an express boat from the council had pulled into Camden the day before, but when Lieutenant James Avery learned of the disaster, he had turned his boat around and returned to Boston. Wadsworth had no idea what Avery's instructions for the expedition might have been. Just as Wadsworth completed his letter to the council, Lieutenant Little of the *Hazard* arrived, reporting that General Lovell was on the Kennebec River. Wadsworth ended his letter saying that his express might meet General Lovell, and if so this letter would be delivered to Lovell. In any event he would remain in "this quarter till I receive orders from the Genl or your honr."[13]

The story of the rout was more than just the escapades of the fleeing militiamen, sailors, and marines. Many acts of hospitality were demonstrated by the people along the routes. For eighteen days John Marsh of Vassalborough boarded and nursed John Bates, a homeward-bound soldier. Edward Watts of Falmouth doctored several sick and wounded soldiers on their retreat from Penobscot. Job Lyman of York gave medicine and tended to Ephraim Pratt, a wounded soldier on his way home. Aaron Porter of Biddeford doctored Samuel Richardson and Mr. Dale, two shipboard marines, who were walking home. John Cox of Falmouth transported fifty-five seamen from the *Tyrannicide, General Putnam,* and *Hazard* from Penobscot to Boston. Mary King of Scarborough supplied 103 meals to the retreating men. Joseph Chadburn of Brunswick fed twenty-eight sailors and two soldiers as they passed through. Captain Abial Lovejoy of Vassalborough, with five other men, took charge of transporting twelve prisoners from Pownalboro to Boston.[14]

Two other groups were involved in the American rout. Earlier, to the east, Colonel John Allan received a dispatch from General Lovell asking for aid. Allan gathered his Indians at Passamaquoddy then set out westward. He arrived at Machias on 5 August, but it was 10 August before he was ready to sortie. That day he received a second request from Lovell for aid. Unfortunately for the Americans at Bagaduce, the wind and fog prevented his leaving. That night he received more pressing news from Passamaquoddy that British vessels were offshore. Colonel Allan corroborated this information before continuing westward. On 12 August he learned that the vessels were trading vessels and not threatening to his force. By 15

August he had divided his force, sending the whites in boats while he led the Indians along the shore in canoes. The two groups were to rendezvous at Eggemoggin Reach, the easternmost channel entering Penobscot Bay. On 16 August Colonel Allan met a strong headwind that separated his canoes during the struggle against the wind.

Then looking seaward he saw vessels stretching eastward. He could not tell if they were his vessels or not. When he arrived at Mount Desert that evening, he learned of the British reinforcement and of the disastrous retreat of the Americans. The next day he sent units out to intercept any of his people who might have arrived at Eggemoggin Reach without knowing the latest news from Bagaduce.[15] Unknown to Colonel Allan, his schooner and brig carrying the Machias militia were the vessels he saw stretching eastward. They reached Deer Isle before learning that the siege was over. Knowing that enemy ships were in Penobscot Bay, the two captains set out for Machias immediately.[16] Colonel Allan reached Naskeag on 18 August. Here he learned that his schooner and brig had arrived and departed the same day. Even at Naskeag he saw smoke from the burning American ships. Allan wrote, "From the Great Quantity of smoke, I imagined the Enemy were Burning the Settlements farther Westward." He had seventy Indians, but most of his provisions and ammunition were on his vessels headed east. There was nothing to do but lead his canoes back to Machias.[17]

The second group, to the west, was Colonel Henry Jackson's regiment of Continental soldiers. Earlier, when the Massachusetts Council received the two letters from General Lovell requesting Continental soldiers, it sent Samuel Adams to Providence, Rhode Island, to ask General Gates for troops. Adams talked with General Gates on 8 August. Ten days later, in Boston, Colonel Jackson's troops embarked for Bagaduce. A 16-gun ship, and two brigs convoyed the Continentals. On 19 August the council received information of the British reinforcement and the expedition's retreat. It immediately sent a vessel after the convoy with the news from Penobscot.[18] The intercepted convoy headed for the nearest port, Portsmouth, New Hampshire. On 22 August Colonel Jackson, at Portsmouth, met Lieutenant Colonel Paul Revere, just arrived from Penobscot. Jackson wrote to the council that, "He [Revere] informs me that the whole of our Shipping is destroy'd, with all the Provisions Ordnance and Ammunition and the whole army Deserted and gone home. I refer you to him for particulars who sets off for Boston this Evening."[19]

The Committee of Safety for Falmouth, on 30 August, summed up its view of the rout: "The return of ye Seamen from Penobscot in ye greatest distress imaginable has obliged us to act as commissary, Quartermaster &c. &c. To furnish them with necessary provisions & to relieve their distresses we have been obliged to issue some impress Warrants; some provisions we have purchased; & some we have borrowed. We have observed ye greatest Economy & order ye necessary confusions would admit of. The men returned without Officers; without Order. We shall transmit your Honors an account of our doings as soon as ye men have done returning."[20]

On 1 September a British vessel sailed into Portsmouth, New Hampshire, under a flag of truce. At first it frightened the townspeople who feared it might be an ultimatum to surrender. Their fear turned to joy when they found out the vessel carried the *Hampden*'s crew, all of whom were released except a Captain Roberts. No explanation was given as to why Roberts was missing from the exchange. The only information was that he would remain aboard and go to New York City.[21]

Bear in mind that the militia came from the three counties in Maine. Generally the militiamen had less distance to travel to reach home than the sailors and marines. Many fleet personnel lived in southern New England and had the longer journey home. It took time for the survivors to reach places where they received transportation. Rumors of the disaster spread everywhere. When the people of Boston heard of the rout, they were shocked. They could not believe the powerful force that had departed Boston two months before was gone. They were in disbelief.

The Massachusetts Council waited for word of the expedition, as did the man on the street and on the Commons. The first official information to reach the council arrived by letter Thursday morning, 19 August 1779. It claimed British reinforcements arrived, destroyed the fleet, and caused General Lovell to raise the siege and retreat with his army into the wilderness. The council did not identify the author of the letter. Probably it was Thomas Berry, for General Lovell assigned him that mission on the morning of 14 August as the transports set out upriver. The council immediately wrote to General Lovell saying, "The Council have this morning been informed that the Enemy at Penobscot were reinforced and had demolished our fleet, & that you were obliged on that account to Raise the Seige at Majorbagaduce Point, & to retreat into the country. Upon the council receiving the above information they thought Proper to pass the inclosed orders for the rule of your conduct in case it should prove true." What followed was a proclamation Lovell should issue to the people to the Eastward to rise up and continue to work against the enemy's occupation of Massachusetts territory.[22]

The council forwarded this letter on to the Navy Board who in turn passed excerpts along to its superior the Marine Committee. The Navy Board's information concerned naval affairs. "Augst 19 An Express Just arrived from Penobscot by which we learn that Reinforcement of the Enemy consisting of one 64, 4 frigates 20 gun Ships of war arrived on the 14th the Army & Navy were retreating up the river the Enemies Ships pursuing had overtaken & destroyed Several Armed ~~Vessells~~ Ships no doubt all will be lost for all were in confusion and the Enemy in the midst of them."[23] Later that same morning, the council received Lovell's letter of 14 August confirming his retreat with the Penobscot Expedition. The council wrote to General Gates to inform him of the situation. In its letter to Gates it quoted from Lovell's note scribbled just as the transports reached Fort Point: "This morning We received a letter from General Lovell dtd ye 14th instant informing that a reinforcement had arrived, and that it was thought expedient with all possible despatch to make a retreat, which he effected without loss, & is now on his way up Penobscot River to to [*sic*] Take Post at Fort Pownal if found convenient: the two Fleets were closing together & the general expressed his great anxiety for the event." The letter to Gates continued, telling him that a boat had departed immediately to warn Colonel Jackson of these events.[24] So on 19 August the council had two letters corroborating the disaster of the Penobscot Expedition. In turn, Colonel Jackson, diverted to Portsmouth, New Hampshire, met Colonel Paul Revere on 22 August and received an eyewitness account of the disaster.

On the same day the council received news of the Penobscot disaster, Brigadier Peleg Wadsworth was in Thomston writing his report of the British reinforcement's arrival. "Being uncertain whether you have been inform'd of the Sad Catastrophe of Your Armament against the Enemy at Magabigwaduce, am under the disagreable Necessity of informing Your Honr that (by information which I depend upon) the Destruction of Your Fleet was compleated on the forenoon of the 16th Inst, & that the Army, five companies excepted, are dispersed to their several homes." He then narrated the events of the faint wind, the flood tide, and as the wind improved the setting in of the ebb tide. The transports, not able to stem the ebb current, "shot into the Eddy on the westerly side of the river & ran ashore about two miles below the Narrows, whilst our ships of war, by the help of much sail and boats, reached a little farther up the whilst this was doing."[25]

Wadsworth continued telling how he was upriver ahead of the "~~first~~ foremost ships" at the Narrows where he decided to place his guns. But on his return to the transports, he found many on fire and all deserted. At this time he learned, "Genl Lovel [*sic*] 'tis said, was ~~on~~ gone up the River in the Hazard, which was then the headmost Vessell." The next morning he "not being able to get Intelligence from the Genl . . . & unable to retain a man on the ground, I [slung] my Pack & March'd directly for Camden."[26]

When General Lovell left the head of navigation to confer with the Penobscots, he had Colonel Davis, Major Todd, Doctor Downer, and five others with him. At the lower town he found the influential Indians were at the upper town, considerably farther up the Penobscot River. Lovell, needing to sign a treaty to salvage his expedition, pushed on up the river. During his conference, he found he must establish a truck house [trading post] on the Kennebec River. This was the most important demand of the Penobscots. After settling all the terms necessary for a treaty, the general hired eight Indians to guide him to the Kennebec.[27]

Meanwhile, the Reverend John Murray, learning of the Penobscot disaster, did all in his power to aid the survivors. He said the "deserters are innumerable" hundreds of families starving in the woods. He searched diligently for General Lovell. He hoped Lovell could bring order to the chaos. Murray set out by boat up the Kennebec to Fort Western to look for Lovell. At Fort Western he found the commodore, Major Gawen Brown, the general's secretary, and several others of the general's family. Yet no one heard from General Lovell since he set out with the Indians. Murray worried about Lovell because "now that every one that under took the longest route is arrived even the women. I have talked with one, that carried her babe not 4 weeks old, & another of 62 that carried bed & provisions." He, and others, feared that the Indians might kill Lovell or turn him over to the British.[28]

But General Lovell was safe, and later his Indian guides brought him to the Kennebec River. In fact, of all the Americans who crossed by land from the Penobscot to the Kennebec, Lovell's party had the easiest journey. In canoes, the Indians took them down the Penobscot River to the Souadabscook. Then they went up that tributary to its headwaters. From there, it was a portage of just over a mile to the Sebasticook River, which flowed into the Kennebec. At the confluence of the Sebasticook and Kennebec was Fort Western.[29]

General Lovell went down to the mouth of the Kennebec and turned east for Georgetown arriving on 28 August. The general felt his business in the area was unfinished and he could not yet return to Boston. While at Georgetown, he wrote his first letter to the council since his 14 August letter when the transports were off Fort Point. He said he would go to Camden to check on General Wadsworth's defensive actions in his absence. He was also eager to view the council's letters sent to Wadsworth, for he understood that the council believed he was a prisoner of either the Indians or the British.[30] The next day, 29 August, Lovell arrived at Townsend and established his headquarters there. He received the council's letter of 19 August ordering him to take the best post possible in Maine to carry out the public service. He received permission to direct Colonel Jackson's regiment to his headquarters. Further, the council empowered him to call upon the militia to meet his needs in securing the eastern counties of Massachusetts against British plundering.

In his return letter he plunged into a recitation of his defensive plans. He planned for three hundred men to be at Camden to cover the country from Pemaquid to Belfast. Lovell wanted Colonel Jackson's regiment stationed at Townsend covering Pemaquid west to Sheepscot River. He planned to have another three hundred troops at Cox's Head at the mouth of the Kennebec River. He intended to construct extensive fortifications at Townsend and at the Kennebec River. For these fortifications he needed two 9-pounders and one 18-pounder at each place, and he wanted three hundred entrenching tools. He suspected the two local artillery companies lacked the training to be effective; therefore, he requested one of Colonel Revere's companies ordered to return to the Eastward immediately.[31]

On 26 August Colonel Revere was the first of the senior officers to reach Boston. He received orders to his former post commanding at Castle Island. Captain Saltonstall returned to Boston 31 August. As had been his custom throughout the campaign, he said nothing publicly. Surprisingly, little information appeared in the papers about the disaster. Later narrators speculated that it was public policy to minimize the bad news or possibly political pressure to wait until the council had complete information on what happened. There were rumors galore but no official explanation.[32]

Still, as the stragglers arrived in Boston, it became difficult to ignore the retreat and rout of the highly touted Penobscot Expedition. During Colonel Revere's absence from Castle Island, volunteers worked improving its fortifications. On 2 September Major John Rice wrote to General Gates: "Upon Lieutenant Colonel Revere's return from Penobscot, he reasum'd the command at Castle Island, which has so disgusted the Volunteers who subscribed for repairing and completing the works, in and about this Town, that they have refused to proceed in this Business until he is removed; they alledge that his conduct upon the Expedition, was very unsoldierlike, & very reprehensible."[33]

The real bombshell was marine Captain Thomas J. Carnes's charges of 6 September to the council. Carnes, the commanding officer of the *General Putnam* marines, brought a complaint against Lieutenant Colonel Paul Revere for his behavior at Penobscot. There followed six charges that included disobedience to his commanding officers. Two charges involved disobeying General Lovell and one instance when Revere refused an order given by General Wadsworth. Another charge was for leaving his men during the retreat. Finally, Carnes presented two vague charges that included neglect of duty and unsoldierlike conduct tending toward cowardice.[34] The day of Carnes's charges, the council relieved Revere of his command and placed him under house arrest. Three days later the house arrest was withdrawn. Revere also received notification from the council that a legislative committee would examine him and other officers. Israel Keith wrote General William Heath that "the indelicacy with which Col. Revere was treated by the Council in the manner of his arrest would have disgraced a sergeant in the army of General Washington."[35] Shortly after that, General Lovell's letter of 29 August arrived. At the end of his recitation of his defensive plans, General Lovell concluded asking the council to give "Lieutenant Colonel Revere a very serious reprimand for his unsoldierlike behavior in returning home without orders."[36]

On 9 September the *Independent Chronicle* of Boston printed the following article:

> As we often have occasion to blame our enemies for publishing false accounts, particularly after they have been worsted in any action, we would by no means put it in their power to find fault with us on similar occasions. We have waited long enough to have had a particular account of the Penobscot expedition from Boston, and it has been promised; but when it will come from that quarter we cannot tell. From the various accounts we have had, the general report stands

thus, that our commanders by sea and land after they had taken a redoubt or two of the enemy's, reconnoitered until the enemy was reinforced with several large ships. Upon appearance of these, two of our vessels made an escape, two afterwards fell into the hands of the enemy and the residue were effectively secured by fire, &c. Our irregular troops made an irregular retreat, it is in imitation of an irregular Brigadier, and a new-fangled Commodore, without any loss, excepting the whole fleet, (saving two vessels) and all the military stores &c. about 70 men who were taken prisoners, a few killed, and a small number that died with fatigue in going through the woods. Thus, it is said ended the Penobscot expedition. The question now is, who is to blame?—Certainly not the under officers and privates.[37]

This article was the turning point. Official recognition of the Penobscot Expedition's disaster took place that day when the House of Representatives decreed that, "Whereas the Failure of the Expedition to Penobscot hath occationed great & universal uneasiness, and it is become necessary that Enquiry should be made immediately into the Causes, thereof." The Committee to Investigate into the Causes of the Failure of the Penobscot Expedition consisted of five members of the House of Representatives and four from the Massachusetts Council. Brigadier General Jonathan Titcomb; the Honorable James Prescott, Esquire; the Honorable Major General Michael Farley, Esquire; Colonel Moses Little; and Major Samuel Osgood, Esquire, were the House of Representatives participants. Generals Artemas Ward and Timothy Danielson, the Honorable William Sever, and Francis Dana, Esquire, were the Massachusetts Council members of the committee. General Ward was chairman of the committee.[38] Strangely enough, with two-thirds of the expedition naval and Massachusetts one of the strongest maritime states among the rebelling colonies, no committee members were naval officers or from the maritime service.

In the days between its formation and its first day of hearings, the committee members familiarized themselves with the council's correspondence with General Lovell. It gathered a list of prospective witnesses. It asked for the expenses incurred by the state from its various staffs. These accounts arrived for the committee between 23 and 25 September and totaled £1,588,668.0.10.[39] Finally it decided the form for its proceedings.

Meanwhile, the military situation to the Eastward wound down. General Gates recalled Colonel Jackson's regiment. Massachusetts, realizing it lacked most everything essential to continue militarily, turned the defense of the Eastward over to the local Committees of Safety and their militia.

Massachusetts recalled General Lovell and his staff. Lovell's family returned to Boston in two groups. Lovell and eight staffers lodged at Mrs. Greeley's house in Falmouth 17 September. They left the next morning and spent that night in Wells. Lovell arrived in Boston on 20 September. General Wadsworth and three others paid Theodore Davis for their transportation from Portsmouth to Boston, arriving 24 September, two days after commencement of the committee's hearings.[40]

Captain Saltonstall neither acknowledged the committee's task nor consented to be a witness. Israel Keith wrote to General Heath that Saltonstall refused "to give an account before white wigs."[41] He said he was to be tried by other authority. Keith continued, "Nothing is more natural than for an old soldier to despise men in civil life who have never smelled powder, and whom he looks upon as cowards. But to be brought to answer for his conduct in the field before such men is intollerable." Yet Saltonstall's name was on the list of witnesses and a notation beside his name said that he "appeared ye 2nd day." However, Saltonstall gave no testimony nor were questions asked of him.[42]

Wednesday 22 September 1779 the committee began its hearings. Thirty-two witnesses, thirteen from the land and nineteen from the naval service, went before the committee. None of the Continental naval officers testified. The procedure was, with few exceptions, for the witness to give a deposition. Sometimes the witness read his deposition to the committee; at other times the committee members read the deposition. If the committee had questions, these followed the deposition. The recurring question, asked of most, regardless of the witness' qualification, was whether the fleet could have defeated the British vessels at Bagaduce before the enemy received its reinforcement. Without exception, the answer was yes, although, some assault captains expressed the danger of unacceptable losses during such an encounter.

Most of the officers' depositions were about their own activity on the expedition. They did not discuss general strategy. But some of the naval officers voiced their opinion of Commodore Saltonstall. George Little, first lieutenant of the *Hazard,* was especially hard on the commodore in recounting their encounter aboard the *Warren* during the rout. Captains Cathcart of the *Tyrannicide* and Williams of the *Hazard* felt that demanding land support as a prerequisite to an attack was a ploy to keep from engaging the enemy. They believed the captains knew that General Lovell could not storm the fort. Captain Hacker of the *Providence* wrote his view outlining how the attack ships should have engaged the enemy. Yet even he felt the need for a land force to assist in the attack. Still, these were officers of auxiliary vessels not subject to engaging the enemy in Bagaduce harbor.[43]

Among the assault captains, Titus Salter of the *Hampden* was emphatic that once they deactivated the Half Moon Battery there was nothing to stop them. Yet at the council of war on the *Warren* on 6 August, even he voted not to attack the enemy vessels alone. Nor did he vote to go in if General Lovell possessed the low ground. Only if the fort was stormed did he vote to attack the enemy vessels. Both Captains N. Brown of the *Hunter* and Carnes of the *Hector* emphasized the risk inherent from the enemy fort and the length of time they would be exposed to its guns.[44]

On 7 October the committee issued its findings in a series of questions and answers. The entire text must be read to grasp the full impact of the committee's conclusion.

The Committee of both houses appointed to enquire into the reasons of the failure of the late Penobscot Expedition have after giving due Notice to the Commanders by Land & Sea & cited such persons as the Committee judged most likely to give the best account of the Reasons of the failure aforesaid proceeded to enquire into the Causes of Said failure—

General Lovells narrative of his procedure with the Councils of War by Land & Sea & the depositions of the several Witnesses delivered in on this enquiry accompany this Report And the Opinion of Your Committee upon the aforesaid Subject will appear as follows—

Question: Is it the opinion of this Committee that they have made sufficient Inquiry into the Causes of the failure of the late Expedition to Penobscot—

Answer: Unanimously Yes—

Question: What appears to be the Principal Reason of the Failure?

Answer: Unanimously, Want of proper Spirit & Energy on the part of the Commodore—

Question: Was General Lovell culpable in not Storming the enemies Principal Fort according to the Requirement of the Commodore & naval Council who insisted upon that as the Condition of our Ships Attacking the Enemies Ships, when at the same time the Commodore informed him that in Case of such an Attack he must call the marines on board their Ships (the last was not made apart of the Condition by the Naval Council)—

Answer: Unanimously, No—

Question: What in the opinion of this committee was the occasion of the total Destruction of our Fleet—

Answer: Principally the Commodore's not exerting himself at all at the time of the Retreat in opposing the Enemies foremost Ships in pursuit—

Question: Does it appear that Genl Lovell throughout the expedition & the Retreat acted with proper Courage and Spirit?

Answer: Unanimously, Yes & it is the opinion of the Committee had he been furnished with all the Men ordered for the service or been properly supported by the Commodore he wou'd probably have reduced the Enemy.

Question: Does it appear that the Commodore discouraged any Enterprizes or offensive measure on the part of our fleet?—

Answer: Unanimously, Yes And tho' he always had a Majority of his Naval Council against offensive operations which Majority was mostly made up of the Commanders of private Armed Vessels yet he repeatedly said, it was matter of favor that he called any Councils & when he had taken their advice he should follow his own opinion—

As the Naval Commanders in the service of the State are particularly Amenable to the Government the Committee think it their Duty to say that each & every of them behaved like brave experienced good Officers throughout the whole of the Expedition.—

Question: What was the conduct of Brigadier Wadsworth during his command?

Answer: Brigadier Wadsworth (the second in Command) throughout the whole Expedition, during the Retreat & after, 'till ordered to return to Boston, conducted with great Activity, Courage, Coolness & prudence.—

The Committee find the number of men ordered to be detached for this Service were deficient nearly one third whether the shameful neglect is chargeable upon the Brigadiers, Colonels or other Officers whose particular duty it might have been to have faithfully executed the Orders of the General Assembly they cannot ascertain—

This document signed by General Ward, as president, then listed the members present: Mr. Dana, Generals Danielson, Titcomb, Farley, and Major Osgood. After the list of members was a note "Hon[orabl]e Mr. Sever not present at all at the Enquiry, & [Colonels] Prescott & Little absent when this report was made."[45]

The next day the House of Representatives resolved "that a copy of this report and the papers accompanying the same be transmitted by the Honorable Council without delay to the Honorable The Congress, that they may take such order thereon, as may seem to them most conducive to Public Justice, and the Secretary is hereby directed to cause the report of the Committee to be published in one of the Boston newspapers, as soon as the Court Martial in Boston upon the Commodore shall be over. Sent up for concurrence /s/ John Hancock, Spkr."[46]

The final decree of the State of Massachusetts was, "Upon this report the General Court adjudged, *that Commodore Saltonstall be ever afterward deprived from holding a commission in the State, and that General Lovell and Wadsworth be acquitted.*"[47] Based on the committee's findings and the state's decree, Massachusetts's congressional representatives appealed to the Continental Congress and the subsequent Constitutional Congress for relief from the expedition's financial burden. Almost fourteen years later, on 29 June 1793, Congress awarded Massachusetts $1,248,000.00 as its share of the cost of the Penobscot Expedition.[48]

Chapter Seven

The Massachusetts
Conspiracy

THE COMMITTEE of inquiry's findings:

> Question: What appears to be the Principal Reason of the Failure?
> Answer: Unanimously, Want of proper Spirit & Energy on the part of the
> Commodore— . . .
> Question: Does it appear that Genl Lovell throughout the expedition & the
> Retreat acted with proper Courage and Spirit?
> Answer: Unanimously, Yes.

How could that be?

Commodore Saltonstall's ships and marines captured Banks' Island. General Lovell's militia made three unsuccessful attempts to land on Bagaduce. Saltonstall's ships scoured the Bagaduce landing area with gunfire before the successful assault. His marines were the first to land. They were the first up the precipice. They were the first to engage and drive the enemy back. Lovell's militia landed later. They reached the midpoint of the incline and rested just as the marines reached the heights. Saltonstall's force planned the attack on Half Moon Battery. His sailors and marines took the battery while the militia broke and fled. Saltonstall's sailors began work on the Westcot Battery before Lovell's troops joined the task. At the council of war on 7 August, Saltonstall suggested either "Strike a bold Stroke, by storming the Enemys works, & going in with the Ships, or raise the Siege." Saltonstall and his captains scouted for a battery site on the east side of Bagaduce River. They fled an enemy boat assault the day before Lovell's force took up the task. Commodore Saltonstall was willing to assault Captain Mowat's vessels at any time, if supported by the land force. At no time did General Lovell agree to storm the enemy fort. Only at the end, when it was too late, did Lovell agree to take his troops to the lower ground behind the fort. How could the gravamen of failure have been reversed and placed on the commodore's shoulders?

It was a Massachusetts conspiracy initiated by General Lovell, who in his letter-reports, in his journal, and in his testimony before the committee effectively painted the worst picture of Commodore Saltonstall and the best picture of his own activities. General Lovell began with some omissions and exaggerations to enhance his image as a competent commander. He drifted into mendacity while pointing out Commodore Saltonstall's failure to support his own effort. Ultimately he resorted to the duplicity of willfully saying different things at different times to the detriment of Saltonstall.

The Massachusetts Committee accepted General Lovell's comments against Commodore Saltonstall for several reasons. First, because Lovell's and the officers' depositions were the committee's only knowledge of the expedition upon which to base its decision. Commodore Saltonstall attended the second day's hearings, but he did not present his views nor challenge those depositions. Further, Saltonstall, an out-of-stater, had no political backing in Massachusetts to aid him. As a citizen of Connecticut, he provided the committee with just the scapegoat it needed to answer the public's demand to know who was responsible for this fiasco. Finally, Saltonstall, as a Continental officer, furnished the State of Massachusetts with the opportunity to saddle the Continental Congress with a share in the expense of the Penobscot Expedition.

General Lovell's first letter to the council was written on 28 July, just after gaining the heights. He told of arriving on 25 July and attempting a landing that evening. Unfortunately for his plan, a strong wind sprang up and he had to call off his assault. He was afraid the wind might keep the second wave from reaching the beach. Thus the first wave on shore would not have support. On 26 July "I took possession with the Marines, supported by General Wadsworth Division of one Island in the harbour, beat them off, took 4 Pieces of Artillery and some Ammunition, the worth Major Littlefield with two Men were drowned by the sinking a Boat by a chance Shot from the Enemy—"[1]

Lovell omitted an account of his two other attempts to land on Bagaduce. In his general orders for 27 July, General Lovell gave thanks to Captains Hacker, Johnson, and Edmunds for their assistance in the landing on Banks' Island and praised the marines for their charge on the enemy. His general orders were for the expedition's consumption. Yet when he wrote to the council he neglected to mention the commodore or the naval part in the attack upon Banks' Island. He overshadowed the role of the marines by stressing General Wadsworth's support. In driving the enemy from the island, Lovell's expression "beat them off" implied more action than took place. According to British sources, there was no engagement. The Royal Marines and British transport seamen fled without offering resistance. Further, Lovell's report of the loss of Major Littlefield and two men in the same sentence with the capture of the battery led the council to assume the loss took place during the assault. In truth, Major Littlefield and his men were lost during the militia's third unsuccessful attempt to land on Bagaduce.

After telling about the erection of a battery on Banks' Island, Lovell reported his landing on Bagaduce on 28 July. "This morning I have made my landing good on the S.W. head of the Peninsula which is one hundred feet high and almost perpendicular very thickly covered with Brush & trees, the men ascended the Precipice with alacrity and after a very smart conflict we put them to the rout." He ended saying, "we are within 100 rod of the Enemy's main fort on a Commanding peice of ground, & hope soon to have the Satisfaction of informing you of the Capturing the whole Army."[2] Again, notice the absence of any mention of the marine and fleet activity in his report. This was in keeping with his general orders of 28 July in which he also ignored the marines and fleet activity.

Three days later, 1 August, Lovell wrote his second report. "My last to you was written in great haste on the 28 Ult. immediately upon my gaining this Ground." He reported that he lost fifty killed and wounded, among them marine Captain Welsh and Captain Hinkley of the Lincoln Militia. "But notwithstanding the seemingly insuperable difficulty of forcing up a Precipice of not less than 200 feet, some part of which was nearly perpendicular, such was the bravery of the troops that they push'd the Enemy off the ground, with so great precipitation that we could not overtake more than eight of them who were made prisoners."[3] He told of ordering artillery & ordnance stores "within point blank shot of the Enemy's grand fort." He noted the difficulty hauling artillery up to the heights. "This last was found to be a Work of great difficulty but the Alacrity of the Troops & the very essential assistance of the Marines surmounted every obstacle & soon brought up four six Pounders & one field piece." By Friday, 30 July, he had a battery of two 18-pounders, one 12-pounder, and one howitzer sixty rods from the enemy's "Citidel."[4]

Lovell did not mention that the commodore's vessels provided the initial cannonading before the landing. Though he did note the death of Captain Welsh and the marines' "essential assistance" in hauling artillery, he did not mention that the marines landed first, were the first to reach the heights, and the first to drive the enemy back. Lovell never mentioned Commodore Saltonstall leading three ships toward the anchored British ships in close line-of-battle across the Bagaduce entrance. Nor did he report that the *Warren* suffered severe battle damage just three hours after his land forces reached the enemy's "Citidel." Instead he wrote: "Meantime the commodore haveing drawn up his heaviest ships close to the Mouth of the river & formed a Line, the Enemy as if from an expectation of an immediate attack from him suddenly abandoned all their Shipping and have sunk most of the transports without the Vessels of War."[5] This statement implied that the enemy shipping feared Commodore Saltonstall's fleet. The inference was that it would be easy for the American men-of-war to destroy the British ships.

General Lovell told of the brig *Diligent*'s capture of the packet from Halifax, including that the packet captain scuttled his dispatches before surrendering, and that the prisoners and deserters from the enemy all claimed that the British expected a speedy reinforcement. Lovell concluded that he must choose between two parts: "either continue a regular Siege with volunteer ships that cannot lie here long inactive; and a body of Militia whose domestic affairs cannot admit of their being long from home; or risk the fate of a Storm." Lovell chose siege.[6] He continued saying, "Since writing the above a detachment under P. Wadsworth this Morning about two Oclock attacked & carried the above mentioned small Redoubt [Half Moon Battery] but it being commanded by the Cannon of their main Fort it was thought proper to abandon it after destroying a small quantity of Provisions there—" After listing the killed and captured and the loss of Major Sawyer, York Militia, he shifted to an account of the close harmony between the troops and the marine department. He concluded with a postscript: "I think the Enemy cannot be attacked by Storm with any probability of Success—their works being exceedingly strong and our Troops (tho brave) are yet undisplined." In Lovell's second letter of the day to Powell, he again said that he could not storm nor did he have the time for a regular siege. Now he requested "a few regular disciplined troops," grenades, mortars, and fire shells. He forwarded these two letters to the council via the Reverend Murray who left aboard the row galley *Lincoln*.[7]

In his general orders of 1 August Lovell thanked the officers and soldiers "both in the Land & Marine department" for the assault on Half Moon Battery. Yet in spite of Lovell's claim of close harmony between the two services, when he wrote to the council he made no mention of the sailors and marines participating in the Half Moon Battery assault. Nor did he mention that the militia panicked and fled while the sailors and marines continued forward. It was Commodore Saltonstall's sea force that captured the battery.

General Lovell's next letter, dated 6 August, told of the enemy sending out small parties that he frequently repulsed. He sent orders to the Eastward for all the militia possible to aid his force at Bagaduce. Then he wrote, "Some of the Officers of the Navy seeing the many difficulties we labour under have expressed a desire to leave us." But he could not entertain such an idea because of the value of the region to the state and the United States. In ending he enclosed two councils of war, both held on that day, one aboard the *Warren,* the other at his headquarters. Major Braddish carried Lovell's letter with its enclosures to Boston.[8]

In the first enclosure, Commodore Saltonstall called a council of war aboard the *Warren,* on 6 August. He presented Lovell's letter of the previous day to the council. In that letter the general said he could go no farther; Lovell wanted to know what the fleet would do. Saltonstall asked if the ships should go in as the general requested. Eight of the assault captains said no. If the general took the lower ground behind the fort and held it, two assault captains would go in. If Lovell stormed the citadel at the same time the ships moved in, nine of the ten assault captains would attack. The tenth assault captain was not present for the council.[9] In the second enclosure, General Lovell called his council of war at his headquarters that same day. Lovell presented Saltonstall's reply to his officers. After hearing the naval officers' views, the land officers unanimously answered they could not storm nor hold the low ground.[10]

There was an interesting reaction by the council to Lovell's letter with its enclosures. It was a precursor of the Lovell-council conspiracy to come. The day before Lovell's letter arrived, the council received General Washington's warning of 4 August that a British fleet had left New York headed for Bagaduce. The council called a meeting and brought the Navy Board Eastern Department members in to participate in the consideration of this news. The council drafted a letter to General Lovell that was completed at midnight. The next morning, 12 August, Lovell's second letter arrived.

Again the council and Navy Board conferred. The only communication the Navy Board had had from Penobscot was Saltonstall's optimistic letter of 1 August citing the close cooperation between the sea and land forces. In contrast, the council received no positive reports from Lovell of the fleet. The general had only negative comments of Saltonstall and the fleet. Lovell's latest report was shocking. The general said he could go no farther until Saltonstall destroyed the enemy vessels. The assault captains said they would attack only if the land force joined the strike. With no understanding of the local situation, neither the Navy Board nor the council could understand why Saltonstall's force did not attack.

The Navy Board wrote to Commodore Saltonstall as follows:

> Major Bradish [*sic*] this morning arrived with dispatches from General Lovell to the Honorable Council.
>
> We don't find that he has brought any for us. The Council however have obliged us with a Communication of General Lovells Letter & the papers Inclosed. Among which we find the result of a Council of War on board the Warren August 1779—[6 August]
>
> We have for Some time been at loss to know why the Enemys Ships have not been Attacked nor does the result of this Council give us any Satisfaction on that head. . . . We think it our duty to direct you to Attack & take or destroy them without delay in doing which no time is to be lost as a Reinforcement are probably on their passage at this time. It is therefore our orders that as soon as you receive this you take the Most Effectual Measures for the Capture or destruction of the Enemies Ships & with the greatest dispatch the nature & Situation of things will admit of—[11]

The Navy Board provided a copy of its letter to the council. Moses Gill drafted the council's reply to General Lovell. It was a hurried, scribbled note with many crossed-out portions. The council sent a copy of the Navy Board's letter to Saltonstall to General Lovell. It noted its approval of the Navy Board's opinion and its orders to the commodore. Interestingly, the council wrote to Lovell to assist Saltonstall, and then, for some reason, crossed out that portion of the letter: "and we expect your Co Opporation in <u>Complying these</u> Carrying Positive orders into effect."[12]

Meanwhile, the council ordered Lieutenant James Avery to be the bearer of the messages for Bagaduce. Avery received orders to deliver his packet personally to General Lovell and receive a receipt noting the day and hour received. He was to carry the packet in a weighted bag to be sunk only as a "last extremity."[13] The Board of War supplied him with "one

Lanthorn [lantern] one Box compass & Six Oars for the Express Boat."
He also received "a gun & Bayonet & one pound of powder & Ball sufficient—he to replace the same upon his return back."[14]

It was obvious neither the council nor the Navy Board was aware of the
naval positions at Bagaduce. Commodore Saltonstall had only one opportunity to report to his superiors. That was on 1 August when the express
row galley *Lincoln* was at Penobscot Bay. Lovell's letters of 28 July and 6
August went to the council unbeknownst to Saltonstall. Therefore, those
in Boston were oblivious to the fleet's need for land force cooperation for a
successful attack on the enemy ships. Lovell's letter and enclosures created
a flurry in Boston that began the thought process of considering the commodore as the cause of all delays. Neither the Navy Board's nor the council's letter influenced the commanders in Bagaduce, for the retreat began
before their letters arrived.

Lovell's next letter to the council was 13 August. It answered the council's letter of 6 August wanting to know what was happening at Bagaduce.
Lovell told the council that he had sent letters the day he landed, others by
Reverend Murray, and his third by Major Braddish. He hoped all had
arrived by the time he wrote this letter. Lovell thought the situation was
critical. He had 950 men, and the enemy had 700 troops and 300 seamen
and marines. The enemy naval force worked wherever needed on land or
aboard ship. He, on the other hand, could not divide his force to satisfy the
naval officers. "You may Judge my Situation when the most important
Ship in the Fleet and almost all the private property Ships are against the
Siege, you will find the Ships were determined to go in if I would take
possession of the Ground in the rear of the Enemy's fort." He knew taking
a position in the rear of the enemy's fort would be dangerous, but the commodore's ships would not go into the harbor otherwise. Thus he consented to send his men to that post. Yet when the time came, he did not send
his troops to the rear of the fort, but instead he "made a tryall of them, and
found by their behaviour before the enemy, it would be inexpedient, I
therefore called a Council of War who were unanimously of my Opinion— The Commodore and Captains then Determined not to go in—"[15]

It was typical of General Lovell to be vague about unpleasant circumstances. He was referring to difficulties with his troops against the British
on 11 August, when the men broke and fled before the enemy. That night
the general held a council that, according to the *Hunter* journal, decided to
raise the siege. Although the minutes of Lovell's council listed the reasons

to raise the siege, it failed to state specifically that the siege was over. General Lovell had difficulty acknowledging his failure to storm the enemy's position, preferring to shift the blame to the commodore. Lovell reported that all his ordnance shells were expended; he had only a few 12-pound cartridges left, and only one-fourth of his small arm cartridges remained. Then he asked the council, if he should have to raise the siege, what should he do? Should he take a post in the Eastward or retire from that country?[16]

His question was followed by a postscript stating that at midnight he received word from Commodore Saltonstall that two of his vessels guarding the mouth of the bay had discovered an approaching fleet believed to be the enemy's reinforcement. "I therefore thought it expedient with all possible dispatch to make a retreat which [was] effected without Loss and am now on my way up Penobscot River to take post at Fort Pownal." If Commodore Saltonstall's fleet should be superior, then he would try to repossess his former position at Bagaduce. "While I am under these misfortunes I hope the Public will suspend their Judgment till a fair and Candid hearing can be had—"[17]

The general forwarded the proceedings of the last five councils of war. The first council of war was aboard the *Hazard* on 7 August. It opened with General Lovell asking what further measures should be taken. Commodore Saltonstall suggested, "We either strike a bold Stroke by Storming the Enemy's Works and going in with the Ships, or raise the Siege."[18] Lovell replied he could not storm in his present condition. After further discussion, the general asked whether the expedition should remain or leave. Thirteen voted to remain including two assault captains and four auxiliary captains. Eight voted to leave including Colonel Revere and seven assault captains.[19]

The next council of war aboard the *Warren* was on 10 August. It determined that the land officers could hold ground eastward of the enemy fort. At this, the naval officers voted to go in and destroy the enemy's ships.[20] The following night Lovell held a council of war at headquarters to discuss the failure of the troops to stand against the enemy that day. All agreed that they could not divide their force against the enemy.[21] At a council of war aboard the *Warren* on 12 August, the naval officers received the militia officers' decision of 11 August. When they found the militia would not hold the ground eastward of the fort, they decided they could not attack the enemy ships in the harbor. The navy captains voted twelve to two not to go into Bagaduce Harbor. Only Captains Waters and Salter agreed to go in.[22] The fifth council of war enclosed was at headquarters on 13 August. Again General Lovell called for a determination of whether to remain or leave. The vote was fourteen to ten to remain. This time Colonel McCobb joined Revere, the commodore, and seven assault captain wanting to raise the siege.[23]

The Massachusetts General Council received five letters from General Lovell in the period from 25 July through 14 August, from the arrival off Bagaduce to the retreat as far as Fort Pownall. Two letters on 1 August stated that he could not storm, that he must employ a siege, and that he needed help. On 6 August he reported that the navy wanted to give up the siege if the land force could not support the ships, and he included two councils of war held that day. On 13 August he again reported his problem with the ships not attacking and, finally, in a postscript dated 14 August, his retreat as far as Fort Pownall. On 19 August the General Council received two brief accounts of the British reinforcement, one probably from Thomas Berry, although not identified by the council, and Lovell's letter of 13–14 August.[24] At this time the members knew only that enemy reinforcements had arrived and an apparently successful retreat was under way.

The General Council's next communication came from General Wadsworth. He wrote from Thomaston on 19 August. He said when he reached Camden he learned that the council's express, Lieutenant Avery, had heard of the disaster, turned around, and headed back to Boston on 16 August. That was the day before he arrived in Camden. Wadsworth had not seen General Lovell since he left the transports in his barge on 14 August; therefore, he was not sure if his account of the catastrophe would be the first one the council received. Wadsworth told of the evacuation of Bagaduce. "The wind being very faint and much against us, prevented our getting far up the river, on the tide of flood, till the coming in of the seabreeze in the afternoon, which bro't in the enemy's Fleet along with it." He told of the *Hampden,* the *Hunter,* and one of the brigs being cut off by the enemy. He related going up the Narrows and finding a place to fortify, "but, on returning, to [my] great surprise, found many of our transports on fire, all deserted, and our troops scattered in the utmost confusion."[25] He said that the next morning he tried to rally the troops to no avail. "Both men and officers had dismissed themselves and marched off the parade faster than they could be brought on." He was not able to receive information or orders from General Lovell, whom he believed was four or five miles up-river. Finally, he swung his pack and marched directly for Camden.[26]

How successful were these letters in preparing the council for Lovell's interpretation of the events at Bagaduce? General Artemas Ward's letter of 8 September 1779 to his former aide-de-camp Colonel Joseph Ward was most revealing:

> The most authentick account yet received of that sad catastrophe, is contained in a letter from Brigadeer Wadsworth to the Council; a copy of which you have inclosed, some parts of which I am of opinion ought not to be told in Gath. [gatherings?] I have the pleasure to inform you that our friend Wadsworth's conduct is spoken of with universal applause, as judicious and brave. Brigadeer Lovell is well spoken of, that he did everything in his power.
>
> The commander of the fleet is cursed, bell, book, and candle, by many; how justly I must at present omit saying. I have been told by one who fell into the enemies hands, and since deceased, that Britains spoke highly in praise of the commander of the land forces as being judicious, &c., in their movements; but that the commander of the fleet they would hang for a coward, if they could catch him. Lieut.-Col. Paul Revere is now under an arrest for disobedience of orders, and unsoldierlike behavior tending to cowardice, &c. As soon as the siege was raised, he made the best of his way to Boston, leaving his men to get along as they could (as it's said). I hope the matter will be thoroughly enquired into, and justice done to every individual officer. I have been told that it has been said by some one in the army, that we wanted advice in planning the expedition, and insinuating thereby that that was the reason why the enterprize failed. They had better spare their reflections, and re-examine their own conduct in all its parts. I think it was well done, and there was as great a prospect of success till the moment the reinforcements arrived, as we could rationally expect.[27]

This letter was written the day before the Committee of Inquiry was formed with General Ward as its chairman. General Ward's letter demonstrated a fully formed biased opinion of the expedition. It certainly was not the mind-set Commodore Saltonstall would want the chairman of the Committee of Inquiry to have.

About the time General Ward wrote his letter, General Lovell's letter of 28 August from Georgetown arrived in Boston. He began his narration following his letter of 14 August. He wrote that the expedition's ships, finding the enemy ships superior, turned, under full sail, and followed after the transports. General Lovell noted that the transports were not able to proceed farther than Sandy Point just above Fort Pownall. When the British ships were within three-fourths of a mile, the troops were landed. Yet the enemy ships, intent on the fleeing American warships paid no attention to his transports until a fire ship stopped their course toward the Narrows. "Early the next morning I went on board the Commodore to Know whether any measures had been determined on by the Shipping & finding no plan for their future operations had been settled." The general said that he and the commodore agreed that he should go upriver to get the other captains to send boats and crews to the *Warren* to assist it in its endeavors to move upstream. Finally, General Lovell, realizing his efforts were of no avail, went upriver to the Lower Town of the Penobscots to hold a council.[28]

General Lovell's letter of 28 August clearly showed his willful duplicity. He did not mention being aboard the *Hazard,* passing his transports at the Narrows, and remaining on the river above the Narrows during the rout at Mill Cove. His letter implied that he was with his troops in the transports when the British ships arrived at the Narrows. (General Lovell's duplicity need not be stated item by item, but a rereading of chapter five's account might be in order.)

It was probably the day after the establishment of the committee, 10 September, that Major Todd arrived in Boston. He had lodged at Mrs. Greeley's place in Falmouth on 8 September. General Lovell gave Todd his letter of 4 September to carry to the council in Boston. At the conclusion of his letter, Lovell wrote, "I make no doubt it would have been to my advantage to have arrived at Boston with the Rest but I doubt not your Honors are sensible of my situation, and as the duty of my country has detained me, I conclude nothing unfavorable in the Meantime will take place— I have forwarded Major Todd with these papers to whom, provided anything is wanting I refer Your Honors, having gone thro' a detail of Affairs."[29] Undoubtedly Lovell's papers were from his journal, especially for 14 August. That would present the retreat and rout from the general's point of view.

It should be remembered that General Ward writing on 8 September said the only "authentick" account was General Wadsworth's letter, and Wadsworth could only report on a portion of the events that occurred during the retreat and rout. Now on 10 September with General Lovell's letter of 28 August and his journal at hand, the General Council had Lovell's version of the events of 14 August. In his journal introduction Lovell wrote: "While it may not perhaps present any new facts in relation to the matter of which it treats, it gives a clearer insight into the details of that unfortunate affair and affords better means of judging with whom the blame should rest."[30] His last entry, an epitome of self-gratulations and aspersions on the fleet, stated:

August 14.—This morning I completed my retreat from Magabigwaduce without the loss of a Man and brought off all the Stores of the Army unmolested by the Enemy. The Transports got under way to pass up the River but it being calm they soon dropt anchor till 12 oclock the wind sprung up at the Southward and blew a tolerable breeze. The Transports then again weigh'd Anchor and to our Great Mortification were soon follow'd by our fleet of Men of War pursued by only four of the Enemy's Ships, the Ships of War passed the Transports many of which got a-Ground, & the British Ships coming up the Soldiers were obliged to take to the shore, & set fire to their Vessells, to attempt to give a description of this terrible Day is out of my Power it would be a fit subject for some masterly hand to describe it in its true colours, to see four Ships pursuing seventeen Sail of Armed Vessells nine of which were stout Ships, Transports on fire, Men of War blowing up, Provisions of all kinds, & every kind of Stores on Shore (at least in small Quantities) throwing about, and as much confusion as can possible be conceived.[31]

General Lovell's 14 August journal entry has become the centerpiece in most historical narratives to prove that Commodore Saltonstall was the gravamen of the expedition's failure. In narration after narration that entry has stood with no analysis of its content.

On 3 September General Lovell received the council's letter of 27 August asking for his account of the retreat. He began his narration of events on 13 August. He recounted that at ten in the evening the commodore told of six ships at the mouth of the bay, which were presumed to be reinforcements for the enemy. Saltonstall said he would know more when his second vessel arrived. At midnight Captain Hallet arrived, confirming that the strangers were enemy vessels. General Lovell immediately ordered a retreat. "On an Island in the entrance of Majabijwaduce River, were two 18 pounders & one 12, under the care of the Officers of the Navy, which were not brought off; I used every endeavour to secure them, by ordering a party for that purpose, but my time was too short, the Enemy's Shipping & boats then being near that place, and that part of our Navy which cover'd this post having drawn off, I dispatched orders for them to desist.—"[32] Again General Lovell belittled the naval operations and implied he did his best to take off the Banks' Island guns. In truth, Lovell and his militia were aboard the transports going upriver at 8:00 A.M. The sailors continued firing to keep the enemy sloops of war in the harbor. Finally, at 10:00 A.M. boats from the *Nautilus* moved to capture Banks' Island. The sailors spiked the guns and returned to their ships, two hours after Lovell left Bagaduce.[33]

Lovell's letter continued and his duplicity became more apparent in his phrasing. "Unexpected to me I observed the Navy underway . . . at 5 Oclock P.M. were along side of us, . . . by sunset the Enemy's Vessells lay abreast of us. . . . I was satisfied these Vessells must fall into their hands; but before I cou'd give my Directions, some of the commanders had Orders from the Commodore to destroy them."[34] After a careful reading of these letters, one could reach several conclusions. First, that General Lovell received little support from Commodore Saltonstall and the private captains in carrying out his wishes. That he tried admirably to achieve the goal of expelling the enemy from Bagaduce, but he struggled equally against a stubborn foe and a spiritless naval commander. Undoubtedly the council's Bagaduce file prepared the committee members to arrive at the conclusion that they reached. What more proof of Saltonstall's guilt was needed for General Ward and the Committee of Inquiry?

If one doubted that the newly created Committee of Inquiry had formed its opinion of the guilt of Commodore Saltonstall by that early date, the committee's next action should dispel that thought. A few days later, when the committee learned that the navy court-martial of Captain Saltonstall would take place on 14 September, the members faced a problem. The Committee of Inquiry was not ready to begin its hearing. What if the navy court-martial tried and found Captain Saltonstall not guilty or guilty of a lesser offense? How could they then find him alone guilty of the failure of the Penobscot Expedition? The Committee of Inquiry asked the General Court to make a special request to the Navy Board Eastern Department to postpone the navy court-martial until 28 September "until the examination of General Lovell & some other officers of the Army had been gone through." The Navy Board approved the Massachusetts General Court's request and forwarded the request and the approval on to the navy court-martial. Captain Sam Nicholson, president of the court-martial, wrote, "To the Honorable the Supream Legislative Body of the States of Massachusetts in General Assembly Convened.— . . . the Court having received a requisition from the Navy Board, together with a resolve of this Honble

Court requesting an adjournment to the 28 inst and taken the same into their Consideration thought proper to adjourn accordingly—."[35]

One further point bolsters the belief that the committee members accepted Lovell's contentions and actively furthered them. Jonathan Parsons wrote that General Jonathan Titcomb, committee member from the House of Representatives, asked him for evidence respecting General Lovell's conduct. In a nota bene to his report he said, "I have omitted the Consideration of anything in the Naval Department, tho I am sure the sole Cause of the Miscarriage was the want of Men & means, and that Commodore Saltonstall must also be accquitted with honor, and I am as ready to do justice to Commodore Saltonstall's Character when called upon." Parsons later wondered what use had been made of his evidence. Unfortunately for his evidence, Parsons's comments on General Lovell's actions were not what the committee wanted to hear, nor did it desire "to do justice to Commodore Saltonstall's Character."[36] So Parsons was not asked for his comments on Saltonstall nor was his letter included among the supporting material submitted by the committee to the Massachusetts General Court.

On 21 September, the day before the committee began its hearings, John Hancock wrote to "His Excellency John Jay Esqr" to tell the Continental Congress of Massachusetts's ill fortune. He related the failure of the Penobscot Expedition to dislodge the enemy. Not only did the state lose "three state vessels of force" but also insured all the others, except the Continental vessels. This financial obligation must be met to fulfill the public faith and credit. Further the drafts from the state's militia to fill the Continental quotas and many other demands of the union "keeps our Treasury exhausted." Therefore, the state requested that Congress allow the state to retain its six million dollars in Continental taxes until it liquidated these debts. Between General Lovell's letter reports, and his diary, and John Hancock's letter, the committee members were receptive to Lovell's coming testimony in his defense.[37]

The committee members gained greater insight into the expedition's expenditures when the accounts were forwarded to them.

Col. Tyler QMG	£27,148.1.2
Speakman Ordnance	£167,827.17.4
Mr. Lucas Provisions	£113,970.2.8
Dr. Downer Medical	£3,571.2.0

Provisions & Stores delivered	£17,150.10.4
Sundries Supplied Ships	£17,919.16.2
List of Ships & amt. 21 trans/8 ships/1 Brig	£1,052,200.
Commissary Department	£85,193.2.4
Bd of War expended	£130,481.17.0
General Lovell's Family expenses traveling	£357.34
[Other expenses not listed]	
Total Expenses	£1,588,668.0.10[38]

By now the committee was convinced of the guilt of Commodore Salton-stall. It was also aware of the significant financial burden of the expedition. Now it was only necessary to find Saltonstall guilty of the expedition's failure in order to shift some of the financial burden to the Continental Congress. The next step was to call the witnesses.

General Lovell was the first witness before the committee on 22 September. His deposition and testimony were in the same vein as his earlier letters. Although General Lovell's testimony essentially repeated information from his letters, his modus operandi was most apparent in his committee presentation.

On the 28th we effected Our landing on the heights in the Morning, about two hours after, to wit about Seven O'Clock we reconoitred & found the Enemy had erected their main Fort from which fir'd in Barbette & had mounted two Cannon the one a 12 and the other a six pounder. . . . The Marines that assisted in landing upon the Peninsula I suppose consisted of 150 Men— If I had judged it prudent to attack the enemy's Works, then supposed the Marines then on shore would have assisted in the attack— I collected the account of the enemies force from the Prisoners we took at our landing—they generally agreed they were about 1000 some more, none less. Upon this, I order'd lines to be thrown for our defence in case of an attack I think there was a rational probability of success if the navy had coopperated with me after I had taken possession of the Heights at Majorbagaduce—by the Navy's coopperating I mean their attacking the Ship[pin]g there was nothing to prevent this, but a Battery of three six pounders, near the Water's Edge unless they could be annoy'd from the main fort which was at ½ a Miles distance, from the Shore & mounted 4.12 pounders, & some 6' pounders

Q: Did you request the Naval Commanders to coopperate with you at the time you effected your landing, or during that Day or any time after—

Ansr: I did not at the time of my landing or during that day—except to furnish the Marines—[39]

Again the general's omissions and exaggerations enhanced his own image and belittled the commodore's. Lovell supposed he had 150 marines, when at the council of war on 27 July Saltonstall promised 227 marines. The general had apparently forgotten that on 28 July, three hours after he took the heights, Commodore Saltonstall led three ships against Captain Mowat's battle line. At the time the Half Moon Battery's guns were four 12-pounders. Saltonstall's *Warren,* in the van, suffered considerable damage that took two days to repair; however at no time did Lovell mention Saltonstall's attack.

General Lovell resumed his testimony on 25 September:

> On the 30 Capt Saltonstall said it was a proposal of his Captain's to go & attack the enemy's Ships on that day Capt Saltonstall said in yt Case he must take all the Marines from on shore for that purpose, to which I objected because I had not got my Cannon mounted in my advance Battery which was incompleat— that the enemy might land from yr Ships if they were attacked & attack me with their whole force in which case I would be in Danger of loosing my Cannon, or being totally defeated.
>
> On the 31st I inform'd Capt Saltonstall that I was ready for his Shipping to opperate, Captain Saltonstall then pointed out the 3 Gun Battery as an obstacle, Upon which I gave Directions to have the battery stormed which was effected about 2 o'Clock the next Morning viz, August 1st which remov'd the obstacle— This Battery mounted 3 6 pounders only at the time.[40]

Lovell failed to mention that Commodore Saltonstall initiated the plan of attack upon Half Moon Battery on 1 August, and that it was the naval force that took the battery. At that time the battery's guns were three 9-pounders. By reducing the size of the enemy guns, Lovell continued to hammer at his theme that Saltonstall was, at the least, timid. Finally, it was clever of Lovell to call Saltonstall captain rather than by his Penobscot Expedition's title of commodore.

General Lovell's testimony continued 26 September:

> When we had reduced the Battery we could not secure our Men from the Enemy's Main Fort & Shipping I requested Commodore Saltonstall to destroy the Shipping he asked me if he destroy'd the enemy's Ships whether I could storm the Enemy's Main Fort. I told him I could not with my land forces only,— But it would put me in a situation to take post in their Rear & sweep all their stock of cattle from them. He then replied, his Ships might suffer, & as that was no place for refitting, he might fall a sacrifice in Case a reenforcment should arrive to the Enemy Upon which Brig Wadsworth went upon the Main

Land to Reconnoitre for a proper place to annoy the Shipping. He return'd & inform'd me he had found a place near Wescott's Point from which the Enemy's Shipping might be annoyed. & their Foraging parties prevented from *Scouting out* upon the quarter—On the 3rd a party on Fatigue were order'd for the purpose of getting up the Cannon & errecting works—On the 4th The Battery was open'd against the Enemy's Shipping but it did not fully answer the intended purpose—finding by this days experience it did not do them any great damage. . . . August 8th This day being very stormy damaged our Amunition very much—We came to a determination to throw up a Battery on the Main Land, on the S. East side of Majorbagaduce—That being the only means Left of destroying the Shipping by the land force in my Opinion—[41]

The fact that the Westcot battery site construction began two days earlier, on 1 August, under Commodore Saltonstall's direction, apparently slipped from General Lovell's memory. General Lovell also failed to mention that the day before he decided to construct the second battery, Commodore Saltonstall and several naval officers examined that site. They fled the site when enemy boat parties attempted to capture them.

Lovell continued describing events from 9 August through 13 August. It was a reiteration of the story he had told many time before. At his conclusion he presented a number of documents to verify his version of the expedition from 5 August though 13 August:

1. His letter of 5 August to Saltonstall saying he could go no further and asking what the fleet would do. Attached to his letter was the fleet's council of war for 6 August. This council of war stated the assault captains would attack the enemy shipping only if supported by the militia. "In Consequence of which I call'd a Council of War a result of which is in the Case— No 2."

2. The militia council of war of 6 August. The militia officers declared they could not storm. They were unanimous in that decision.

3. A letter General Lovell sent to the commodore via a committee of General Wadsworth, Colonel Mitchell, and Lieutenant Colonel Revere to continue discussing a solution.

4. The result of the conference where Saltonstall asked for a joint council of war. [Revere's journal said, "We wait on the Commodore. He says he is not willing to confer but will meet Genl Lovell in a general Council; we agree to meet on board the Hazard."]

5. The joint council of war aboard the *Hazard* on 7 August. This was when Commodore Saltonstall wanted to storm or raise the siege. Raising the siege was put to a vote and thirteen were for staying and eight for raising the siege. There was no comment or vote for storming the fort.

6. A copy of Captain Hacker's letter submitting a plan of attack against the enemy vessels.

7. The joint council of war on 10 August when both groups of officers decided to attack.

8. The militia council of war on 11 August after the militia's disastrous display before the enemy.

9. The naval council of war on 12 August when the naval officers determined not to go into Bagaduce without militia support. The vote was two to attack and twelve not to attack.

10. The joint council of war on 13 August when the militia officers revoked their refusal to support the naval attack. Then, in a vote to continue or raise the siege, ten wanted to raise the siege and fourteen voted to remain.

General Lovell buttressed his testimony with this flurry of documents.[42]

General Wadsworth was among the last to testify, doing so on 29 September. He was supportive of his commander, General Lovell. Wadsworth began:

> The failure of the expedition under Enquiry seems to me to be owing principally to the Lateness of our Arival Before the Enemy, the Smallness of our Land Forces, & the uniform Backwardness of the Commander of the Fleet.... With respect to what took place at Townsend, I subscribe to General Lovells Representation, with this Addition, that at least; one fourth part of the troops then appear'd to me to be Small Boys & old men, & unfit for the Service. I also subscribe to General Lovells Representation of our Arival & during our Continuance on the Heights of Magabigwaduce untill the Evacuation.

About the rout at the Narrows he said, "At this time the Foremost of our Vessels of War were passing the transports, & there appear'd to me to be a Fair Opportunity of Saving our whole Fleet, had some of our heaviest Ships been order'd to form a Line a Little below our Transports to have Stop'd the Enemys foremost ships in their pursuit. The Wind was then dying away for the Evening & the Tide of Ebb very strong, so that their heavier Ships could not have got up to their Assistance till the next tide."[43] What did Wadsworth mean when he said, "a Fair Opportunity of Saving our whole Fleet"? He could not have meant that by forming a line and holding off the enemy's foremost ships the American fleet would defeat the British force. Except for the *Warren*'s 18- and 12-pounders, only two of the privateer ships had 9-pounders. Of the remaining five vessels, four had 6-pounders, and one 4-pounders. The two other privateers had been captured earlier. The British, with their larger guns, could stand off and pummel the American ships. In the resulting conflict combat casualties would take place, and eventually the Americans would have to surrender, becoming prisoners of war. As for the tide and wind, General Wadsworth may have been confused at the end of a very busy day, for on 14 August the low tide was at 6:42 P.M. Thus slack tide would have been from 6:12 to 7:12 that evening. Captain Daniel Waters of the *General Putnam* reported, "At 7 o'clock we entered the narrows at 10 o'clock came to anchor above the narrows slight wind."[44] If Waters could sail up the narrows, assisted by the rising flood tide from 7 to 10, obviously the British ships in the rear could have assisted their foremost ships.

If Wadsworth meant save the transport fleet, it would only place the Mill Cove rout farther up the Penobscot River with the same headlong flight to return home. Wadsworth observed the Mill Cove rout. He knew that once the militia landed it considered its duty over; it was time to leave. The reality of the situation was that the arrival of British reinforcements doomed the expedition. Yet Wadsworth's opinion of saving the fleet was another telling point for the conspiracy. After telling of the rout in more detail, he concluded and signed his deposition. Then he added:

> The Uniform Backwardness of the Commander of the Fleet appear'd in the several Councils of War at which I was present; Where he always held up the Idea that the Damage that his Ships would receive in attempting the Enemys Shiping would more than counterbalance the Advantage of Destroying them. Since the destruction of those Ships would not give us the Possession of the Enemy immediately. It was urged by the General that this was a necessary Step towards their Reduction. His Answer was in General, what would be achiev'd by his Going in to the Enemys Shiping, & towards the latter part of the siege the Storming of their principal fortress by Land was made the Condition of his attacking them by sea. I believe that the Enemys Ships might have been destroy'd at any time during the Siege (wind & tide permitting) especially after the reduction of the Battery on the first of August. /s/ P. Wadsworth B General.[45]

Wadsworth's addition to his deposition was a summation of the accusations against Commodore Saltonstall.

Based on the evidence accepted by the committee, its findings were not too extreme. But had these distinguished gentlemen sought the true events of the expedition rather than a scapegoat, they might have paid closer attention to the evidence presented. They might have questioned General Lovell on his account of the rout at the Narrows. According to three detailed depositions of officers, militia Major William Todd, volunteer Captain Waterman Thomas, and navy Lieutenant George Little of the *Hazard*, Lovell was safely up the Penobscot River aboard the *Hazard* during the fiasco at Mill Cove. The only time the general was on shore, after leaving Bagaduce, was at the head of navigation. According to Captain Philip Brown, the general helped him launch a boat to bring sailors ashore during the final burning of the expedition's vessels.

Lovell's letter of 11 August to Commodore Saltonstall was yet another example of his guile. On that day Lovell wrote, "In this alarming posture of affairs, I am once more obliged to request the most speedy service in your department; . . . The destruction of the Enemy's ships must be effected at any rate, although it might cost us half our own; . . . The information of the British ships at the Hook (probably sailed before this time) is not to be despised; not a moment is to be lost; we must determine instantly."[46] The news that Sir George Collier took seven men-of-war from New York to reinforce General McLean came out of New York on 1 August. Sir George Collier stopped at Staten Island to load two regiments to serve as marines.[47] Two days later General George Washington received a letter from Lord Stirling dated 2 August that the warships had put to sea. Washington sent an extract of the letter to the Massachusetts Council.[48] On 11 August the council received Washington's letter. At midnight President Powell prepared copies of the initial letter and Washington's letter for General Lovell.[49] If the letter left Boston on 12 August, how could Lovell know its contents a day earlier when he tried to prod Saltonstall into action? Almost certainly some member of the committee remembered Washington's letter and the council's warning to Lovell.

Apparently General Lovell broadcast his letter of 11 August throughout the expedition, possibly to increase pressure on Commodore Saltonstall. John Calef reported that the British found a copy of Lovell's letter to Saltonstall aboard the captured *Hunter*. Calef had it in his journal that was published in 1781.[50] Americans recovered Lovell's letter of 11 August from one of the expedition's scuttled transports, probably the general's headquarters vessel, the *Sally*.[51] Obviously Lovell wrote it before the rout developed.

How did General Lovell receive his information on the same day that the Massachusetts General Court received Washington's warning? Two possibilities are plausible. One is that some vessel sailing from New York observed the British fleet and entered Penobscot Bay to report this information to the Americans; although, there are no reports in extant records of such a happening. More probably, Lovell just made up the statement about the British at the Hook to prod Commodore Saltonstall into action and the dates were just a coincidence. After all, everyone knew that the British headquarters in New York would be the most probable source for reinforcements. If Lovell did not know about Sandy Hook, any of his naval captains could tell him of Sandy Hook and its abbreviation to "the Hook."

This last possibility has merit because that same day, 11 August, he wrote in his journal, "We have lately had many Councils of War some for the Ships going in, others for evacuating the present post. But I cou'd not consistant with my Duty to my Country give my Vote for leaving so important a station as I now possess as it is the only Ground on the peninsula which is of equal height with their fort. & as I have received no positive information of any Fleet of the Enemy being destined for this place."[52]

The next day, 12 August, General Lovell wrote in his journal: "Another Council of War. [This was a naval council of war held at sunset aboard the *Warren* on 12 August in reply to the militia council of war held at headquarters on 11 August wherein the militia officers unanimously determined that they could not "hold a part of the rear of the enemy's fort, and the present lines at the same time." The naval captains then voted twelve to two not to go into Bagaduce harbor without land support.[53]] The Captains of some private Ships of War are very uneasy & with pain I must add the Commodore so very desirous of leaving a Post of so much consequence to the States but in particular to this State that I am in pain from the consequences, if I shou'd give my Consent to leaving so important a piece of Ground as I now hold, only on a report of some Ships sailing Eastward from N. York & they shou'd not arrive I cou'd never forgive the Injury I did my country." [General Lovell concluded with no thought of what might happen to the American vessels if the British force were superior.] He continued: "if a superior Fleet does arrive I can but retreat to some convenient place up the river tho at the same time I wish it in my power to act more offensively than I do."[54]

The following day, 13 August, before the British reinforcements arrived, a joint council of war voted on the question of evacuating or remaining; the tally was ten for leaving and fourteen for remaining. General Lovell voted to remain, and in his addendum to his letter of 3 September to the Massachusetts Council he explained his vote as follows: "On the 13th by 5

OClock, many were for evacuating the post as will appear by N10 but as I soon expected advice from Boston, and every moment a reinforcement by Colonel Allen & Porter, and my orders being of such a Tenor I did not consider myself at Liberty to retreat with out an Order from Council, I cou'd not give my Vote for leaving so important a post, as I had rec'd no information of any renforcement on their Way to join the Enemy."[55]

For three consecutive days at the end of the siege General Lovell reiterated that he received no information of reinforcements for the enemy. Therefore, it was apparent that his letter to Commodore Saltonstall on "The information of the British ships at the Hook (probably sailed before this time) is not to be despised; not a moment is to be lost; we must determine instantly" was a ploy to get Saltonstall to sail against the British without support from Lovell's land forces.

When Lovell's presentations are examined closely, not once did he offer a positive statement of Commodore Saltonstall. The general's case was simple: Saltonstall caused the failure. The commodore failed to attack the enemy ships or defend the transports. Lovell reiterated his case in all his presentations.

Politically and financially it was to the state's benefit to reach its finding that Commodore Saltonstall bore all the blame for the Penobscot disaster. To this end the committee asked most witnesses if they thought the expedition's ships could destroy the enemy vessels without support from the militia. All replied that it was possible. Only Captains Nathan Brown of the *Hunter* and John Carnes of the *Hector* qualified their yes answer. Both mentioned how costly it would be for the fleet to go in alone. Had the committee questioned their qualifications further, it might have learned of the technological limitations of square-rigged ships and of the fleet guns' inability to fire on the enemy fort. Assaulting Captain Mowat's ships in Bagaduce Harbor called for cooperation between the land and sea forces, which did not happen until too late.

Chapter Eight

Paul Revere's Tribulations

COLONEL PAUL REVERE arrived in Boston 26 August. That same day the council issued orders for him to resume his command at Castle Island, although he did not receive these orders for another three days.[1] Sometime in early September, marine Captain Thomas J. Carnes from the *General Putnam* went before the council leveling charges against Lieutenant Colonel Paul Revere. The following day Revere learned of Carnes's actions and immediately wrote the council. He begged the council "that in a proper time there may be a strict inquiry into my conduct, where I may meet my accusers face to face." The colonel said he had learned one charge was that he did not land with his men on the assault on Bagaduce. He vehemently denied this. Again he demanded to face his accuser before the council.[2]

Revere's letter brought results. The council instructed Captain Carnes to put his accusations in writing. Carnes complied:

Gentlemen: —Being requested to lodge a complaint against Lt. Colonel Revere for his behavior at Penobscot, which I do in the following manner, viz.:—

First. For disobedience of orders from General Lovell in two instances, viz, when ordered to go on shore with two 18 pounders—and one 12, and one four, and one howitzer, excused himself.

Second. When ordered by Major Todd at the retreat to go with his men and take said cannon from the Island, refused, and said his orders were, to be under the command of Gen. Lovell during the expedition to Penobscot, and that the siege was raised, and he did not consider himself under his command.

Thirdly. In neglect of duty in several instances.

Fourthly. In unsoldierlike behavior during the whole expedition to Penobscot, which tends to cowardice.

Fifthly. In refusing Gen. Wadsworth the Castle barge to fetch some men on shore from a schooner which was near the enemy's ships on the retreat up the river.

Sixthly. For leaving his men, and suffering them to disperse and taking no manner of care of them.

Sept. 6. 1779   T. J. Carnes.[3]

That same day the council relieved Colonel Revere of his command and placed him under house arrest in Boston. Three days later, 9 September, the council informed him that he would stand before an inquiry into the expedition, and it released him from house arrest.[4]

On 22 September 1779, when the committee began hearing witnesses, its members had two issues before them. They needed to decide the cause of the failure of the expedition and to determine the validity of the charges directed against Colonel Paul Revere. The proceedings to determine the two issues were as different as could be. The conspiracy against Captain Saltonstall was a one-sided presentation. Saltonstall was absent, and no one acted in his behalf. Whereas, Colonel Revere was an active participant whenever the question of his conduct came before the committee. Also, he had witnesses to substantiate his position. Thus, although the hearings were an investigation, not a court-martial, the proceedings took on the give-and-take of a court-martial.

Revere waited impatiently for the accusation against him to come before the committee. It was six days before Major Todd gave his deposition. On his first day of testimony, Todd said that during the retreat General Lovell ordered Colonels Mitchell and Revere to bring their forces up the Penobscot River. Neither colonel did so.[5]

The next day, 29 September, Major Todd returned to continue his statement. He said that several times General Lovell sent him to bring Colonel Revere to the general's marquee. In all, he visited Revere's tent four times but only found him one time. He told of General Lovell being surprised at Colonel "Revere's inattention to his duty." Todd told of Revere's frequent absences from camp. He said Revere's own officers reported he was aboard the transports. Todd concluded by saying, "I heard Genl Wadsworth say in Genl Lovell Marque, that if the siege continued seven years (if it was possible to avoid it) he should not ask him to take any command—"[6]

When the committee listened to marine captain Carnes, it heard damning statements. Captain Thomas Carnes began by saying that the night before the assault Colonel Revere had orders to land as a reserve corps and to keep close to the rear of the assault troops. The reserve corps landed to the left of his position and he could see the artillerymen, but at no time did he see Colonel Revere. He did not see Revere, or his reserve corps, until the troops had gained possession of the heights and the lines laid out at the summit. Captain Carnes said that Colonel Revere left his men on shore and went back to the transport for both breakfast and dinner. Then toward evening Revere brought all his men back aboard the transport for the night. He claimed Revere continued this procedure for the next several days. The night the battery was erected at the edge of the woods, the colonel was nowhere in sight. Finally, General Wadsworth asked for Revere several times before requesting Captain Cushing to cut out the embrasures. Carnes said that many of the guns were brought ashore and hauled up the incline by sailors and marines. He charged Revere with failing to supervise gun installations. A few days later when General Lovell could not find Colonel Revere he issued a general order for him to move ashore. Even after the general sent Revere a letter, Carnes said he seldom saw Revere.

During periods of cannonading, Carnes found Revere away from the battery being fired. He was in another breastwork a hundred yards away spotting the shots. Revere told his men when their shots were accurate or poorly placed, but he never gave any instructions to his men. Captain Carnes watched Revere several times when he directed his piece personally, and he thought it was impossible "that a colonel of artillery should make such a bad shot, and know no more about artillery."[7] Although this information was not mentioned in the record, Captain Thomas Jenner Carnes had served in Colonel Richard Gridley's artillery regiment in 1775. The British captured him at Fort Washington in November 1776, and Carnes was among the prisoners exchanged in 1777. He then served in the Eastern Company of the New Jersey Artillery in the Continental service. He resigned in March 1779 and joined the marines. Thus Carnes was familiar with artillery service.[8]

General Wadsworth was the next officer to testify. When he recounted his trouble with Colonel Revere during the retreat, he said there was a small schooner carrying most of the provisions. The ebb tide was drifting the schooner down toward the enemy. The general ordered a number of boats to tow her across the current. They were not successful, but they did manage to take off the crew. One of the boats was Colonel Revere's barge. Colonel Revere told Wadsworth that he had "no right to command either him or the Boat & gave orders to the contrary." Yet the barge was sent to the schooner. The general promised Revere "an arrest as soon as the Army should be Collected."[9] General Wadsworth said the reason Lieutenant Colonel Revere gave for not sending the barge was it had all his private baggage and he did not want to lose it. Wadsworth then asked him "whether he came there to take Care of his private Baggage, or to serve the State."[10] Upon the completion of General Wadsworth's deposition, General Wadsworth was cross-examined by the committee, Revere, Carnes, and the committee again.

The committee asked:

> Q. Do you recollect asking for Col[onel] Revere, and asking Capt Cushing to cut out the embrasures, as mentioned in Capt Carnes's Deposition?
>
> A. I am not positive that I asked for him, but had thoughts in my mind why I had not seen him there at the firing the Batteries—I believe I asked Capt Cushing's advice about making the embrasures I well remember that the next day Col[onel] Revere clear them out—
>
> Q. Whether Col[onel] Revere was missing on Shore?
>
> A. I saw him but seldom on shore during the first week after our landing.

Questioned by Revere:

> Q. Do you recollect my carrying you to a place & showing it as a proper one for getting up the Cannon & Artillery Round[?]
>
> A. I remember being on the Bank with Col[onel] Revere and finding on a place to get up the Cannon, where we afterwards got them up.
>
> Q. Do you remember sending for me to go to an Island to the Eastward of Hacker's Island to find a post to annoy the enemy shiping?
>
> A. I remember you went with me, I don't recollect sending for you, but don't think it improbable.

Questioned by Captain Carnes:

> Q. Did you say or hear Genl Lovell say that if the Siege Continued seven years, if it was possible to avoid it, he would not order Col[onel] Revere to take any Command.
>
> A. I have no recollection of the sort, or even that it ever was in my mind—If I had said it, 'tis probable it would have left some traces in my mind—

Questioned again by the committee:

> Q. Did you during the Seige discover any inattention or backwardness to duty in Col[onel] Revere?

A. I did not see him so frequently in Camp as I expected his way in my Mind in the time of it. His sentiments & Opinions where there was a division of Voices, was always different from Mine. I remember that he was against Taking Post to the East of the Enemy's Main Fort.[11]

The next day, 30 September, Acting-Lieutenant Philip Marett of the *Sky Rocket* said he was ashore several times during the initial landing and Colonel Revere always appeared active and diligent. On the retreat, he recalled Colonel Revere passed his ship a little after sundown. When Captain Burke asked him to come aboard for some grog, Revere replied he could not stop for he was collecting his men.[12]

The next deposition was of Captain James Brown of the brig *Samuel.* At the conclusion of Captain Brown's testimony, Captain Carnes asked Brown if he remembered when Major Bronville carried a billet from General Lovell to Revere ordering him to encamp on shore with his men. "I can not, but think 'twas after the 30th—Certain I am 'twas several days after our landing—I can not positively say 'twas not before the 30th." Then Colonel Revere asked Brown how often he came aboard the ordnance brig after his baggage went ashore. Brown replied "very seldom, you was not onboard every day & when You came 'twas on particular business. . . . I particularly remember that you several days, saw'd of[f] the fuzes of the Shells, which you said were too long & seem'd always anxious to be on shore as soon as possible, & refused to stay & drink coffee & dine when I had asked [you]."[13]

The last witness on the twenty-ninth was Doctor J. Whipple, who was called by Colonel Revere to answer Captain Carnes's charges. He stated that he did not know about Captain Carnes's statement that Revere was part of a reserve corps. Yet he did see the order to the colonel to send cannon, with proper manning, to shore. Dr. Whipple knew that Revere carried out that order. The doctor could not testify as to whether Revere returned to the transport to eat his meals on the first days, nor could he comment on the fourth charge of unsoldierly behavior. As to Colonel Revere's bravery, Dr. Whipple did not know that the colonel had been under any trial for that trait. The next day Whipple returned to add that on the evening of 30 July Colonel Revere told him he had sent the corps' tents ashore. Further, he said that he and Colonel Revere were with General Lovell in the general's tent on 29 July. Whipple signed his statement and swore under oath to its truthfulness.[14]

Adjutant General Jeremiah Hill was the next witness. After his deposition the committee asked him if he knew that Colonel Revere received the order of 30 July for Revere and his corps to encamp on shore. Hill answered, "I do not know but the orders fully were deliver'd out by me at the usual time." He continued saying that after arriving in Boston, Revere asked him about the orders. When Revere said he never knew of them, Hill showed him a copy of the orders.[15] Captain Carnes then requested that Captain Gilbert Speakman, commissary of ordnance, present his written deposition concerning the conduct of Colonel Revere. Speakman began by saying that the two officers had different duties and so he could not give a detailed account of the colonel. Yet he related what he remembered of his time with Colonel Revere. A few days after the landing Captain Speakman remembered that orders were received on the transport for some artillery. Colonel Revere sent for one of his officers to go ashore to carry out the request. Revere did not believe the orders were directed at him personally. He felt it must be a mistake; therefore, he called for his barge to take him ashore to check with General Lovell. When he returned from visiting the general he sent Captain Cushing ashore with the required pieces. Some days later, Speakman recalled that some of the general's staff came out to the transport to borrow Colonel Revere's barge. The colonel replied, "He wanted it himself—& said he brought that Barge for his own use & not for the General's."[16]

At another time Speakman was at the general's marquee and General Lovell asked him if he knew where Colonel Revere was. He answered that the colonel was on the brig. General Lovell, surprised at his absence, asked Major Todd to write and order Colonel Revere to attend to affairs at the marquee. When Revere received the letter he was in bed. He was surprised at such an order. Revere got up, dressed, and went ashore. When he returned he said from the tone of Todd's letter he thought the general was put out with him, but on going ashore he found that General Lovell made light of the incident.

Finally, Captain Speakman related the events of 14 August at the beginning of the retreat. General Lovell sent Major Todd to order Colonel Revere to remove the guns on Hacker's Island. Revere said he could not comply because he had no boat. After the transports made sail, Revere said he did not go to Hacker's Island because he didn't know if General Lovell had the right to order him to go. Revere took out some papers, read them, and said, "his orders were to be under the Command of Genl Lovell during the Penobscot Expedition and as the siege was rais'd, he considered the expedition was at an end, and therefore did not consider himself any longer under Genl Lovell's command." At noon Colonel Revere went ashore and Captain Speakman never saw him again until the Court of Inquiry in Faneuil Hall.[17]

When questioned by Colonel Revere, Speakman noted that the men ordered to assist Revere in removing the guns from Hacker's Island never did arrive. The committee then asked Speakman about the time General Lovell sent his letter for Revere to come ashore. The captain was not sure but he thought it was after the general's marquee was moved to its second location. This led the committee to question several other witnesses on the subject. Mr. Marston was vaguer than Speakman, but he too thought that it was not written until the marquee had been moved. Major Todd said he wrote it not before 30 July. Major Bronville, who delivered the letter, was sure it was before 31 July.[18] The next deponent was Lieutenant Andrew McIntyre of the artillery. Colonel Revere asked him, "Do you know whether I gave orders on the 30th to Capt Cushing for him with his Company to encamp on shore in future?" McIntyre answered, "Such orders were given rather before 8 o'clock in the morning."[19]

On 1 October, Colonel Paul Revere cross-examined General Lovell as follows:

Q. Did you on the 28th of July, the day you landed on Magabigwaduce, see me, with the Corps I commanded.

A. Yes

Q. Do you remember that some time after (the same day) you ordered me personaly to send to the Island for the Howitzer, Field-piece, Gun, and apparatus, and to call on Col Davis for Boats & men

A. Probably I did but do not remember the circumstances

Q. Do you remember, that about sundown, the ~~same~~ of the 28th evening, I waited on you, and informed you; that I had found a part of the Bank not near so high as that we came up, upon which you directed me to gitt two 18 pounders on shore, and to call on Capts Williams, Holmes, Halet and Cathcart for men to assist me

A. Yes, I gave such orders, but it lies in my mind it was about 10 o'clock

Q. Do you remember the next morning, I met you near the lines, and that the militia were at work, when you took me by myself, and told me that you had reconnitred the Enemys works, and found them stronger than you expected;

that it never would do to storm them with the men you had, and that I must be expeditious as possible in getting my canon on shore for we must aproach them.

A. I believe it is so but don't recolect ye circumstance.

Q. Was there a day from the time we landed on Magabigwaduce to the day we retreated up the river, but what you saw me at least twice a day.

A. I do not recolect everyday but remember see you oftn.

Q. Did you ever send, or give me an Order Verbally which I did not obey

A. No except on the day after we retreated

Q. Did you on the Evening of the 29th of July send me Billet of this impart, to wit, the General is surprised that he had not seen Col[onel] Revere & desires he would wait upon him immediately—

A. Such a Billet was sent but I cannot recollect the time when and the Col[onel] waited upon me immediately & satisfied me that he had been well employed. I now think it was not later than the 28th

Q. Did you by your order of the 28th of July mean to include the whole Army?

A. I did

The answers [to] the above questions were sworn to by Genl Lovell before Court Oct 1st.[20]

Colonel Paul Revere weighed the testimonies presented to the committee. He felt it best to present his defense in detail, overlooking nothing brought before the committee. For that purpose he submitted a lengthy letter, more than 3,240 words, commencing his narrative in February 1779. It was a long rambling missive.

He told of the difficulties in February when his regiment was reduced to three companies. The council desired Revere to accept command of the reformed regiment. Other officers turned against him when he retained his commission while some of them gave up their commissions. This led to a rift between Captain William Todd and Revere. Todd told General Artemas Ward that he thought Revere had drawn rations for thirty more men than were assigned at Castle Island. General Ward told him to complain to the council. At the appointed time Revere arrived at the place for the investigation, but no articles were brought against him. From then on Captain Todd did whatever he could to injure Revere. After Colonel Revere received orders to go to Penobscot, he heard that Captain Todd was going to be one of General Lovell's brigade majors. Revere told the general how disagreeable Todd was to him, and he said he would only speak to Todd in the line of duty.

Having laid the groundwork for the enmity between the two officers, Revere delved into minute details to answer every charge mentioned before the Committee of Inquiry. In answer to the charge that he did not land with his men the first day, Revere noted the testimonies of Captains Perez Cushing, Amos Lincoln, and Colonel Joshua Davis. Revere explained further that the reason he remained aboard the first two nights was that most of his guns were aboard ship, and his orders were to command all the artillery. By being aboard he was ready to send to shore whatever was needed almost instantly. He took exception to the belief that he remained aboard beyond 29 July. Again he cited the depositions of several of his officers that all moved ashore on 30 July.

Colonel Revere agreed that the sailors and marines carried cannons ashore but not because the artillerymen were laggards. He noted that without help his forty-man detail could never get the 18-pounders up the bank. In addition, his men were busy bringing up the utensils necessary to use the guns, such as the hammers, spurges, worms, powder, and wads.[21] He pointed out General Wadsworth's answer to Captain Carnes's question if he had said or heard General Lovell say "that if the Siege Continued seven years, if it were possible to avoid it he would not order Col[onel] Revere to take any Command." General Wadsworth answered that he had no recollection of that. In addition, he said it was not in his mind—and if he did say it "tis probable it would have left some trace in my mind."[22]

With regard to his being aboard ship frequently to avoid duty ashore, Revere brought out the testimony of Captain James Brown of the transport *Samuel* that he was an infrequent visitor and was always aboard only for some duty for the artillery. In fact, Captain Brown said he refused to remain aboard ship long enough to drink coffee or dine with the him.[23]

Colonel Paul Revere felt General Wadsworth's charge of disobedience was a case of misunderstanding. As he related it, he ordered Lieutenant Phillips to take the men and bring his barge to him. The barge and General Wadsworth arrived at the same time. When General Wadsworth insisted on sending the barge to aid the schooner, Revere refused at first, then changed his mind and sent the barge to the schooner. When the barge returned to shore, the general wanted it to try and tow the endangered schooner. According to Revere, he asked the general to find another boat for the task, and Wadsworth went off to find another boat. Revere thought the two departed good friends. He waited half an hour, and when the general did not return, Revere went to look for his men who had moved on. Thinking they had gone upriver, Revere set out in that direction He never saw General Wadsworth until he got back to Boston.

Another point of contention for Colonel Revere was General Wadsworth's comment that Revere's opinions were always different from his own. Revere ventured that he thought that during the councils of war one was supposed to give one's honest opinion. If he was incorrect, then it bode ill for future officers to speak in such councils. Revere asked the committee to check the councils of war. He pointed out that he agreed with comments made in the first five that he attended. Only at the two councils of war on 7 and 13 August, when votes were taken whether to continue or raise the siege, did he differ with General Wadsworth. Still Revere could not understand why he was singled out. For on 7 and 13 August seven and nine others voted the same as he did.

Paul Revere delved at great length to prove that at the time of the rout he did go upstream as directed by General Lovell. Both Captain Lieutenant Thomas Newcomb and Lieutenant Nicholas Phillips said he went twenty miles up the Penobscot River to Grants Mills and remained there all day. He left the river only after learning the ships were to be burnt the following day. At the bottom of that page he placed an asterisk with the comment that Captain John F. Williams of the *Hazard* told of seeing him on the *Vengeance* on 15 August. [As the *Vengeance* was burned at Hampden, according to Colonel John Brewer, then Grants Mills was somewhere in the vicinity of Hampden.[24]] Continuing, Revere pointed out that there was nothing in the evidence to indicate that General Lovell carried any troops up the river to fortify; further, the evidence presented showed that General Lovell himself did not go to the head of navigation until late at night. Of all the senior field officers, he was the only one that went up the river as ordered.[25]

Finally Revere addressed his leaving the Penobscot River without orders. He had already proved that he alone of the field officers had gone upriver, but he asked: "Where could I have found the General or Brigadier, if it had been necessary to have got orders? The first went 100 miles up the Penobscot River, and the other down, and I crossed the woods to Kennebec river." Once again Revere referred to his orders "to obey General Lovel [*sic*], or other my Superior Officers during the continuance of the Expedition." He continued, "Surely no man will say, that the Expedition was not discontinued, when all the shipping was either taken or burnt; the Artillery and Ordnance stores all destroyed." He did, he said, what he thought right.[26]

On 7 October the committee issued its findings. It assigned to Captain Saltonstall the failure of the Penobscot Expedition. It exonerated Generals Lovell and Wadsworth. It found the Massachusetts state naval officers "behaved like brave experienced good Officers throughout the whole of the Expedition." The committee concluded that "the number of men ordered to be detached for this Service were deficient nearly one third whether the shameful neglect is chargeable upon the Brigadiers, Colonels or other Officers whose particular duty it might have been to have faithfully executed the Orders of the General Assembly they cannot ascertain"[27] In spite of having removed Revere from his command, placing him under house arrest, and devoting considerable attention to the alleged charges against him, the committee made no specific mention of Colonel Revere in its findings. Omitting Revere from its findings was especially confusing because in General Artemas Ward's letter of 8 September 1779 he wrote: "Lieut-Col. Paul Revere is now under arrest for disobedience of orders, and unsoldierlike behavior tending to cowardice. . . . I hope the matter will be thoroughly enquired into, and justice done to every individual officer."[28] Apparently neither General Ward nor the committee wanted to dilute the findings against Commodore Saltonstall by acknowledging any suspicions of misconduct by other officers.

This finding was not what Colonel Revere wanted published. The next day Revere wrote to the council and the House of Representatives begging they direct the committee to sit again. He had endured public humiliation by his arrest and from the charges alleged. He had presented himself for examination and proved his innocence. Yet the committee had "neither condemned [nor] acquitted him." Further he had additional evidence to present, and "as several of his Chief Evidences are going to Sea" he must be heard immediately. If his petition could not be met, he requested "your Honors would Order that a Court Martial should be appointed for his tryal, agreeble, to the Continental Regulations."[29] That same day the House of Representatives ordered Colonels Thacher, Garrish, and Brown to act as a committee to enquire into the matter. On 19 October the new committee summoned its witnesses to meet on 11 November at the East Lobby of the State House to give testimony "on the conduct of Colonel Revere."[30] The sheriff of Suffolk County notified Captains Alexander

Holmes, John Hallet, and William Burke; Mr. Watson, captain of the marines of the *Charming Sally;* James Nevers, second lieutenant of the *Tyrannicide;* and Joseph Cunningham, second lieutenant of the *Hazard.* All were to report at 9 A.M. in the East Lobby. Oddly enough Colonel Revere was ordered to appear at 10 A.M.[31]

At the enquiry, Colonel Revere presented his daily diary from 21 July to 19 August. The diary showed the day-to-day workings of a dedicated and conscientious officer. The new committee then heard depositions from the witnesses. Captain Holmes reported seeing Colonel Revere busy getting up the cannons on 28 and 29 July. Gunner Thomas Wait Foster of the *Warren* said of Revere he was not backward and he was always busy trying to find out the strength of the enemy. Others told the same information about the colonel.[32]

Five days later, 16 November, the new committee handed down its verdict in the same question-and-answer format as the first committee:

Qust 1 Was Liet Col[onel] Paul Revere culpable for any of his conduct during his stay at Bagaduce, or while he was in or upon the River Penobscot? Answer Yes.

2. What part of Liet Col[onel] Paul Revere's conduct was culpable? Answer: in disputing the orders of Brigadier General Wadsworth respecting the Boat, and in saying that the Brigadier had no right to command him or his boat.

3. Was Liet Col[onel] Paul Revere's conduct justifiable in leaving the River Penobscot and repairing to Boston with his men, without particular orders from his superior officers? Answer. No, not wholly justifiable.

4. Does anything appear in evidence to the disadvantage of any of the Militia Officers during the Expedition to Penobscot or on the retreat therefrom? Answer. No, Excepting Col[onel] Jonathan Mitchell, who by his own confession left the River Penobscot without leave from any superior officer, and returned to North Yarmouth, the place of his habitation.

All which is humbly submitted. /s/ Artemas Ward[33]

This finding reduced the number of charges against Revere but did find him guilty of culpable behavior in two instances.

Colonel Revere was not happy. This report seemed to confirm the gossip in Boston. Further, the report kept him from drawing his back rations. Yet reducing the original charges from six to two was encouraging. Revere felt that there were mitigating circumstances not yet examined. Thus on 4 January 1780 he again petitioned the General Court. "It is reported thro the State, that I have been broke and cashered (I have heard of it more than once) and lay under disgrace that the malice of my enemies can invent, and it will remain so till the Facts are published. I would once more Pray your Honors that you would grant me a Tryal by a Court Martial. I further pray your Honors, that you would Order the Commissary General, to deliver me my back Rations, for by reason of my being confined to Boston, I have not been able to get any, since the last day of June, except what I drew at Penobscot. I have been maintaining a Family of Twelve ever since." The committee unanimously opposed his petition for a court-martial. But the General Court ordered the commissary general of the state to issue Revere his back rations.[34]

The persistent Revere sent another petition to the General Court on 8 March 1780. This time the court acted upon his request. On 18 March it empowered the council to appoint a court-martial. The court-martial with Colonel Edward Procter as president and William Tudor as judge advocate had eleven other members. Colonel Procter was reluctant to hold a court-martial. He attempted to decline the duty because of his long relations with the defendant. When his request to be relieved failed, Procter simply never called the court into session.[35]

It was 22 January 1781 before Revere renewed his plea for a court-martial. The General Court tabled his petition until the next session of the court in 1782. Finally, without further action by Colonel Revere, his court-martial met on 19 February 1782. This time there were no delays to the proceedings. The court found the first charge of refusing his boat to General Wadsworth supported. Yet it considered that almost immediately after refusing Revere did employ his boat as ordered; therefore, it acquitted him of this charge. As to the second charge, it found the whole army in confusion, scattered, and dispersed. The court found that no regular orders were or could be given, and also acquitted him on that count. The court-martial then opined that Lieutenant Colonel Paul Revere be acquitted "with equal Honor as the other Officers in the same Expedition."[36]

The fight between Revere and Todd now shifted to the *Boston Globe.* On 18 March 1782 a letter signed by "Veritas" brought up all the original charges against Revere. On 25 March Revere answered "Veritas" exposing him as Todd. Revere was too verbose for a single issue, and his letter spilled over to the 1 April issue, which included copies of several court depositions. Todd and Carnes retaliated in an answer in the 8 April issue. Revere responded in kind in the 15 April issue. This last salvo ended the public struggle between the three.[37]

Ironically, in 1863 General Peleg Wadsworth's grandson Henry Wadsworth Longfellow placed Revere firmly in the pantheon of Revolutionary War heroes with his poem "Paul Revere's Ride."

Chapter Nine

A Court~Martial
Shrouded in
Mystery

MANY NARRATORS of the Penobscot Expedition believed that Captain Saltonstall was cashiered from the Continental Navy by the Massachusetts Committee of Inquiry's findings with regard to the failure of the Penobscot Expedition. That is not true. As a Continental officer, Captain Saltonstall was not under the jurisdiction of the State of Massachusetts. His conduct fell under the Rules for the Regulation of the Navy of the United Colonies, adopted by the Continental Congress on 28 November 1775. The articles of 1775 consisted of forty paragraphs referred to as *The Blue Book*. They were quite general in their terms, with few details defining the duties of officers.[1] When Captain Saltonstall commented about the committee's hearing, "he said he was to be tried by another authority," he was referring to the Continental Navy's court-martial.[2] The extensive collection of both official and unofficial contemporary sources provided interesting glimpses into the Penobscot Expedition. Yet the affairs of Captain Saltonstall were shrouded in mystery. Contemporary sources concerning Saltonstall were few, too few to provide more that a sketchy outline of his court-martial.

On 2 September the Navy Board wrote to the Marine Committee that Captain Saltonstall had arrived in town two days earlier. It reported that the officers and men were arriving daily. Lieutenant Philip Brown of the *Diligent* came in on the evening of 1 September, and it expected Captain Hoysteed Hacker momentarily. It announced that as soon as the officers arrived, it would appoint a court of inquiry. The board charged the court to inquire into the loss of the ships and the conduct of the captains. Yet the board cautioned that "we must still Suspend our Judgment on that unhappy event untill the truth is properly investigated."[3]

On 7 September the Navy Board issued its warrant for a court-martial for Captain Dudley Saltonstall. Captain Samuel Nicholson, of the frigate *Deane* in Boston harbor, was appointed president of the court. The trial began Tuesday, 14 September, eight days before the Massachusetts committee began hearing its witnesses. In preparation, the court issued a number of citations for witnesses to appear for both Captain Saltonstall and the United States. The witnesses arrived expecting the trial to proceed normally. Unfortunately for the witnesses and Saltonstall, just before the court began, the Massachusetts General Assembly asked the Navy Board to delay its proceedings. The Navy Board said the Massachusetts General Assembly asked it to postpone the court-martial until 28 September because the General Assembly wanted its Committee of Inquiry to examine General Lovell and some other army officers first.[4] The Navy Board agreed to comply with the General Assembly's request and forwarded it and its concurrence on to the court. The members of the court, deferring to the request of these two august bodies, adjourned until 28 September. Through this delay, the state committee was nearing the end of its interrogation of witnesses before the naval court-martial began.[5]

When the court announced its adjournment, Captain Saltonstall objected, saying the delay deprived him of evidence in support of his defense because "the greater part of them [are] ready for the seas & resolved to embrace the first wind."[6] Captain Saltonstall suggested that the naval court-martial request the Massachusetts General Court, which could exercise jurisdiction over the witnesses, to retain them in port. The court-martial, demonstrating what it felt to be a spirit of impartiality, accepted Saltonstall's suggestion. Thus it made a plea to the General Court to retain those witnesses. The court-martial had no doubt "that the love of justice & attention to candor, which has always been characteristic of your proceedings," would make the following captains available for the naval proceedings:

Capt. John Carnes	Salem
Capt. Nath. West	[Salem]
Capt. Nath. Brown	[Salem]
Capt. Edmonds [*sic*]	Beverly
Capt. Thomas Thomas	Newburyport
Capt. Alex. Homes [*sic*]	Boston
Capt. Wm. Burke	Boston

Captain Sam Nicholson, president of the court, signed the letter. The court received the letter on 20 September.[7] The court's actions with regard to retaining the witnesses are unknown.

The delay of Captain Saltonstall's trial was more serious than just losing witnesses. It allowed the state committee to reach its findings midway through the navy court-martial. Public opinion in Boston over the committee's findings might well have influenced the court-martial being held in Boston harbor aboard the frigate *Deane*. Further, the delay allowed the court-martial's judge advocate to gather information about his case from the committee's proceedings.

On 28 September 1779 George Richards, judge advocate for the court-martial, presented his indictment:

To the President and Members of a Court Martial now Convened on boarde the Deane Frigate for the trial of Dudly [*sic*] Saltonstall, Esqr

Articles of Accusation and Charges Exhibited against the said Dudly Saltonstall Esqr Captain in the American Navy, late Commander of the Continental Frigate Warren.

Article 1. W[h]ere in Dudly Saltonstall stands charged with General breach of Orders bearing date Navy Board Eastern Department Boston July 13, 1779 he the said Dudly Saltonstall not having to the utmost of his power Captivated, Taken killed or destroyed the Enemies force either by Sea or Land as per attested Copy of his Orders will fully appear that he was strictly joined to do by all ways and means possible.

Article 2d: The said Dudly Saltonstall is further charged & accused of Capital Neglect of duty & flagrant misconduct in the following particulars

1. That he did not from time to time transmit to the Honble Navy Board of this department regular accounts of his Conduct and the operations of the force under his command by sea, having neglected to embrace some opportunities by which a safe Conveyance would have been afforded to Letters, Messages or other Dispatches

2d That he did not furnish the Captains and Commanders of vessels under his sole direction with written Orders and Instructions from time to time which were in fact absolutely Necessary for the better governing themselves and more particularly was guilty of great neglect of duty in not furnishing the Captains and Commanders of Vessels with any orders or Instructions after the Enemy's reinforcement appeared in Sight but permitted all the Captains and Commanders of Vessels to act discretionary and secure themselves and their shipping as they thought best.

3dly That when in sight of the Enemy he did not hearten and encourage the

Officers and Men under his Command but at all times spoke discouraging Respecting our strength and the force of the Enemy all which Conduct is in violation of the Rules and Regulations for the governing the Navy in that Case provided.

4th That after the Reinforcement of the Enemy appeared in sight he did not attempt to save and secure the Continental Frigate Warren under his Command, together with the Continental Vessels of War as also those belonging to the State of Massachusetts but by adding one ill timed delay to another neglected the means at first in his power having neither fortifyed nor ran so high up the River as might have been effected—

5th The said Dudly Saltonstall stands charged with Incapacity, Irresolution and timidity highly unbecoming the Commander of any forces in that he did not make a proper disposition and arrangement of the force under his Command to Attack the Enemies Shipping or to defend themselves advantageously in Case of being attacked on the Contrary having suffered the Enemies Boats to Come upon his Rear & to Capture Vessels almost under his Stern—

6th The said Dudly Saltonstall stands charged with neglect of duty and misconduct in quitting deserting & leaving the Frigate Warren under his Command on the Evening of the 15th instant when the Enemies ships were within Gun shot as also for landing his Men and leaving the Frigate at that critical time with only two Officers and four Midshipmen to defend her in Case of being attacked by the Enemies Boats.

All which Articles of Accusation & charges of Misconduct are exhibited to the Court Martial now Convened to be prosecuted against the said Dudly Saltonstall Esqr upon proper evidence legally adduced
Geo Richards Nav Jud Advoc
Boston, September 28 1779[8]

The next day, 29 September 1779, the Navy Board wrote to the Marine Committee, informing them of the impending court-martial: "Capt Saltonstall, whose Tryal is but just coming on, having been postponed upon the Special Request of the General Court of this State."[9] The articles of accusation and charges bore a strong resemblance to the Massachusetts committee's findings. The committee report said, "Question: Does it appear that the Commodore discouraged any Enterprizes or offensive measure on the part of our Fleet?— Answer: Unanimously, Yes."[10] This became article 2, charge 3: "That when in sight of the Enemy he did not hearten and encourage the Officers and Men under his Command but at all times spoke discouraging Respecting our strength and the force of the Enemy." Again, the committee wrote: "Question: What in the opinion of this Committee was the occasion of the total Destruction of our Fleet—Answer: Principally the Commodore's not exerting himself at all at the time of the Retreat in opposing the Enemies foremost Ships in pursuit"[11] Article 2, charge 4, read: "That after the Reinforcement of the Enemy appeared in sight he did not attempt to save and secure the Continental Frigate Warren under his Command, together with the Continental Vessels of War as also those belonging to the State of Massachusetts." Charge 5 added that "he did not make a proper disposition and arrangement of the force under his Command to Attack the Enemies Shipping or to defend themselves advantageously in Case of being attacked." Further, the testimony of Captain Waterman Thomas and of navy Lieutenant George Little in the committee's hearing told how General Lovell asked the commodore to bring his ships up the Penobscot River to the head of navigation and fortify.[12] Article 2, charge 4, specified that Saltonstall "by adding one ill timed delay to another neglected the means at first in his power having neither fortifyed nor ran so high up the River as might have been effected—"

Yet it would have been difficult for the court-martial to arrive at a guilty verdict. For example, article 1 charged Saltonstall with "not having to the utmost of his power Captivated, Taken killed or destroyed the Enemies force either by Sea or Land as per attested Copy of his Orders."[13] In the first place, neither of the two members of the Navy Board in Boston at that time, William Vernon and James Warren, had naval experience or a maritime background. Although they had no conception of the circumstances in Bagaduce nor of the technical limitations of Saltonstall's assault ships, they left no discretion to Commodore Saltonstall as to how he should proceed. When the Navy Board, learning of the British reinforcement, wrote to Saltonstall that if "you are obliged to retire, as we presume you would [be to] avoid having their Ships in your Rear while a Reinforcement appears in front," it was clear the board did not grasp the geographical positions of the two fleets. Further, the board acknowledged that the commodore had the right to react to local circumstances.[14]

In his defense Saltonstall could bring evidence of cannonading the enemy ships, taking Banks' Island, providing gun support for the landing on Bagaduce, his marines gaining the heights of Bagaduce, engaging Captain Mowat's force three hours after his marines reached the heights, his ship being seriously damaged during the encounter with Mowat, attacking Half Moon Battery, and selecting a battery site at Westcot and another battery site above Haney's point. Also, he could develop the British defenses and the danger his force faced if he assaulted the harbor without land support to the satisfaction of his peers. Through the councils of war, he could state that every time the land force agreed to support his assault ships he was ready to enter Bagaduce harbor. Thus the commodore did do all in his power to captivate, take, kill, or destroy the enemy forces by sea or land. If the court-martial heard such evidence it would undoubtedly acquit Captain Saltonstall of article 1.

Article 2, charge 1, stated that "he did not from time to time transmit to the Honble Navy Board . . . accounts of his Conduct and the operations of the force under his command by sea." Captain Saltonstall did transmit an account of his conduct at the only time he knew of a dispatch vessel being sent to Boston. When the dispatch row galley *Lincoln* departed for Boston on 1 August it carried his report to the Navy Board. When General Lovell twice dispatched his own messengers before the retreat, there is no evidence that Saltonstall knew of Lovell's communications. This article and charge merited an acquittal.

Article 2, charge 2, encompassed two accusations. First, "That he did not furnish the Captains and Commanders of vessels under his sole direction with written Orders and Instructions from time to time which were in fact absolutely Necessary for the better governing themselves." Eleven councils of war were held at Bagaduce. Nine were attended by Saltonstall and his captains. The two not attended by sea officers took place on 6 August and 11 August at Lovell's headquarters and dealt with militia problems. The minutes of the councils of war were recorded. Captain Salter felt there were too many councils of war. "It is impossible for me to say how many Councils of War were held at different Times, but upon finding them not to the Purpose I desired that Yea and Nay might be counted and every Persons Name mentioned."[15] Besides these formal councils of war Commodore Saltonstall met with his officers on 31 July to discuss the danger that Half Moon Battery presented to his ships and the action to counter it. On 7 August he took several of his captains with him to evaluate a new battery site north of Haney's Point. Again on 9 August when Saltonstall found out the Bagaduce River and the South Bay were deep enough for his ships to sail out of gun range of the British fort, he held an informal meeting with his captains to discuss the impact of this knowledge on their actions. It was decided that if the land force would attack simultaneously, the assault ships would enter the harbor. This was immediately conveyed to General Lovell. Clearly Commodore Saltonstall did furnish written orders, instructions, and informal meetings to keep his subordinates informed.

Second, that he "was guilty of great neglect of duty in not furnishing the Captains and Commanders of Vessels with any orders or Instructions after the Enemy's reinforcement appeared in Sight but permitted all the Captains and Commanders of Vessels to act discretionary and secure themselves and their shipping as they thought best." Under the stress of the arrival of the enemy reinforcement, Commodore Saltonstall held his final council of war on 14 August. Fleet maneuvers were beyond the capability of his heterogeneous fleet. Plans for action were brought up and discussed, until flight up the Penobscot River became the solution. With vessels ill prepared to maneuver in unison, the commodore believed the safety of each vessel resided in the captain's ability.

Article 2, charge 3 stated "That when in sight of the Enemy he did not hearten and encourage the Officers and Men under his Command but at all times spoke discouraging Respecting our strength and the force of the Enemy all which Conduct is in violation of the Rules and Regulations for the governing the Navy in that Case provided." Undoubtedly this charge stemmed from the contrasting views of General Lovell and Commodore Saltonstall concerning sending the assault ships into Bagaduce Harbor. Lovell felt there could be no further progress against the enemy until Captain Mowat's vessels were destroyed. Yet as the general told the committee, even after Saltonstall destroyed the enemy ships he could not storm the enemy's fort "with his land forces only." Saltonstall replied that "his Ships might suffer, & as that was no place for refitting, he might fall a sacrifice in case a reenforcement should arrive."[16]

During testimony before the Committee of Inquiry, all witnesses answered yes to the question, Could the sea force defeat Mowat's vessels alone? Yet the five councils of war in which the sea officers voted to go in or not revealed a different viewpoint. The councils listed the votes of all the sea captains, but only the assault captains' views were important to the mission because they would be responsible for carrying out the attack. (See table 4.)

The committee dealt with the discrepancy between the affirmative answers in testimony and actual votes in the councils of war by stating, "And tho' he [Saltonstall] always had a majority of his Naval Council against offensive operations which Majority was mostly made up of the

Table 4. Assault Captains' Votes in Councils of War, July–August 1779

Date	Assumptions	Votes
29 July	No land support	No (unanimous)
6 August	No land support	7 No
	If militia stormed	Yes (unanimous)
	If militia took low ground	2 Yes
	If militia stormed at time	7 Yes
10 August	With militia support	9 Yes (unanimous)
12 August	Without militia support	2 Yes, 8 No
13 August	With militia support	Yes (unanimous)

Source: Councils of War, 29 July, and 6, 10, 12, and 13 August, Papers of the Continental Congress, 1774–1789, National Archives, Massachusetts State Papers, 1775–1787, roll 47, vol. 2:129, 130, 134, 136, 140, RG 360.

Commanders of private Armed Vessels."[17] The crux of the charge for the court-martial depended on whether the members believed that the final success justified the expected losses. Without the court's testimony, the assumption of guilt or innocence cannot be determined for this charge.

Article 2, charge 4, had two parts. First, "That after the Reinforcement of the Enemy . . . he did not attempt to save and secure the Continental Frigate Warren . . . the Continental Vessels of War . . . [and] those belonging to the State of Massachusetts." Due to the superiority of the enemy fleet, Captain Saltonstall determined to save his crews. He did this by gaining distance (and thus time) between his vessels and the enemy. His plan also kept the enemy from capturing and utilizing his armed vessels. The two assault ships that refused to follow his plan met a different ending. The *Hunter's* crew escaped by beaching the ship and fleeing into the woods, but the enemy gained the ship intact. The *Hampden's* crew fought before striking its colors, and the enemy gained both the ship and crew. It would be hard to fault Commodore Saltonstall for his actions under those circumstances.

Second, "by adding one ill timed delay to another neglected the means at first in his power having neither fortifyed nor ran so high up the River as might have been effected—" The phrase "adding one ill timed delay to another" is too meaningless to defend against. There was no extensive development at the head of navigation. A few settlers struggled against the wilderness. What was the advantage of using sailors to fortify a wilderness with no means to acquire supplies, armament, or reinforcement? Especially with a superior force of ships and troops a few miles downriver chasing them. Again, knowledge of the local circumstances would dictate an acquittal of this charge.

Article 2, charge 5, was another two-pronged charge. First, Saltonstall "did not make a proper disposition and arrangement of the force under his Command to Attack the Enemies Shipping." On 28 July Saltonstall led four ships against the enemy's defense of Bagaduce harbor and failed. He proposed and on 1 August participated in eliminating the British Half Moon Battery. He also planned, on 1 and 7 August, to erect batteries against the British position in Bagaduce harbor. During his four councils of war in August he agreed to enter the enemy harbor if he had support from the land force.

Second, he did not defend his force "advantageously in Case of being attacked." Again this was a meaningless phrase designed to proliferate charges against him. If the court-martial had received pertinent information about the reality of his situation it must have found in his favor.

Article 2, charge 6, was another proliferation of charges, but in this case the accusations were ridiculous. First, he was accused of quitting his ship "when the Enemies ships were within Gun shot." The enemy boats, not ships, were below the burning transport *Samuel*, and it was not established that the boats were within gun shot range. Further, in a retreat, what was the crime of leaving the field within or without gunshot range? Second, he was charged with landing his men "with only two Officers and four Midshipmen to defend her in Case of being attacked by the Enemies Boats." What rule or regulation was violated by leaving two officers and four midshipmen aboard the *Warren* when his ship was not under attack?

Unfortunately for posterity, navy judge advocate George Richards's indictment is the extant record of the court-martial of Captain Saltonstall. Without the court-martial record, assumptions about the proceedings can only be speculations.

On 28 October 1779 the Navy Board Eastern Department sent a report to its superior, the Continental Marine Committee, which included this tantalizing bit of information: "The Court Martial upon tryal of Capt Dudley Saltonstall closed their business on monday Last. [That would be

Monday 25 October 1779.] The papers respecting this unhappy & in glorious Event we have Sent for the Inspection of Congress."[18] The Navy Board ended its letter without a hint as to the outcome of Saltonstall's court-martial. Why the court-martial papers were sent directly to Congress instead of being forwarded to the Marine Committee as was standard procedure is another mystery. On 5 August 1778 the Marine Committee wrote to the Navy Board: "You will in future send forward the proceedings at large of all Courts Martial."[19] A year later, on 24 August 1779, the Marine Committee wrote concerning another case: "[if] it is your Opinion that the good of the service requires their being brought to trial, you will order a Court Martial for that purpose and transmit to us a Copy of the Proceedings."[20] Why, in Captain Saltonstall's case, did the Navy Board deviate from the norm and bypass the Marine Committee? Could it have been that the Massachusetts legislature wanted the navy court-martial to reach Congress before it sent its Committee of Inquiry's report to Congress? This is certainly possible. On 20 November 1779 Artemas Ward, as president of the council, wrote: "Pursuant to a Resolution of the General Assembly you have inclosed the Report of a Committee appointed by them to enquire into the Reasons of the failure of the Late Expedition to Penobscot together with the Papers accompaning this Report which are transmitted to Congress that they may be inabled to take such Order thereon as they shall Judge most condusive to Public Justice."[21]

The naval court-martial ended 25 October. It should be remembered that the day after the Committee of Inquiry ended its hearings the Massachusetts House of Representatives resolved that "the Secretary is hereby directed to cause the report of the Committee to be published in one of the Boston newspapers, as soon as the Court Martial in Boston upon the Commodore shall be over. Sent up for concurrence /s/ John Hancock, Spkr."[22]

On 2 November, just a week after the court-martial ended its hearings, Jonathan Parsons, who had been with the expedition, wrote to Jeremiah Wadsworth, "In Edds & gills last weeks paper I see the determination of a Court Martial whereby Commodore Saltonstall is judged incapable of holding a Commission in the american Service, what Evidence was laid before the gentlemen who determined in that matter I am at a loss to conceive."[23] (Evidently Jonathan Parsons was a longtime reader of the *Boston Gazette*, for he referred to that paper by the names of the two original owners, Benjamin Edes and John Gill. The two had published the paper

from 1755 to 1775. In 1779 the masthead read "Benjamin Edes, and Sons.")
Though seemingly the court-martial of Captain Saltonstall would be
important news after the disaster at Penobscot Bay, Benjamin Edes made
no mention of Saltonstall or his court-martial in his *Boston Gazette* for 25
October or 1 November 1779.[24] Parsons almost certainly got his information from another source. John Gill, still active as printer to the General Assembly and of the *Continental Journal,* wrote briefly about Saltonstall's court-martial in his paper on Thursday, 28 October 1779. "We hear
the Court-martial on Capt. *Saltonstall,* late commander of the Continental frigate Warren, finished last Friday [22 October], and that the said Saltonstall was by said Court broke and declared unfit to serve the United
States in the naval department forever."[25] Who released this information
to Gill three days before the official ending of the court, 25 October, is
unknown, but the terminology used in Gill's article is not that generally
followed by courts-martial. The norm would be to state all the articles and
charges preferred against the accused followed by a statement of guilty or
not guilty for each offense. Interestingly, the statement "declared unfit to
serve the United States in the naval department forever" echoed the lan-
guage used by the General Assembly when it decreed "*that Commodore
Saltonstall be incompetent ever afterward to hold a commission in the service of
the State.*"[26] Such phrases as "forever" and "ever afterward" are phrases of
endlessness not usually found in courts-martial. It may be that John Gill,
as printer to the General Assembly, was privy to information not available
to the press or the general public.

Regardless of where Jonathan Parsons read about Saltonstall's court-
martial, he speculated that "by popular Clamour I am led to conclude that
the whole matter turned on Commodore Saltonstalls not taking possession of the Enemies Ships lying in the mouth of the Harbour at *Bagaduce.*"
He then launched into a long, impassioned defense of Saltonstall and ended by saying the commodore "was absolutely right, that is acted rationally,
and the very arguments improved against him do but evince his superior
ability to manage & direct in these matters—" In his postscript he told Jeremiah Wadsworth that, like the state enquiry, the naval court-martial had
failed to call upon him for evidence.[27]

Navy Judge Advocate George Richards's indictment is the only extant
record of Captain Saltonstall's court-martial. Yet other references to the
court-martial pop up with little substantive information, like will-o'-the-
wisps. For example, on 24 November 1779, Dudley Saltonstall petitioned

the Continental Congress concerning "his trial for loss of frigate Warren." This is a tantalizing bit of information. Did his court-martial boil down the articles and charges to a single charge of "loss of frigate Warren"? What was the basis of Saltonstall's petition? Congress received his petition on 1 December 1779 and immediately sent it to the Marine Committee.[28] On 10 December 1779 the Board of Admiralty, Philadelphia, wrote to the Navy Board Eastern Department that Congress had done away with the Marine Committee and replaced it with the Board of Admiralty. It then added "the Proceedings of the Court Martial on the trial of Captain Dudley Saltonstall is not yet come to hand altho by your letter of the 28th of October last you gave reason to expect them, pray let them be forwarded to us and furnish him with a copy if required."[29] Obviously the Board of Admiralty had received Saltonstall's petition, but until it received a copy of the proceedings of his court-martial, it was in no position to judge the merits of his petition.

The next month, 25 January 1780, the Admiralty Board sent an interesting letter to the Navy Board in Boston. First it stated: "I am directed to transmit to you the enclosed copy of a Resolve of Congress passed the 25th instant relative to the officers of the Continental Navy not in Actual Service, and to which a due regard is expected." The letter then continued to seek Captain Saltonstall's court-martial. "The Board is dayly in expectation of an answer to their Letters of the 10th ultimo, which they imagine has been hitherto delayed by the inclemency of the weather." Later it again referred to the commodore stating: "Captain Saltonstal[1] informed the Board that you had lately received the Model of a vessel built in Holland upon a New Construction—they wish you to send it here when convenient. /s/ John Brown Secy."[30] After explaining that naval officers not on "actual service" still merited respect, the admiralty referred to Saltonstall by his navy rank. This indicated that, until it received the court-martial, it continued to view Captain Saltonstall as not on actual service. Further, Saltonstall may have felt his petition presented a sound argument in mitigation for his loss of the *Warren,* for he wanted the Continental Navy to hurry its ship construction, probably so that he could return to sea.

The official paper trail of Commodore Saltonstall's court-martial ends with the Admiralty Board's letter of 25 January 1780. The only substantive finding from his trial was his petition to Congress concerning "his trial for loss of frigate Warren." Apparently Saltonstall was unaware of General Lovell's duplicity or the magnitude of the Massachusetts Conspiracy. Had he and his family known of the enormous miscarriage of justice done to him, the Connecticut branch of the family would have had enough political power to challenge the Massachusetts finding. But apparently his family and friends were not aware of Dudley Saltonstall's status. On 20 April 1780 Silas Deane wrote to his brother Barnabas Deane asking for information about their brother-in-law. Silas Deane ended his letter saying, "My compliments to all friends, in particular to General Saltonstall's family. I wrote him and son Dudley by Capt. Rogers of Brantford, but received no answer. Just tell me what became of D. Saltonstall's affair."[31]

* * *

A brief review of Captain Dudley Saltonstall's actions and decisions demonstrate his ability and competence during the Penobscot Expedition. Initially he assessed the naval situation and determined that Bagaduce Harbor was dangerous for his square-rigged ships to assault, calling it "that damned hole." It was his planning, his use of the small vessels, and his marines that achieved the capture of Banks' Island. He provided gun support for the fourth and successful landing on Bagaduce, with his marines leading the way. Even though the British vessels moved deeper in the harbor, he attempted to assault them. Yet his first assessment was correct. Due to the geography, wind, and technological limitations of his vessels, he could not sail close enough to successfully engage the enemy. He planned the attack on Half Moon Battery, which his sailors and marines captured but could not hold. With the British vessels deeper in the harbor anchored in their third position, he planned the Westcot Battery on the mainland to engage the enemy. On 7 August, Commodore Saltonstall proposed that the expedition launch an all-out assault or give up the siege. When the land officers refused to do either, he planned to establish another battery to assault the enemy ships. From 7 August through 13 August he was willing to assault the enemy, if he had the cooperation of the land force. When the British reinforcements arrived, his plan to flee up the Penobscot to obtain time and distance from the enemy to destroy his vessels and save his crews was the proper solution. The fate of the *Hunter* and the *Hampden* validate his solution. While Commodore Saltonstall was not as flamboyant as a Farragut or a Bull Halsey, his decisions were sound within the context of his situation. He was a competent naval officer.

Parsons, in his letter to Jeremiah Wadsworth, also offered his advice to the captain. "Its my opinion that it would be advisable for Commodore

Saltonstall to push to Sea in a private Ship the heaviest he can get the Command of, and as his connections are able to serve him & thereby serve themselves, I think there can be no difficulty in his getting a very good Ship— he as all that are accquainted with him know him to be as good a Commander as any, and the Penobscot expedition has not hurt his Character with me."[32]

Whether Captain Saltonstall knew of Parsons's letter is not clear, but after a time of inactivity, he did go to sea to recoup his reputation. He wrote to Adam Babcock, the owner of the brigantine *Minerva*, requesting permission to convert her into a cruiser or privateer and command her. Babcock answered, "It is perfectly agreeable to me that you should command the Brigt. as cruiser rather than as merchantman, and chiefly that you may regain the character with the world which you have been most cruelly and unjustly robbed of in a manner as new and unusual as it was barbarous and tyrannical. You never lost it with me, and this I believe you never doubted."[33] This was high praise coming from Adam Babcock who was part owner of the *Hampden*, which was lost in the Penobscot Expedition. Paul Revere became one of the investors in Saltonstall's venture.[34]

The brigantine *Minerva*, commissioned 21 May 1781, carried a crew of 120 with sixteen guns. Captain Saltonstall's cruise as a privateer was successful. On 24 June he engaged the British schooner *Arbuthnot* of ten guns en route from New York to Newfoundland. The *Arbuthnot*'s cargo was tobacco. Saltonstall sent his prize into New London. A week later he encountered the 16-gun British vessel *Hannah*. The *Hannah* was en route from London to New York. After an hour's engagement Captain Saltonstall was victorious. The *Hannah*'s cargo was valued at eighty thousand pounds.[35] Yet his success was small compensation compared to the enormous character assassination dealt him by the Massachusetts Conspiracy. After the war Saltonstall returned to merchant marine sailing to the West Indies. He died in Haiti in 1796.

* * *

The assault on his character did not end with the Committee of Inquiry.

Around the time of the nation's bicentennial a number of articles and a few books were written about the Penobscot Expedition. Of the many sampled for this study, not one investigated the technological limitations of Saltonstall's ships with respect to entering Bagaduce harbor in the face of the competent British defenses. As for the Committee of Inquiry's hearings, a few mentioned that the committee whitewashed the Massachusetts officers but nonetheless employed the committee's finding that Commodore Saltonstall bore the brunt for the failure. Not one of these works investigated the depths of the committee's perfidy toward its obligation to seek justice in its inquiry. Few of the narrators dealt with the navy court-martial, and those that did were satisfied that it was held and assumed it reached the same conclusion as the Massachusetts committee.

After hearing a lecture demonstrating this study's thesis, a lady from the audience said she lived in Castine and she had never heard anyone defending Saltonstall. She said, "You know in Castine we called him Commodore Sit and Stall." It is hoped that after 222 years the exposure of the Massachusetts Conspiracy will restore to the commodore his rightful name.

Appendix

Mathematical Charts
and Calculations

Assumptions: (a) Distances are in nautical miles (6076.12 feet per mile).
                (b) There is negligible current.
                (c) The channel is 600 yards wide.
                (d) The ship is traveling into the wind.

$$(1) \quad T(d) := 34983.52 \cdot \frac{d}{6076.12}$$

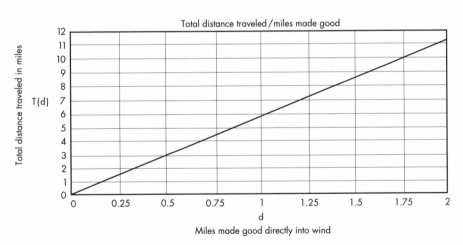

To travel one mile under the stated conditions, a ship would have had to travel 5.76 nautical miles.

(2) $N(d) := 6076.12 \cdot \dfrac{d}{317.39}$

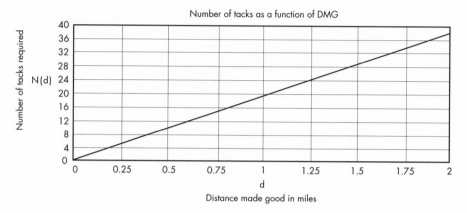

To travel one mile under the stated conditions, a ship would have had to tack 19.14 times.

(3) $H(r) := \dfrac{5.76}{r}$

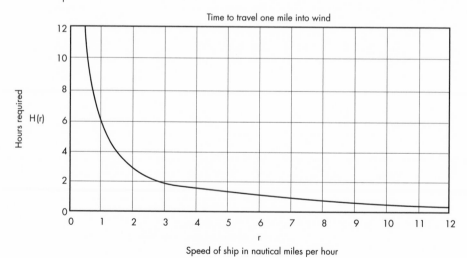

A ship traveling at 2 nautical miles per hour under the stated conditions would require 2.88 hours to travel one mile.

Notes

Chapter 1. Bagaduce

1. Esther Forbes, *Paul Revere and the World He Lived In* (Boston: Houghton Mifflin Company, 1942), 133–35; Revere's illustration is opposite page 146.

2. Majabigwaduce "variously spelled, with little to choose among most of its forms, the very worst excepted, has long been applied to the Castine peninsula. ... [I believe] the original word, replaced by an Abnaki form, was Micmac Indian; that it meant a big tidal salt bay; and that it referred to the whole Bagaduce River, so called, not merely to Castine Harbor." Fanny Hardy Eckstrom, *Indian Place-Names of the Penobscot Valley and the Maine Coast* (Orono: University of Maine, 1941, 1974 printing), 193, 198. Contemporaries of the Penobscot Expedition used Bagaduce to indicate the Castine peninsula.

3. Colonel John Brewer to Judge David Perham, date unknown, "Penobscot Expedition against Castine," *Bangor (Maine) Daily Whig and Courier,* 19 August 1846.

4. Council of War, 7 August 1779, Papers of the Continental Congress, 1774–1789, National Archives, Massachusetts State Papers, 1775–1787, roll 47, vol. 2, 132, RG 360.

5. Leland J. Bellot, *William Knox: The Life and Thought of an Eighteenth-Century Imperialist* (Austin: University of Texas Press, 1977), 4, 24, 39, 56–57.

6. David Russell Jack, "Calef, John, M.D.," *Biographical Data Relating to New Brunswick Families, Especially of Loyalist Descent,* 2d ed. (St. John, N.B.: New Brunswick Museum, 1965), 1:154–55; E. Alfred Jones, *The Loyalists of Massachusetts, Their Memorials, Petitions, and Claims* (London: Saint Catherine Press, 1930), 70–71; Robert W. Sloan, "New Ireland: Men in Pursuit of a Forlorn Hope, 1779–1784," *Maine Historical Society Quarterly* 19 (fall 1979): 74.

7. Samuel F. Batchelder, "The Life and Surprising Adventures of John Nutting, Cambridge Loyalist, and His Strange Connection with the Penobscot Expedition of 1779," *Cambridge Historical Society Publications* 5 (January–October 1910): 55–63.

8. Sloan, "New Ireland," 74.

9. Batchelder, "Life and Surprising Adventures of John Nutting," 68; Webster's New Biographical Dictionary of Infopedia 2.0, s.v. "Ward, Artemas"; *Biographical Directory of the United States Congress, 1774–1981* (Washington, D.C.: GPO, 1989), 2005.

10. David Harris Willson, *A History of England* (N.Y.: Holt, Rinehart and Winston, 1967), 561.

11. Massey to Gen. William Howe, Great Britain, Royal Commission on Historical Manuscripts, *Report on American Manuscripts in the Royal Institution of Great Britain,* 4 vols. (London: Mackie, 1904–9), 1:209.

12. Batchelder, "Life and Surprising Adventures of John Nutting," 71.

13. Bellot, *William Knox,* 163.

14. Batchelder, "Life and Surprising Adventures of John Nutting," 74–75; Bellot, *William Knox,* 163–67, 177.

15. Batchelder, "Life and Surprising Adventures of John Nutting," 56–76; *Report on American Manuscripts,* 1:284.

16. Batchelder, "Life and Surprising Adventures of John Nutting," 76–78.

17. Clinton to McLean, New York, 13 April 1779, *Report on American Manuscripts,* 1:415–16.

18. Charles Bracelen Flood, *Rise and Fight Again: Perilous Times along the Road to Independence* (New York: Dodd, Mead, 1976), 157.

19. U.S. Navy, Naval History Division, *Naval Documents of the American Revolution* (Washington, D.C.: GPO, 1964–), 1:297–332; Chester B. Kevitt, compiler, *General Solomon Lovell and the Penobscot Expedition,* 1779 (Weymouth, Mass.: Weymouth Historical Commission, 1976), 173. Kevitt's compilation is a particularly valuable source because in chapter 2 he juxtaposes the journals of Massachusetts Militia general Solomon Lovell and Dr. John Calef, British surgeon. In chapter 3 he presents selected letters and documents from other participants during the Penobscot Expedition.

20. Batchelder, "Life and Surprising Adventures of John Nutting," 59, 76.

21. Hank Taft and Jan Taft, *A Cruising Guide to the Maine Coast,* 2d ed. (Camden, Me.: International Marine Publishing, 1991), 159.

22. Robert Carver Brooks, "Notes and General Comments—The Penobscot Expedition, 1779, and the Massachusetts Conspiracy," typescript, July 1999, p. 8. This represents Brooks's critique of the first draft of this work; the typescript is in my possession.

23. Five-day journal by an unidentified source, *Nova-Scotia Gazette* (Halifax), 6 July 1779, supplement.

24. Ibid.; McLean to Sir Henry Clinton, 26 June 1779, in Kevitt, *General Solomon Lovell,* 62–63; McLean to Lord George Germain, 26 August 1779, in John E. Cayford, *The Penobscot Expedition: Being an Account of the Largest American Naval*

Engagement of the Revolutionary War (Orrington, Me.: C and H Publishing, 1976), app. G, 73–76.

25. Mowat to Buck, 15 June 1779, Jonathan Buck Papers, Bucksport Public Library, Bucksport, Maine.

26. *Nova-Scotia Gazette* (Halifax), 6 July 1779.

27. Cushing to Massachusetts Council, 19 June 1779, in Kevitt, *General Solomon Lovell*, 60–61; Massachusetts Archives Collection ["Felt Collection"], Records, 1629–1799, Revolutionary Period (1775–80), Penobscot Expedition, 1779, 145:542, Massachusetts Archives, Boston.

28. Brewer to Perham, *Bangor (Maine) Daily Whig and Courier*, 19–20 August 1846.

29. Germain to General George Clinton, Whitehall, 2 September 1778, letter no. 11, American Manuscripts (Guy Carleton Papers), 1775–1783, transcripts, vol. 7, no. 27, 239–41, Public Archives of Canada, Ottawa.

30. McLean to Germain, 26 August 1779, in Cayford, *Penobscot Expedition,* app. G, 73–75; Batchelder, "Life and Surprising Adventures of John Nutting," 79; William Lawrence, "Sergeant Lawrence's Journal," in George A. Wheeler, ed., *History of Castine, Penobscot, and Brooksville, Maine* (Bangor, Me.: Burr and Robinson, 1875), doc. 7.

31. Henry Mowat, "A Relation of the Services in Which Capt. Henry Mowat Was Engaged in America from 1759 to the End of the American War in 1783," *Journal of History* 3 (1910):334–43, 337, 339.

32. Wheeler, *History of Castine,* 304–7.

33. *Nova-Scotia Gazette* (Halifax), 6 July 1779.

34. "A Castine Summer—1779," *Wilson Museum Bulletin* (fall 1975):1. This letter, written in 1779 by a young woman living in what is now Castine, is among the Samuel Adams papers in the New York Public Library; it was reprinted in the *Wilson Museum Bulletin*. At least one page and the signature are missing, but from internal evidence, it is believed to have been written by Jane Goldthwait from Majabigwaduce Hospital Headquarters, 20 August 1779; she was the youngest daughter of Thomas Goldthwait. Colonel Goldthwait was commander of Fort Pownall (Fort Point) for a number of years before it was burned in 1775. The Goldthwaits then probably lived near the site of the fort until the summer of 1779 when they were "mob'd" and accepted British protection. The letter was apparently written to Jane's half-sister, Catherine Goldthwait, then thirty-five years old, not yet married. Jane herself was twenty-four.

Vernal Hutchinson, *When Revolution Came: The Story of Old Deer Isle in the Province of Maine during the War for American Independence* (Ellsworth, Me.: Ellsworth American, 1972), 74–75.

35. *Documentary History of the State of Maine,* ed. James Phinney Baxter, 2d series (Portland, Me.: Bailey and Noyes, 1913), 16:304, 362–63.

36. McLean to Henry Clinton, Bagaduce, 26 June 1779, *Report on American Manuscripts*, 1:460.

37. Ibid., 1:453–58.

38. A German, Johan Jakob Dieß, had land on what is now known as "Dice's Head," and there were many Anglicized versions of Dieß's name in contemporary accounts.

39. McLean to Henry Clinton, Bagaduce, 23 August 1779, *Report on American Manuscripts*, 2:15; Mowat, "A Relation of the Services," 49; Batchelder, "Life and Surprising Adventures of John Nutting," 79; John Calef, *The Siege of Penobscot by the Rebels* (1781; reprint, New York: New York Times, 1971), 17 June–17 July. Because of the many editions of the Calef publication, dates for journal entries are cited rather than page numbers.

40. "A Castine Summer," 1–2.

41. Ibid., 2.

42. Calef, *Siege of Penobscot*, 18–19 July; Mowat, "A Relation of the Services," 50.

43. Calef, *Siege of Penobscot*, 19–20 July; Wheeler, *History of Castine*, 291–92, 323; Hutchinson, *When Revolution Came*, 77–78.

44. Calef, *Siege of Penobscot*, 21 July; Wheeler, *History of Castine*, 323; HM *Albany* log, 21 July 1779, British Admiralty Records, Ships' Logs, Public Records Office, London.

45. A spring was a hawser usually led out one of the after gun ports and attached to the anchor ring before letting it go. With an equal strain on the cable and hawser the vessel will ride to a bridle and may be cast in any particular direction; *A Naval Encyclopaedia: Comprising a Dictionary of Nautical Words and Phrases* (Philadelphia: L. R. Hamersly, 1881), 35; John Harland, *Seamanship in the Age of Sail* (Annapolis, Md.: Naval Institute Press, 1984), 276.

46. Mowat, "A Relation of the Services," 339–40; Calef said Mowat had three transports, but Mowat listed four, Calef, *Siege of Penobscot*, 24 July.

47. Mowat, "A Relation of the Services," 339.

48. Brewer to Perham, *Bangor (Maine) Daily Whig and Courier*, 19 August 1846.

49. Ibid.

Chapter 2. Massachusetts's Answer

1. Committee report to General Court, 24 June, in Kevitt, *General Solomon Lovell*, 62; the general court's acceptance, 24 June, in *Documentary History*, 16:305.

2. John J. Currier, *History of Newburyport, Massachusetts, 1764–1905* (Newburyport, Mass.: Author, 1906), 590–92.

3. Ibid., 592.

4. Ibid., 593.

5. Ibid.

6. Ibid., 594; Massachusetts Archives Collection, 145:519.

7. Currier, *History of Newburyport,* 594.

8. Massachusetts Council to Continental Navy Board in Boston, 30 June, in Kevitt, *General Solomon Lovell,* 63–64.

9. Continental Navy Board to Massachusetts Council, 30 June, ibid., 64.

10. Kenneth Scott, "New Hampshire's Part in the Penobscot Expedition," *American Neptune* 7 (July 1947):200–202.

11. Kevitt, *General Solomon Lovell,* 153–58.

12. Massachusetts Council to Lovell, 1 July; Massachusetts Council to Saltonstall, 3 July, ibid., 64–65, 69.

13. New London County Historical Society, "Brief Biographies of Connecticut Revolution Naval and Privateer Officers, Dudley Saltonstall," pt. 4, vol. 1 of *Records and Papers of the New London County Historical Society* (New London, Conn.: New London County Historical Society, 1893), 65.

14. U.S. Navy, *Naval Documents,* 5:1029; William J. Morgan, *Captains to the Northward: The New England Captains in the Continental Navy* (Barre, Mass.: Barre Gazette, 1959), 50–51.

15. U.S. Navy, *Naval Documents,* 8:269.

16. Saltonstall to John Hancock, in *The Remembrancer, or Impartial Repository of Public Events,* 17 vols. (London: J. Almon, 1775–84), 5:135; Gardner W. Allen, *A Naval History of the American Revolution,* 2 vols. (Boston: Houghton Mifflin, 1913), 1:188, 201; Morgan, *Captains to the Northward,* 45, 51, 76–77.

17. Saltonstall to Barnabas Deane, 17 November 1777, Jacob B. Gurley Papers, Collection of Naval Manuscripts, 1734–1782, 12a, 12b, Connecticut State Library, Hartford; *Naval Encyclopaedia,* 105.

18. *Warren-Adams Letters: Being Chiefly a Correspondence among John Adams, Samuel Adams, and James Warren . . . 1743–1814,* 2 vols. (Boston: Massachusetts Historical Society, 1917–25), 1:368, 372, 2:8; *Out-Letters of the Continental Marine Committee and Board of Admiralty, August 1776–September 1780,* ed. Charles Oscar Paullin, 2 vols. (New York: Naval History Society, 1914), 2:28, 57.

19. Samuel Eliot Morison, *John Paul Jones: A Sailor's Biography* (Boston: Little, Brown, 1959), 42–43.

20. Currier, *History of Newburyport,* 595.

21. Council to Suffolk County Sheriff, 2 July; Council to Essex County Sheriff, 3 July, in Kevitt, *General Solomon Lovell,* 65, 69–70.

22. Saltonstall's account to Navy Board Eastern Department, Gurley Papers, 6b, 6c.

23. Navy Board Eastern Department to Marine Committee of the Continental Congress, 14 July 1779, letter 175, Navy Board Eastern District, Letter Book, New York Public Library, microfilm ZZ-145; Kevitt, *General Solomon Lovell,* 68–69.

24. Kevitt, *General Solomon Lovell,* 70; Orders of the Board of War, 5, 7 July, and Council to the Board of War, 8 July, *Documentary History,* 16:325, 326–29, 337–38.

25. Extract of a letter from Penobscot, 22 August, in *Nova-Scotia Gazette* (Halifax), 14 September 1779.

26. Gates's disclaimer noted in Douglas Southall Freeman, *George Washington: A Biography* (New York: Scribner, 1948–57), 5:122, n. 3; Hazard letter, Jamaica Plain, 22 March 1780, *Massachusetts Historical Society Proceedings* 4 (1860):129; James Thacher, *A Military Journal during the American Revolutionary War, from 1775–1783* (Boston: Cottons and Barnard, 1827), 166.

27. Massachusetts Council to Lovell, 2 July, in Kevitt, *General Solomon Lovell*, 66.

28. Navy Board to Saltonstall, 13 July, ibid., 72–73.

29. Navy Board to Marine Committee, 14 July 1779, Navy Board Eastern District, Letter Book.

30. Hill, 95, RG 360.

31. Lovell journal, 28 July, in Kevitt, *General Solomon Lovell*, 27–29; Lovell to Powell, 28 July, ibid., 80–81. Because General Lovell's journal appears in many publications, hereafter cited as Lovell journal and date.

32. *Documentary History*, 17:298; Lovell journal, 22 July.

33. Paul Revere to General William Heath, 24 October 1779, Massachusetts Historical Society, *Collections* (Boston: Massachusetts Historical Society, 1904), ser. 7, pt. 2, 4:319.

34. Lovell journal, 22 July.

35. Allan R. Millett and Peter Maslowski, *For the Common Defense: A Military History of the United States of America* (New York: Free Press, 1984), 76–77.

36. Edgar S. Maclay, *A History of American Privateers* (New York: D. Appleton, 1899), 119.

37. *Naval Encyclopaedia*, 722, 759.

38. Howard I. Chapelle, *The History of the American Sailing Navy: The Ships and Their Development* (New York: Norton, 1949), 15; Colby Mitchell Chester Papers, "Study of Commodore Dudley Saltonstall and the Penobscot Bay Expedition in 1779," 22–23, MSS78410, Naval Historical Foundation Collection, Library of Congress.

39. Chapelle, *History of the American Sailing Navy*, 14, 38–39; *Naval Encyclopaedia*, 294–95; Chester Papers, "Study of Commodore Dudley Saltonstall," 30.

40. *Naval Encyclopaedia*, 838; U.S. Navy, *Naval Documents*, 7:101, 347, 1117; Chester Papers, "Study of Commodore Dudley Saltonstall"; Massachusetts, Secretary of the Commonwealth, *Massachusetts Soldiers and Sailors of the Revolutionary War*, 17 vols. (Boston: Wright and Potter, 1896–1908), 2:647.

41. Philip Chadwick Foster Smith, *Fired by Manley Zeal* (Salem Mass.: Peabody Museum of Salem, 1977), 99–100.

42. All the ship captains' records, except for Saltonstall's and Salter's, were found in *Massachusetts Soldiers and Sailors* in the volumes concerned; Navy Board

to Marine Committee, 10, 16 June, letters 157, 158, Navy Board Eastern District, Letter Book.

43. Paul Revere, Diary from 21 July to 19 August 1779, 50–55, RG 360; Massachusetts Archives Collection, 145:246–49; Revere's diary also published in Elbridge H. Goss, *Life of Colonel Paul Revere*, 2 vols. (Boston: J. G. Cupples, 1891), 22 July; Revere to Heath, 24 October 1779, Massachusetts Historical Society, *Collections*, 4:320.

Chapter 3. Assault

1. Lovell's Orders, 24 July, in Kevitt, *General Solomon Lovell*, 75–77.
2. Downs, 37, Cathcart, 79, Morris, 91, RG 360.
3. Hill, 95, ibid.; Lovell journal, 24 July.
4. *A Detail of Some Particular Services Performed in America, 1776–1779*, 106; *Albany* log, 25 July.
5. Mowat, "A Relation of the Services," 339; Calef, *Siege of Penobscot*, 25 July.
6. Philip Brown, 59, RG 360.
7. The island had several names, Nautilus, Cross, and Banks' Island.
8. Downs, 37, RG 360.
9. Cathcart, 79, ibid.
10. *Albany* log, 26 July; "Journal of the Attack of the Rebels . . . in Penobscot-Bay," 26 July, *Nova-Scotia Gazette* (Halifax), 14 September 1779; "Copy of a Journal Found on Board the Hunter Continental Ship of 18 Guns," *Nova-Scotia Gazette* (Halifax), 2 November 1779; and "Operations in Maine in 1779, Journal Found on Board the Hunter, Continental Ship, of Eighteen Guns," entry for 25 July, *Historical Magazine* (February 1864):51.
11. Hill, 95, RG 360; Moore to his father, 24 August 1779, in Beatrice Brownrigg, *The Life and Letters of Sir John Moore* (Oxford: B. Blackwell, 1923), 15.
12. Calef, *Siege of Penobscot*, 25 July.
13. Ibid., 28 July.
14. Nathan Goold, "Colonel Jonathan Mitchell's Cumberland County Regiment: Bagaduce Expedition, 1779," *Collections of the Maine Historical Society*, ser. 2, 10:52; Lovell journal, 25 July.
15. Calef, *Siege of Penobscot*, 25 July.
16. *Albany* log, 26 July; Cathcart, 79, Johnston, 105, RG 360; "Journal of the Attack," 26 July, *Nova-Scotia Gazette* (Halifax), 14 September 1779.
17. John Brewer, "A Short Statement of What Took Place at Majabigwaduce, . . ." 82–83, in John E. Godfrey Collection, misc. box 7/1, Maine Historical Society, Portland, Me.; Brewer to Perham, *Bangor (Maine) Daily Whig and Courier*, 19 August 1846.
18. Council of War, *Warren*, 26 July, 127, RG 360.
19. *Albany* log, 27 July.

20. Williams, 41, RG 360.

21. Johnston, 105, ibid.

22. Thomas Philbrook, "Narrative," in Hope Rider, *Valour, Fore and Aft: Being the Adventures of the Continental Sloop "Providence," 1775–1779, Formerly Flagship "Katy" of Rhode Island's Navy* (Annapolis, Md.: United States Naval Institute Press, 1977), app. F, 228.

23. *Albany* log, 27 July.

24. "Operations in Maine in 1779," entry for 26 July; Cathcart, 79, RG 360.

25. Cathcart, 79, RG 360.

26. Mowat, "A Relation of the Services," 51.

27. Ibid.; Calef, *Siege of Penobscot*, 26 July; Lovell journal, 26 July; Philbrook, "Narrative," 229; Goss, *Life of Colonel Paul Revere*, 27 July.

28. Headquarters, Transport Sally, 27 July, Massachusetts Archives Collection, 145:437.

29. *Albany* log, 27 July; Johnston, 105, RG 360; Philbrook, "Narrative," 229.

30. Massachusetts Archives Collection, 145:50–51.

31. Council of War, *Warren*, 27 July, 128, RG 360.

32. Ibid., 79.

33. Hill, 95, Gawen Brown, 35, ibid.

34. Davis, 84, ibid.

35. Cathcart, 82, ibid.

36. Ibid.; Downs, 37, ibid.; "Operations in Maine in 1779," entry for 28 July.

37. McLean to Collier, 26 August, in Cayford, *Penobscot Expedition*, app. G, 74.

38. Ibid., 73–76; McLean to Clinton, 23 August, *Report on American Manuscripts*, 2:15; Moore to his father, 24 August 1779, in Brownrigg, *Life and Letters*, 15–16.

39. Downs, 37, RG 360.

40. William Reidhead, "William Reidhead's Journal, 1779," 28 July, *Bangor Historical Magazine* 5 (July 1889–June 1890); Lawrence included 27 and 28 July in one entry of 27 July, Lawrence, "Sergeant Lawrence's Journal," 27 July.

41. Joseph Williamson, "Sir John Moore at Castine during the Revolution," *Collections of the Maine Historical Society*, ser. 2, 2:403–9.

42. Gawen Brown, 35, Hill, 95, Todd, 115, RG 360; extract of a letter from Majorbagaduce, dated 3 August 1779, in *Pennsylvania Gazette* (Philadelphia), 25 August 1779.

43. Wadsworth to William D. Williamson, 1 January 1828, quoted in Flood, *Rise and Fight Again*, 182; Goss, *Life of Colonel Paul Revere*, 28 July; Todd, 115, Gawen Brown, 35, RG 360.

44. Revere to Heath, Massachusetts Historical Society, *Collections*, 4:321.

45. McLean to Sir Henry Clinton, 23 August 1779, *Report on American Manuscripts*, 2:15.

46. Brewer to Perham, *Bangor (Maine) Daily Whig and Courier,* 20 August 1846; Wheeler, *History of Castine,* 332.

47. Wheeler, *History of Castine,* 323.

48. Cathcart, 81, RG 360; Goss, *Life of Colonel Paul Revere,* 28 July.

49. Lovell to Powell, 28 July, in Kevitt, *General Solomon Lovell,* 80–81; Lovell said he "dispatch'd an Express by way of Falmouth to you," Lovell to Powell, 13 August 1779, in Kevitt, *General Solomon Lovell,* 106; Wadsworth said there were two whaleboats sent, Wadsworth to Williamson, 1 January 1828, in *Collections of the Maine Historical Society,* ser. 2, 2:157; account of James Fosdick, Massachusetts Archives Collection, 145:422; John Allen to Powell, 10 September, 5, RG 360; Brooks, "Notes and General Comments," 13.

50. Massachusetts Archives Collection, 145:543.

51. Headquarters, Heights on M., 28 July, ibid., 145:438–39.

52. Calef, *Siege of Penobscot,* 28 July; gammoning is the lashing over the bowsprit to secure the bowsprit, *Naval Encyclopaedia,* 308; the foremast, main topmast, and mizzen topgallant mast, all ultimately depend for their security on the integrity of the bowsprit and forestay, Harland, *Seamanship in the Age of Sail,* 298.

53. Philip Brown, 59, RG 360.

54. Kevitt, *General Solomon Lovell,* 35.

55. McLean to Sir Henry Clinton, 23 August 1779, *Report on American Manuscripts,* 2:16.

56. *Albany* log, 28, 29 July; Calef, *Siege of Penobscot,* 29 July; William Hutchings, "The Narrative of William Hutchings," in Wheeler, *History of Castine,* 325.

57. Captains Williams and Cathcart said this took place at the council of war on 30 July, 41 and 81, RG 360; yet the proper date was 29 July, as there was no council on 30 July. Council of War, *Warren,* 129, RG 360.

58. Council of War, *Warren,* 29 July, ibid.

59. McLean to Lord Germain, 26 August 1779, in Cayford, *Penobscot Expedition,* app. G.

60. Lovell's defense, Committee of Inquiry, 25 September, in Kevitt, *General Solomon Lovell,* 129.

61. Calef, *Siege of Penobscot,* 30 July; "Journal of the Attack," 30 July, *Nova-Scotia Gazette* (Halifax), 14 September 1779.

62. *Naval Encyclopaedia,* 303; Adams to Josiah Quincy, 29 July 1775, U.S. Navy, *Naval Documents,* 1:1004.

63. Navy Board to Saltonstall, 23 July, letter 181, Navy Board Eastern District, Letter Book; Philip Brown, 59, RG 360.

64. Philip Brown, 59, RG 360.

65. Lovell's defense, Court of Inquire, 25 September, in Kevitt, *General Solomon Lovell,* 129; "Operations in Maine in 1779," entry for 31 July.

66. It should be remembered that the *Albany's* log went from meridian to meridian. Thus the weather stated under 31 July was the weather during this assault.

67. The American account may be found in Lovell journal, 1 August; Downs, 37, Salter, 112, RG 360; "Operations in Maine in 1779," entry for 1 August; William Moody, "The Journal of Drummer Moody of Col. Mitchell's Regiment," 31 July, in Goold, "Colonel Jonathan Mitchell's Cumberland County Regiment"; Goss, *Life of Colonel Paul Revere,* 1 August; the British account is taken from journal, *Nova-Scotia Gazette* (Halifax), 1 August; Calef, *Siege of Penobscot,* 31 July; *Nautilus* log, 1 August; *Albany* log, 31 July; Lawrence, "Sergeant Lawrence's Journal," 31 July; Reidhead, "William Reidhead's Journal," 1 August; Hutchings, "Narrative of William Hutchings," in Wheeler, *History of Castine,* 324.

The eighteen prisoners joined the eight captured during the original assault, plus the crewmen taken from the British schooner brought in by the *Diligent* on 28 July, Lovell journal, 28 July; Philip Brown, 59, RG 360.

68. *Albany* log, 1 August; Salter, 112, RG 360; Calef, *Siege of Penobscot,* 1 August.

69. Lawrence, "Sergeant Lawrence's Journal," 2 August; Reidhead, "William Reidhead's Journal," 2 August.

70. Headquarters, 1 August, Massachusetts Archives Collection, 145:443–44.

71. Lovell journal, 1, 3 August; Calef, *Siege of Penobscot,* 2 August.

72. Lovell to Powell, 1 August, in Kevitt, *General Solomon Lovell,* 83–87.

73. Massachusetts Archives Collection, 145:373; Navy Board to Saltonstall, 10 August, letter 188, Navy Board Eastern District, Letter Book.

74. Allan to Powell, 10 August, 5, RG 360; Colonel Augustin Mottin De La Balme, Journal of Trip to Maine, May–September 1779, 42, item 21846 in the Haldimand Papers, Library of Congress.

Chapter 4. Siege

1. Waters, 53, RG 360; Lovell journal, 2 August.

2. Lovell journal, 3 August; Calef, *Siege of Penobscot,* 2 August; Moody, "Journal of Drummer Moody," 3 August; Massachusetts Historical Society, *Collections,* index lists Lieutenant William Dennis.

3. Extract of a letter from Majorbagaduce, dated 3 August 1779, in *Pennsylvania Gazette* (Philadelphia), 25 August.

4. Lovell to Saltonstall, 11 August, in Kevitt, *General Solomon Lovell,* 100; Lovell journal, 3 August.

5. Lawrence, "Sergeant Lawrence's Journal," 2–3 August; Reidhead, "William Reidhead's Journal," 2–3 August; Calef, *Siege of Penobscot,* 3 August; *Albany* log, 3 August, but this log covered from noon to noon, so its entry "Early this morning discovered the Rebels erecting a Battery on advantagious ground to the left of the River and about 3/4 of a mile above the Men of War," would indicate the event was observed on 4 August; *Nautilus* log, 4 August.

6. Lovell journal, 4 August; Calef, *Siege of Penobscot,* 4 August; *Albany* and *Nautilus* logs, 4 August.

7. Lawrence, "Sergeant Lawrence's Journal," 4 August; Lovell journal, 4 August; Calef, *Siege of Penobscot,* 4 August.

8. Calef, *Siege of Penobscot,* 5 August.

9. Calef's map of Bagaduce (Calef, *Siege of Penobscot*) did not show a canal nor did the map of Lt. George W. D. Jones, 7th Regiment, with Collier's force, titled "Sketch of the Neck and Harbour of Majabigwaduce," in Douglas W. Marshall and Howard Henry Peckham, *Campaigns of the American Revolution: An Atlas of Manuscript Maps* (Ann Arbor: University of Michigan Press, 1976); Hill, 95, Todd, 115, RG 360; Hutchings, "Narrative of William Hutchings," in Wheeler, *History of Castine,* doc. 9, 271–76; statement of Wadsworth, in Kevitt, *General Solomon Lovell,* 142.

10. Wadsworth, 76, RG 360.

11. Davis, 84, ibid.

12. Lovell to Saltonstall, 5 August, in Kevitt, *General Solomon Lovell,* 89.

13. Council of War, *Warren,* 6 August, 130, RG 360, also found in Kevitt, *General Solomon Lovell,* 90–91; "Operations in Maine in 1779," entry for 6 August.

14. Council of War, Headquarters, 6 August, in Kevitt, *General Solomon Lovell,* 91–92; Goss, *Life of Colonel Paul Revere,* 6 August.

15. Lovell journal, 6 August; account of David Braddish, Massachusetts Archives Collection, 145:410.

16. "Operations in Maine in 1779," entry for 9, 12 August.

17. Nathan Brown, 28, RG 360.

18. John Carnes, 29, ibid.

19. Salter, 112, ibid.

20. Jonathan Parsons, Newburyport, Mass., to Jeremiah Wadsworth, Esq., Philadelphia, 2 November 1779, Connecticut State Library, Hartford.

21. Jack Coggins, "Peril on the Penobscot," in *Ships and Seamen of the American Revolution* (Harrisburg, Pa.: Stackpole Books, 1969), 134–35; Richard Bailey, interview by author, tape recording, 17 October 1998, aboard HMS *Rose,* Jacksonville, Fla.

22. For more complete details see chapter 13, "Working Ship in A Tideway," Harland, *Seamanship in the Age of Sail.*

23. Parsons to J. Wadsworth, 2 November 1779; Hacker to Lovell and Saltonstall, 8 August, in Kevitt, *General Solomon Lovell,* 94–96.

24. *Encyclopaedia Britannica,* 15th ed., s.v., "technology of war"; U.S. Department of Commerce, Penobscot River navigation chart 13309, 24th ed., 19 November 1988; "Operations in Maine in 1779," entry for 9 August.

25. Chester Papers, "Study of Commodore Dudley Saltonstall," 34–35.

26. Elliot Rappaport, interview by author, tape recording, 14 June 1997, Marine Maritime Academy, Castine, Maine.

27. Robin Walbridge, interview by author, 30 October 1997, aboard HMS *Bounty,* Jacksonville, Fla.

28. Penobscot River navigation chart 13309; Bailey, interview.

29. Captain Austin Becker, interview by author, 29 July 2000, aboard the Continental sloop *Providence,* sailing from Castine to Bucksport, Maine.

30. Calef, *Siege of Penobscot,* 6 August.

31. Council of War, *Hazard,* 7 August, 132, RG 360.

32. Ibid.; Kevitt, *General Solomon Lovell,* 94–95; "Operations in Maine in 1779," entry for 7 August; Revere's defense, Massachusetts Archives Collection, 145:339.

33. Revere to Heath, 24 October 1779, Massachusetts Historical Society, *Collections,* 4:318–26.

34. Lovell journal, 7 August; Calef, *Siege of Penobscot,* 7 August; *Nautilus* log, 7 August; *Albany* log, 8 August; "Operations in Maine in 1779," entry for 7 August; Lawrence, "Sergeant Lawrence's Journal," 7 August; Reidhead, "William Reidhead's Journal," 7 August; Philbrook, "Narrative," 230; "Journal of the Attack," 7 August, *Nova-Scotia Gazette* (Halifax), 14 September 1779.

35. Philbrook, "Narrative," 230; "Operations in Maine in 1779," entry for 8 August; Lovell's defense before the investigating committee in Kevitt, *General Solomon Lovell,* 138.

36. Hacker to Lovell and Saltonstall, 8 August 1779, in Kevitt, *General Solomon Lovell,* 94–96.

37. Davis, 84, RG 360.

38. Calef, *Siege of Penobscot,* 5 and 8 August.

39. Waterman Thomas, 67, RG 360.

40. Carnes, 29, ibid.

41. "Operations in Maine in 1779," entry for 9 August.

42. Council of War, *Warren,* 10 August, 134, RG 360.

43. Ibid.; "Operations in Maine in 1779," entry for 10 August.

44. Morris, 91, RG 360; Dudley Saltonstall, Gurley Papers, 4c.

45. Downs, 37, RG 360.

46. Hill, 95, ibid.; Moody, "Journal of Drummer Moody," 11 August; Hutchinson, *When Revolution Came,* 86; Lovell's Returns, 8 and 12 August, Massachusetts Archives Collection, 145:83, 101.

47. James Morris, 91, RG 360.

48. The Hook mentioned was Sandy Hook, New York, Lovell to Saltonstall, 11 August, in Kevitt, *General Solomon Lovell,* 99–101.

49. Lovell journal, 11 August.

50. Reidhead, "William Reidhead's Journal," 11 August; Lawrence, "Sergeant Lawrence's Journal," 11 August.

51. Council of War, Headquarters, 11 August, 135, RG 360.

52. "Operations in Maine in 1779," entry for 11 August.

53. Lovell to Massachusetts Council, 13 August, in Kevitt, *General Solomon Lovell,* 107.

54. Council of War, *Warren,* 12 August, 140; Cathcart, 81, RG 360.

55. Kevitt, *General Solomon Lovell,* 101–3; Lovell to Massachusetts Council, addendum to letter of 3 September, ibid, 119.

56. Goss, *Life of Colonel Paul Revere,* 12 August; Davis, 84, Speakman, 63, RG 360.

57. McLean letter, 26 August 1779, in Cayford, *Penobscot Expedition,* app. G; Lawrence, "Sergeant Lawrence's Journal," 12 August; Reidhead, "William Reidhead's Journal," 12 August; Lt. George W. D. Jones's map "Sketch of the Neck and Harbour of Majabigwaduce" showed the battery.

58. Extract of a letter from Belfast, dated 12 August 1779 in *Pennsylvania Gazette* (Philadelphia), 25 August 1779.

59. Calef, *Siege of Penobscot,* 13 August.

60. Council of War, Headquarters, 13 August, 139, RG 360.

61. Cushing, 39, Davis, 84, ibid.; *Nautilus* log, 13 August.

62. During the interview with Captain Walbridge of HMS *Bounty,* he provided a tide and current chart for Castine from 28 July to 19 August 1779, which coincided with the tidal information supplied by Admiral Chester's narrative (Chester Papers, "Study of Commodore Dudley Saltonstall," #136); the wind from the *Albany* and *Nautilus* logs, 13 August.

63. Lovell journal, 13 August; *Albany* log, 13 August; John Carnes, 29, RG 360.

64. *Albany* log, 13 August.

65. Salter, 112, RG 360.

66. Hallet, 33, Philip Brown, 59, ibid.

67. Collier to Philip Stephens, Secretary of the Admiralty, *Remembrancer, or Impartial Repository,* 8:354.

68. Collier to Stephens, 20 August, in Cayford, *Penobscot Expedition,* app. E; Allen, *Naval History,* 2:432–33.

69. Collier to Stephens, 20 August, in Cayford, *Penobscot Expedition,* app. E; Saltonstall to Lovell, 13 August, in Kevitt, *General Solomon Lovell,* 106; Lovell to Massachusetts Council, 13 August, 3 September, in Kevitt, *General Solomon Lovell,* 106–8, 115–19.

70. Council of War, 7 August, 132, RG 360.

Chapter 5. Retreat and Rout

1. Saltonstall to Lovell, 13 August, in Kevitt, *General Solomon Lovell,* 106; Hill, 95, McCobb, 47, Mitchell, 31, RG 360; *Albany* log, 13 August.

2. McLean to Germain, 26 August, in Cayford, *Penobscot Expedition,* app. G.

3. Thomas, 67, Cushing, 39, RG 360.

4. *Albany* log, 13 August; *Nautilus* log, 14 August.

5. Waters, 53, RG 360.

6. Cathcart, 79, Hallet, 33, Council of War, *Warren,* 14 August, 140, ibid.

7. Salter, 112, ibid.

8. Berry to Council, 14 August, Massachusetts Archives Collection, 145:115.

9. Davis, 84, RG 360.

10. Brooks, "Notes and General Comments," 3.

11. Lovell to Powell, 14 August, actually it was the postscript of his 13 August letter, Massachusetts Archives Collection, 145:139; Todd, 118, RG 360; *Albany* log, 13 August.

12. *Nautilus* log, 14 September.

13. Todd, 118, RG 360.

14. *Albany* log, 14 August; McLean to Henry Clinton, 23 August 1779, *Report on American Manuscripts,* 2:14; *Naval Encyclopaedia,* s.v. "warping," 834; Brooks, "Notes and General Comments," 15.

15. Goss, *Life of Colonel Paul Revere,* 14 August; Davis, 84, RG 360.

16. P. Brown, 59, RG 360.

17. *Blonde* log, as printed in Allen, *Naval History,* 2:433.

18. *Republican Journal* (Belfast, Maine), 3 December 1889; Collier to Clinton, 19 August, *Report on American Manuscripts,* 2:12–13.

19. Collier to Clinton, 19 August, *Report on American Manuscripts,* 2:12–13.

20. Salter, Massachusetts Archives Collection, 145:44–47; *Blonde* log, in Allen, *Naval History,* 2:433–34.

21. Studding-sails were light sails set outside the regular sails in fair wind and moderate weather for more propulsion, *Naval Encyclopaedia,* 712.

22. Todd, 115, Little, 87, RG 360.

23. Ibid.

24. Davis, 84, ibid.

25. Hill, 95, ibid.; Lovell to Massachusetts Council, 28 August, in Kevitt, *General Solomon Lovell,* 110; *Blonde* log, in Allen, *Naval History,* 2:433; *Albany* log, 14 August.

26. Waters, 53; Davis, 84, RG 360.

27. Davis, 84, Cushing, 39, ibid.

28. Davis, ibid; James Brown, 57, ibid.

29. Hill, 95, ibid.

30. Wadsworth, 71, ibid.

31. Watterman Thomas, 67, ibid.

32. Wadsworth, 71, ibid.; Wadsworth to Williamson, 1 January 1828, *Collections of the Maine Historical Society.*

33. Wadsworth to Council, 19 August, Massachusetts Archives Collection, 145:135.

34. Wadsworth, ibid., 145:278.

35. Wadsworth, 71, RG 360.

36. *Albany* log, 14 August; "Defense Update," Maine Public Broadcasting Network, 1982; Little, 87, RG 360.

37. Letter from David Perham giving Colonel Brewer's account of the expedition against Penobscot in 1779, doc. 10 in Wheeler, *History of Castine*, 331. Brewer said it happened on 14 August but it must have been 15 August.

38. Davis, 84, Waters, 53, RG 360.

39. Waters, 53, Todd, 115, Thomas, 67, Little, 87, ibid.

40. Little, 87, Thomas, 67, ibid.

41. Little, 87, ibid.

42. Ibid.

43. Ibid., Waters, 53, ibid.

44. Little, Massachusetts Archives Collection, 145:221; Thomas 67, RG 360.

45. McLean to Henry Clinton, 23 August, in Bagaduce, *Report on American Manuscripts*, 2:16.

46. *Albany* log, 14 and 15 August; *Blonde* log, in Allen, *Naval History*, 2:434.

47. P. Brown, 59, Williams, 41, RG 360.

48. Williams, 41, Cathcart, 79, ibid.

49. P. Brown, 59, ibid.

50. Ibid.

51. Thomas, 67, ibid; *Naval Encyclopaedia*, 424.

52. Todd, 115, Morris, 91, RG 360.

53. Morris, ibid; *Albany* log, 15 and 16 August.

54. Wadsworth, 71, RG 360.

55. *Albany* log, 17 August; *Nautilus* log, 17 August.

56. Brewer to Perham, *Bangor (Maine) Daily Whig and Courier*, 19 August 1846.

Chapter 6. Homeward Bound and the Accounting

1. Moody, "Journal of Drummer Moody," 14–15 August.

2. Ibid., 16–26 August.

3. Philbrook, "Narrative," 231; Philbrook's brackets.

4. Rider, *Valour, Fore and Aft*, 194.

5. John C. Dann, ed., *The Revolution Remembered: Eyewitness Accounts of the War for Independence* (Chicago: University of Chicago Press, 1980), 412–13.

6. Goss, *Life of Colonel Paul Revere*, 15, 16, 19 August; Phillips and Newcomb, Massachusetts Archives Collection, 145:345, 342.

7. Currier, *History of Newburyport*, 595–96.

8. Hutchinson, *When Revolution Came*, 89–90.

9. Brewer to Perham, *Bangor (Maine) Daily Whig and Courier*, 19–20 August 1846.

10. Ibid; Massachusetts Archives Collection, 145:545.

11. Brewer to Perham, *Bangor (Maine) Daily Whig and Courier,* 20 August 1846.

12. Wadsworth to Burke, Camden, 17 August, Massachusetts Archives Collection, 145:133.

13. Wadsworth to Council, Thomston, 19 August, ibid., 135.

14. There were twenty pages listing people reimbursed for their acts of kindness in Massachusetts Archives Collection, vol. 145, pages 542–43, 545–46, and 548–49 provide a sample.

15. Allan to Powell, 10 September 1779, RG 360.

16. Hutchinson, *When Revolution Came,* 91–92.

17. Allan to Powell, 10 September 1779, RG 360.

18. Lovell to Powell, 1 August, two letters, in Kevitt, *General Solomon Lovell,* 83–87; Massachusetts Council to Gates, 8 August, 19 August, Massachusetts Archives Collection, 145:84, 139.

19. Massachusetts Archives Collection, 57:347, excerpted from Scott, "New Hampshire's Part in the Penobscot Expedition," 210.

20. Committee of Safety, Falmouth, to Massachusetts Council, 30 August, in Kevitt, *General Solomon Lovell,* 114.

21. Weare Papers, 7:34, New Hampshire Historical Society, 1863, reprinted in Scott, "New Hampshire's Part in the Penobscot Expedition," 207.

22. Council to Lovell, 19 August, Massachusetts Archives Collection, 145:134.

23. Navy Board to Marine Committee, 18 August, with postscript of 19 August, letter 200, Navy Board Eastern District, Letter Book.

24. Council to Gates, 19 August, Massachusetts Archives Collection, 145:139; Lovell's letter of 14 August was his postscript to his letter of 13 August not a separate letter, Massachusetts Archives Collection, 145:105.

25. Wadsworth to Council, Thomaston, 19 August 1779, Massachusetts Archives Collection, 145:135.

26. Ibid.

27. Lovell to Council, 28 August, in Kevitt, *General Solomon Lovell,* 110–12.

28. Murray to Powell, 21 August, Massachusetts Archives Collection, 145:141; F. H. Tarkson to Powell, 28 August quoting Murray's letter of 25 August, *Documentary History,* 17:43–44.

29. Eckstrom, *Indian Place-Names,* 11, 13.

30. Lovell to Council, 28 August, Georgetown, in Kevitt, *General Solomon Lovell,* 110–12.

31. Lovell to Council, 29 August, Townsend, ibid., 112–13.

32. Navy Board to Marine Committee, 2 September, letter 210, Navy Board Eastern District, Letter Book.

33. Rice to Gates, 2 September, Gates Papers, New-York Historical Society, extract taken from Flood, *Rise and Fight Again,* 245.

34. Thomas Carnes to Council, 6 September, in Kevitt, *General Solomon Lovell,* 17.

35. Revere to Heath, 24 October 1779; Keith to Heath, 26 September 1779, Massachusetts Historical Society, *Collections,* 4:318–26.

36. Lovell to Council, 29 August, in Kevitt, *General Solomon Lovell,* 112–13.

37. *Independent Chronicle* (Boston), 9 September 1779, 3; excerpt from Scott, "New Hampshire's Part in the Penobscot Expedition," 211.

38. Committee Appointed to Investigate the Failure of the Penobscot Expedition, 9 September, in Kevitt, *General Solomon Lovell,* 123–24; Massachusetts Archives Collection, 145:167.

39. Massachusetts Archives Collection, 145:180–206b.

40. Payments to Greeley, Kimball, and Davis, Massachusetts Archives Collection, 145:206-6a-6b.

41. Keith to Heath, 26 September 1779, Boston, Massachusetts Historical Society, *Collections,* 4:317–18.

42. Ibid.; Massachusetts Archives Collection, 145:179; Kevitt, *General Solomon Lovell,* 13.

43. Little, 87, Cathcart, 79, Williams, 41, RG 360; Hacker to Lovell and Saltonstall, 8 August, in Kevitt, *General Solomon Lovell,* 94–96.

44. Council of War, *Warren,* 6 August, 130; N. Brown of the *Hunter,* 28, Carnes of the *Hector,* 29, RG 360.

45. "Report of Committee on Expedition," in Kevitt, *General Solomon Lovell,* 14–16; only a portion of the report was in Massachusetts Archives Collection, 145:350–51 and it had a note on the top margin "This Report can be found in full in Court Records Vol. 40, page 65/66"; the report found in 25–26, RG 360, also included the notation of those absent from either the hearings or the final report, and was dated 7 October 1779. Those absent were not included in *The Proceedings of the General Assembly and of the Council, of the State of Massachusetts-Bay, relating to the Penobscot Expedition . . . ,* which is appended to Calef, *Siege of Penobscot.*

46. House of Rep. to the Council, 26, RG 360.

47. William D. Williamson, *History of the State of Maine,* 2 vols. (Hollowell, Me.: Glazier, Masters, 1832), 2:479; emphasis in original.

48. Kevitt, *General Solomon Lovell,* 21.

Chapter 7. The Massachusetts Conspiracy

1. Lovell to Powell, 28 July, in Kevitt, *General Solomon Lovell,* 80–81.

2. Ibid.

3. Lovell to Powell, 1 August, ibid., 83–87.

4. Ibid., 84.

5. Ibid., 85.

6. Ibid., 85–86.

7. Lovell to Powell, 1 August, two letters, ibid., 83–87.

8. Lovell to Powell, 6 August, ibid., 89–90.

9. Council of War, *Warren,* 6 August, 130, RG 360.

10. Council of War, Headquarters, 6 August, in Kevitt, *General Solomon Lovell,* 91–92; Goss, *Life of Colonel Paul Revere,* 6 August.

11. Navy Board to Saltonstall, 12 August, Massachusetts Archives Collection, 145:98–98a; Kevitt, *General Solomon Lovell,* 103–4.

12. Council to Lovell, 12 August, Massachusetts Archives Collection, 145:99, 410.

13. Council to Avery, 12 August, ibid., 418.

14. Council to Board of War, 12 August, ibid., 416.

15. Lovell to Council, 13 August, ibid., 103–4.

16. Kevitt, *General Solomon Lovell,* 107.

17. Lovell to Council, 13 August, 14 August, this last was the postscript of the first letter, Massachusetts Archives Collection, 145:103–4, 105; Kevitt, *General Solomon Lovell,* 106–8.

18. Cited in Council of War, *Hazard,* 7 August, 132, RG 360.

19. Ibid.

20. Council of War, *Warren,* 10 August, 134, ibid.

21. Council of War, Headquarters, 11 August, 135, ibid.

22. Council of War, *Warren,* 12 August, 136, ibid.

23. Council of War, Headquarters, 13 August, 139, ibid.

24. Council to Lovell, 19 August; Council to Gates, 19 August, Massachusetts Archives Collection, 145:135, 139.

25. Wadsworth to Council, 19 August, Massachusetts Archives Collection, 145:133; John Vance Cheney, "Revolutionary Letters, Third Paper: Major-General Artemas Ward and Others," *Scribner's Monthly* 11 (November 1875–April 1876):716–17.

26. Cheney, "Revolutionary Letters," 716–17.

27. Artemas Ward to Joseph Ward, Boston, 8 September 1779, in Cheney, "Revolutionary Letters," 716.

28. Lovell to Council, 28 August, in Kevitt, *General Solomon Lovell,* 110–12.

29. Payment to Mrs. Greeley, Falmouth, 8 September, Massachusetts Archives Collection, 145:205a; Lovell to Council, 4 September, in Kevitt, *General Solomon Lovell,* 123.

30. Harriette Merrifield Forbes, *New England Diaries, 1602–1800: A Descriptive Catalogue of Diaries, Orderly Books, and Sea Journals* (1923; reprint, New York: Russell and Russell, 1967), 187.

31. Lovell journal, 14 August, in Kevitt, *General Solomon Lovell,* 50.

32. Lovell to Council, 3 September, and its addendum, ibid., 115–21.

33. *Nautilus* log, 14 August.

34. Lovell to Council, 3 September, in Kevitt, *General Solomon Lovell*, 116–17.

35. Navy Board to Marine Committee, 29 September 1779, NA M247, r. 44, no. 145, RG 360; Massachusetts Archives Collection, 145:169–70.

36. Jonathan Parsons to J. Wadsworth, 2 November 1779, Connecticut State Library, Hartford.

37. Hancock to Jay, 21 September, Massachusetts Archives Collection, 145: 171–72.

38. Ibid., 180–206b.

39. Lovell's defense, 22 September, 27–28, RG 360.

40. Lovell's testimony, 26 September, 28, ibid.

41. Ibid.

42. Lovell's defense, 29–31, ibid.

43. Statement of General Wadsworth, in Kevitt, *General Solomon Lovell*, 141–44.

44. Waters, 53, RG 360.

45. Statement of General Wadsworth, 29 September, 74, ibid.

46. Lovell to Saltonstall, 11 August, in Kevitt, *General Solomon Lovell*, 99–101.

47. Major Lee to Major General Lord Stirling, 1 August, Newark, ibid., 87–88.

48. Washington to Council, 3 August, West Point, ibid., 88–89.

49. Council to Lovell, 11 August, ibid., 98–99.

50. Calef, *Siege of Penobscot*, title page and 40–41.

51. Ibid., 40.

52. Kevitt, *General Solomon Lovell*, 46.

53. Council of War, *Warren*, 12 August, 135, RG 360.

54. Kevitt, *General Solomon Lovell*, 47.

55. Ibid., 120.

Chapter 8. Paul Revere's Tribulations

1. *Massachusetts Soldiers and Sailors*, 13:121–22.

2. Joseph Williamson, "The Conduct of Paul Revere in the Penobscot Expedition," *Collections of the Maine Historical Society*, ser. 2, 3:380–81.

3. Extracted from ibid., 381; Kevitt, *General Solomon Lovell*, 17; in Massachusetts Archives Collection, 145:766.

4. Revere to Heath, 24 October 1779, Massachusetts Historical Society, *Collections*, 4:325.

5. Todd, Massachusetts Archives Collection, 145:235.

6. Todd, ibid., 237.

7. Thomas Carnes, ibid., 274.

8. *Massachusetts Soldiers and Sailors*, 4:111; *Official Register of the Officers and*

Men of New Jersey in the Revolutionary War Compiled under Orders of Theodore F. Randolph, Governor, by William S. Stryker, Adjutant General (Baltimore: Genealogical Publishing, 1967), 320.

9. Wadsworth, Massachusetts Archives Collection, 145:275–82a.

10. Ibid.

11. Ibid.

12. Marett, ibid., 145:250.

13. James Brown, ibid., 145:273.

14. In his deposition there is no indication of Whipple's rank, but in Revere's letter of defense (Massachusetts Archives Collection, 145:336–40), he referred to him as doctor (337).

15. Massachusetts Archives Collection, 145:300.

16. Ibid., 322–25.

17. Ibid.

18. Ibid.

19. Ibid., 311a.

20. Ibid., 320–21.

21. Ibid., 336–40.

22. Ibid., 278, 336–40.

23. Ibid., 273.

24. Brewer to Perham, *Bangor (Maine) Daily Whig and Courier,* 19 August 1846.

25. Massachusetts Archives Collection, 145:336–40.

26. Ibid.

27. Committee findings, 25–26, RG 360.

28. Artemas Ward to Joseph Ward, 8 September 1779, in Cheney, "Revolutionary Letters," 716.

29. Massachusetts Archives Collection, 145:346.

30. Ibid., 366, 372.

31. Ibid., 369, 372.

32. Ibid., 346, 372a, and 373.

33. Ibid., 375.

34. Extracted from Kevitt, *General Solomon Lovell,* 18–19; Revere to General Court, 22 January 1781, *Documentary History,* 18:97–98.

35. *Documentary History,* 18:97–98; Proceedings of Court-Martial in Case of Paul Revere, ibid., 18:428–30.

36. Proceedings of Court-Martial in Case of Paul Revere, *Documentary History,* 18:428–30.

37. Frederic Grant Jr., "The Court-Martial of Paul Revere," *Boston Bar Journal* 21 (May 1977):10–11.

Chapter 9. A Court-Martial Shrouded in Mystery

1. U.S. Navy, Bureau of Naval Personnel, *Naval Justice. October 1945* (Washington, D.C.: GPO, 1945), 18.

2. Keith to Heath, 25 September 1779, Boston, Massachusetts Historical Society, *Collections,* 4:318.

3. Navy Board to Marine Committee, 2 September, Navy Board Eastern District, Letter Book.

4. Navy Board to Marine Committee, 29 September 1779, M247, r. 44, no. 145, RG 360.

5. Nicholson to General Assembly, Massachusetts Archives Collection, 145: 169–70; also extracted in Kevitt, *General Solomon Lovell,* 13–14.

6. Nicholson to General Assembly, Massachusetts Archives Collection, 145: 169–70; also extracted in Kevitt, *General Solomon Lovell,* 13–14.

7. Kevitt's extraction did not list the officers desired.

8. Saltonstall, court-martial, Gurley Papers, 7a, 7b, 7c.

9. Navy Board to Marine Committee, 29 September 1779, M247, r. 44, no. 145, RG 360.

10. Kevitt, *General Solomon Lovell,* 15; 25–26, RG 360.

11. Report of the Committee, 25–26, RG 360.

12. Thomas, 67, Little, 87, ibid.

13. Saltonstall, court-martial, Gurley Papers, 7a, 7b, 7c.

14. Navy Board to Saltonstall, 12 August, Massachusetts Archives Collection, 145:98.

15. Salter deposition, 112, RG 360.

16. Lovell deposition, in Kevitt, *General Solomon Lovell,* 137.

17. Report of the Committee, 25–26, ibid.

18. Letter 246, 28 October 1779, Navy Board Eastern District, Letter Book.

19. *Out-Letters of the Continental Marine Committee,* 1:280.

20. Ibid., 2:100–101.

21. Massachusetts Council to Congress, 20 November 1779, 19, RG 360.

22. House of Representatives to the Council, 26, RG 360.

23. Parsons to J. Wadsworth, 2 November 1779.

24. *Boston Gazette,* 25 October and 1 November 1779.

25. *Continental Journal* (Boston), 28 October 1779.

26. W. Williamson, *History of the State of Maine,* 2:478; emphasis in original.

27. Parsons to J. Wadsworth, 2 November 1779.

28. Secretary of Congress, Register of Letters, 1779–81, M247, r. 197, i185, v2, p. 5, RG360; *Journals of the Continental Congress, 1774–1789,* Wednesday, 1 December 1779 (Washington, D.C.: Library of Congress, 1904–37), 15:1334.

29. Admiralty Board to Navy Board Eastern Department, 10 December 1779, M332, r. 6, no. 249, RG 360; *Out-Letters of the Continental Marine Committee,* 2:136.

30. Admiralty to Navy Board, 25 January 1780, M332, r. 6, no. 258, RG 360; *Out-Letters of the Continental Marine Committee,* 2:150–51.

31. S. Deane to B. Deane, Williamsburg, 20 April 1780, *The Deane Papers,* vol. 4 (New York: New-York Historical Society, 1890), 132.

32. Parsons to J. Wadsworth, 2 November 1779.

33. Leverett Saltonstall, *Ancestry and Descendants of Sir Richard Saltonstall: First Associate of the Massachusetts Bay Colony and Patentee of Connecticut* (Cambridge: Riverside Press, 1897), 232.

34. Scott, "New Hampshire's Part in the Penobscot Expedition," 211–12; E. Forbes, *Paul Revere,* 360.

35. *Minerva,* brigantine, bond for letter of marque, 21 May 1781, M247, r. 203, i196, p. 73, RG 360; Louis F. Middlebrook, *Maritime Connecticut during the American Revolution 1775–1783,* 2 vols. (Salem, Mass.: Essex Institute, 1925), 2:163–64.

Bibliography

Allen, Gardner W. *A Naval History of the American Revolution.* 2 vols. Boston: Houghton Mifflin, 1913.

Bangor (Maine) Daily Whig and Courier, 19–20 August 1846.

Batchelder, Samuel F. "The Life and Surprising Adventures of John Nutting, Cambridge Loyalist, and His Strange Connection with the Penobscot Expedition of 1779." *Cambridge Historical Society Publications* 5 (January–October 1910):55–98.

Bellico, Russell. "The Great Penobscot Blunder." *American History Illustrated* 13 (December 1978):4–9, 44–48.

Bellot, Leland J. *William Knox: The Life and Thought of an Eighteenth-Century Imperialist.* Austin: University of Texas Press, 1977.

Biographical Directory of the United States Congress, 1774–1981. Washington, D.C.: GPO, 1989.

Boston Gazette, 25 October, 1 November 1779.

Bourne, Russell. "The Penobscot Fiasco." *American Heritage* 25 (October 1974):28–33, 100–101.

Brewer, John. "Penobscot Expedition against Castine." *Bangor (Maine) Daily Whig and Courier,* 19, 20 August 1846.

———. "A Short Statement of What Took Place at Majabigwaduce. . . ." In John E. Godfrey Collection. Misc. box 7/1, pp. 82–83. Maine Historical Society, Portland, Me.

Brooks, Robert Carver. "Notes and General Comments—The Penobscot Expedition, 1779, and the Massachusetts Conspiracy." Typescript, July 1999.

Brownrigg, Beatrice. *The Life and Letters of Sir John Moore.* Oxford: B. Blackwell, 1923.

British Admiralty Records. Ships' Logs. Public Records Office, London.

Buck, Jonathan. Papers. Bucksport Public Library. Bucksport, Maine.

Carleton, Guy. Papers. American Manuscripts, 1775–1783. Vol. 7, no. 27, 239–41. Transcripts. Public Archives of Canada, Ottawa.

Caesar, Gene. "The Cowardly Career of Paul Revere." *True: The Man's Magazine* (March 1962):33–34, 92–99.

Calef, John. *The Siege of Penobscot by the Rebels*. 1781. Reprint, New York: New York Times, 1971.

"A Castine Summer—1779." *Wilson Museum Bulletin* (fall 1975).

Cayford, John E. *The Penobscot Expedition: Being an Account of the Largest American Naval Engagement of the Revolutionary War*. Orrington, Me.: C and H Publishing, 1976.

Chapelle, Howard I. *The History of the American Sailing Navy: The Ships and Their Development*. New York: Norton, 1949.

Cheney, John Vance. "Revolutionary Letters, Third Paper: Major-General Artemas Ward and Others." *Scribner's Monthly* 11 (November 1875–April 1876): 712–19.

Chester, Colby Mitchell. Papers. "Study of Commodore Dudley Saltonstall and the Penobscot Bay Expedition in 1779." MSS78410. Naval Historical Foundation Collection. Library of Congress.

Coakley, Robert W. "American Military History: The Early Period, 1607–1815." In *A Guide to the Study and Use of Military History*, ed. John E. Jessup Jr. and Robert W. Coakley. Washington, D.C.: GOP, 1979.

Coggins, Jack. "Peril on the Penobscot." In *Ships and Seamen of the American Revolution*. Harrisburg, Pa.: Stackpole Books, 1969.

Continental Journal (Boston), 28 October 1779.

Cooper, James Fenimore. Vol. 1 of *The History of the Navy of the United States of America*. Upper Saddle River, N.J.: Literature House, 1970.

———. *Naval History of the United States of America*. Philadelphia: Thomas, Cowperthwait, 1847.

Currier, John J. *History of Newburyport, Massachusetts, 1764–1905*. Newburyport, Mass.: Author, 1906.

Dann, John C., ed. *The Revolution Remembered: Eyewitness Accounts of the War for Independence*. Chicago: University of Chicago Press, 1980.

The Deane Papers. Vol. 4. New York: New-York Historical Society, 1890.

"Defense Update." Maine Public Broadcasting Network, 1982.

A Detail of Some Particular Services Performed in America, 1776–1779. New York: N.p., 1835.

Documentary History of the State of Maine. Vols. 16–19. Ed. James Phinney Baxter. 2d ser. Portland, Me.: Bailey and Noyes, 1913.

Doudiet, Ellenore W. *Majabigwaduce, Castine, Penobscot, Brooksville*. Castine, Me.: Castine Scientific Society, 1978.

Eckstrom, Fanny Hardy. *Indian Place-Names of the Penobscot Valley and the Maine Coast*. Orono: University of Maine, 1941, 1974 printing.

Elliott, Peter J. "The Penobscot Expedition of 1779: A Study in Naval Frustration." Master's thesis, University of Maine, Orono, 1974.

Failbisy, John D. "Penobscot 1779: The Eye of a Hurricane." *Maine Historical Society Quarterly* 19 (fall 1979):91–117.

Flood, Charles Bracelen. *Rise and Fight Again: Perilous Times along the Road to Independence.* New York: Dodd, Mead, 1976.

Forbes, Esther. *Paul Revere and the World He Lived In.* Boston: Houghton Mifflin, 1942.

Forbes, Harriette Merrifield. *New England Diaries, 1602–1800: A Descriptive Catalogue of Diaries, Orderly Books, and Sea Journals.* 1923. Reprint, New York: Russell and Russell, 1967.

Fowler, William M. "Disaster in Penobscot Bay." *Naval War College Review* 31 (winter 1979):75–80.

———. "Saltonstall, Dudley." In *American National Biography*, ed. John A. Garraty and Mark C. Carnes, 19:221–22. New York: Oxford University Press, 1999.

Freeman, Douglas Southall. Vol. 5 of *George Washington: A Biography.* New York: Scribner, 1948–57.

Goold, Nathan. "Colonel Jonathan Mitchell's Cumberland County Regiment: Bagaduce Expedition, 1779." *Collections of the Maine Historical Society,* ser. 2, vol. 10.

Goss, Elbridge H. *Life of Colonel Paul Revere.* 2 vols. Boston: J. G. Cupples, 1891.

Grant, Frederick, Jr. "The Court-Martial of Paul Revere." *Boston Bar Journal* 21. (May 1977):5–13.

Gurley, Jacob B. Papers. Collection of Naval Manuscripts, 1734–1782. Connecticut State Library, Hartford.

Hale, Edward Everett. "The Penobscot Expedition, 1779." In *Narrative and Critical History of America,* ed. Justin Winsor, 6:603–4. Boston: Houghton Mifflin, 1884–89.

Harland, John. *Seamanship in the Age of Sail: An Account of the Shiphandling of the Sailing Man-of-War, 1600–1869, Based on Contemporary Sources.* Annapolis, Md.: Naval Institute Press, 1984.

Hayward, Walter S. "The Penobscot Expedition." In *Essays in Modern English History in Honor of Wilbur Cortez Abbot.* Cambridge: Harvard University Press, 1941.

Hazard, William. Letter. Jamaica Plain, 22 March 1780. *Massachusetts Historical Society Proceedings* 4 (1860):129.

Hutchings, William. "The Narrative of William Hutchings." In *History of Castine, Penobscot, and Brooksville, Maine,* ed. George A. Wheeler, Document 9. Bangor, Me.: Burr and Robinson, 1875.

Hutchinson, Vernal. "Siege of Penobscot." In *When Revolution Came: The Story of*

Old Deer Isle in the Province of Maine during the War for American Independence, 67–90. Ellsworth, Me.: Ellsworth American, 1972.

Independent Chronicle (Boston), 9 September 1779.

Jack, David Russell. "Calef, John, M.D." Vol. 1 of *Biographical Data Relating to New Brunswick Families, Especially of Loyalist Descent.* 2d ed. St. John, N.B.: New Brunswick Museum, 1965.

Jones, E. Alfred. *The Loyalists of Massachusetts, Their Memorials, Petitions, and Claims.* London: Saint Catherine Press, 1930.

Jones, George W. D. "Sketch of the Neck and Harbour of Majabigwaduce." In Douglas W. Marshall and Howard Henry Peckham, *Campaigns of the American Revolution: An Atlas of Manuscript Maps.* Ann Arbor: University of Michigan Press, 1976.

Journals of the Continental Congress, 1774–1789. Vol. 15. Washington, D.C.: Library of Congress, 1904–37.

Kevitt, Chester B, compiler. *General Solomon Lovell and the Penobscot Expedition, 1779.* Weymouth, Mass.: Weymouth Historical Commission, 1976.

La Balme, Augustin Mottin de. "Journal of Trip to Maine, May–September 1779." Item 21846 in the Haldimand Papers, Library of Congress.

Lawrence, William. "Sergeant Lawrence's Journal." In *History of Castine, Penobscot, and Brooksville, Maine,* ed. George A. Wheeler, Document 7. Bangor, Me.: Burr and Robinson, 1875.

Leamon, James S. "Crisis on the Penobscot." In *Revolution Downeast: The War for American Independence in Maine.* Amherst: University of Massachusetts Press, 1993.

Maclay, Edgar S. *A History of American Privateers.* New York: D. Appleton, 1899.

Massachusetts Archives Collection ["Felt Collection"]. Records, 1629–1799. Revolutionary Period (1775–80). Vol. 145, Penobscot Expedition, 1779. Massachusetts Archives, Boston.

Massachusetts Historical Society. *Collections,* ser. 7, pt. 2, vol. 4. Boston: Massachusetts Historical Society, 1904.

Massachusetts. Secretary of the Commonwealth. *Massachusetts Soldiers and Sailors of the Revolutionary War.* 17 vols. Boston: Wright and Potter, 1896–1908.

Mayhew, Dean R. "The Bagaduce Blunder: Commodore Saltonstall and the Penobscot Expedition." *Mariner's Mirror* 61 (February 1975):27–30.

Middlebrook, Louis F. *Maritime Connecticut during the American Revolution 1775–1783.* 2 vols. Salem, Mass.: Essex Institute, 1925.

Millett, Allan R., and Peter Maslowski. *For the Common Defense: A Military History of the United States of America.* New York: Free Press, 1984.

Moody, William. "The Journal of Drummer Moody of Col. Mitchell's Regiment." In "Colonel Jonathan Mitchell's Cumberland County Regiment," *Collections of the Maine Historical Society,* ser. 2, 10:143–74.

Morgan, William J. *Captains to the Northward: The New England Captains in the Continental Navy.* Barre, Mass.: Barre Gazette, 1959.

Morison, Samuel Eliot. *John Paul Jones: A Sailor's Biography.* Boston: Little, Brown, 1959.

Mowat, Henry. "A Relation of the Services in Which Capt. Henry Mowat Was Engaged in America from 1759 to the End of the American War in 1783." *Journal of History* 3 (1910):334–43.

Munson, Gorham. "Fifes and Drums on the Penobscot." In *Penobscot: Down East Paradise.* Philadelphia: Lippincott, 1959.

National Archives. Massachusetts State Papers, 1775–1787. RG 360.

A Naval Encyclopaedia: Comprising a Dictionary of Nautical Words and Phrases. Philadelphia: L. R. Hamersly, 1881.

Navy Board Eastern District. Letter Book. 23 October 1778–29 October 1779. New York Public Library.

New London County Historical Society. "Brief Biographies of Connecticut Revolution Naval and Privateer Officers, Dudley Saltonstall." Pt. 4, vol. 1 of *Records and Papers of the New London County Historical Society.* New London, Conn.: New London County Historical Society, 1893.

Nielson, Jon M. "Penobscot: From the Jaws of Victory—Our Navy's Worst Defeat." *American Neptune* 37 (October 1977):288–305.

Nova-Scotia Gazette (Halifax), 6 July, 14 September, 2 November 1779.

Official Register of the Officers and Men of New Jersey in the Revolutionary War Compiled under Orders of Theodore F. Randolph, Governor, by William S. Stryker, Adjutant General. Baltimore: Genealogical Publishing, 1967.

"Operations in Maine in 1779, Journal Found on Board the Hunter, Continental Ship, of Eighteen Guns." *Historical Magazine* (February 1864):51–54.

Out-Letters of the Continental Marine Committee and Board of Admiralty, August 1776–September 1780. Ed. Charles Oscar Paullin. 2 vols. New York: Naval History Society, 1914.

Parsons, Jonathan. Letter, 2 November 1779. Connecticut State Library, Hartford.

Pennsylvania Gazette (Philadelphia), 25 August 1779.

"Penobscot: The Battle No One Ever Heard Of." Maine Public Broadcasting Network, 1980.

Philbrook, Thomas Weld. "Narrative." In *Valour, Fore and Aft: Being the Adventures of the Continental Sloop "Providence," 1775–1779, Formerly Flagship "Katy" of Rhode Island's Navy,* ed. Hope S. Rider, 228–31. Annapolis, Md.: Naval Institute Press, 1977.

Proceedings of the General Assembly and of the Council, of the State of Massachusetts-Bay, Relating to the Penobscot Expedition. In *The Siege of Penobscot by the Rebels,* John Calef, appendix. 1781. Reprint, New York: New York Times, 1971.

Reidhead, William. "William Reidhead's Journal, 1779." *Bangor Historical Magazine* 5 (July 1889–June 1890):226–31.

The Remembrancer, or Impartial Repository of Public Events. 17 vols. London: J. Almon, 1775–84.

Republican Journal (Belfast, Maine), 3 December 1889.

Rider, Hope S. *Valour, Fore and Aft: Being the Adventures of the Continental Sloop "Providence," 1775–1779, Formerly Flagship "Katy" of Rhode Island's Navy.* Annapolis, Md.: Naval Institute Press, 1977.

Royal Commission on Historical Manuscripts. *Report on American Manuscripts in the Royal Institution of Great Britain.* 4 vols. London: Mackie, 1904–9.

Saltonstall, Leverett. *Ancestry and Descendants of Sir Richard Saltonstall: First Associate of the Massachusetts Bay Colony and Patentee of Connecticut.* Cambridge: Riverside Press, 1897.

Scott, Kenneth. "New Hampshire's Part in the Penobscot Expedition." *American Neptune* 7 (July 1947):200–212.

Shaw, Henry I. "Penobscot Assault—1779." *Military Affairs* 17 (summer 1953):83–94.

Sloan, Robert W. "New Ireland: Men in Pursuit of a Forlorn Hope, 1779–1784." *Maine Historical Society Quarterly* 19 (fall 1979):73–90.

Smith, Charles R. "Success at Sea and Disaster at Penobscot." In *Marines in the Revolution: A History of the Continental Marines in the American Revolution, 1775–1783.* Washington, D.C.: History and Museums Division, Headquarters, USMC, 1975.

Smith, Philip Chadwick Foster. *Fired by Manley Zeal: A Naval Fiasco of the American Revolution.* Salem, Mass.: Peabody Museum of Salem, 1977.

Symonds, Craig L. "The American Naval Expedition to Penobscot, 1779." *Naval War College Review* 24 (April 1972):64–72.

———. *A Battlefield Atlas of the American Revolution.* Cartography by William J. Clipson. Baltimore: Nautical and Aviation Publishing, 1986.

Taft, Hank, and Jan Taft. *A Cruising Guide to the Maine Coast.* 2d ed. Camden, Me.: International Marine Publishing, 1991.

Thacher, James. *A Military Journal during the American Revolutionary War, from 1775 to 1783.* Boston: Cottons and Barnard, 1827.

U.S. Navy. Bureau of Naval Personnel. *Naval Justice. October 1945.* Washington, D.C.: GPO, 1945.

———. Naval History Division. *Naval Documents of the American Revolution.* Washington, D.C.: GPO, 1964–.

Wadsworth, Peleg. Letter to William D. Williamson, 1 January 1828. *Collections of the Maine Historical Society,* ser. 2, vol. 2.

Wallace, Willard. *East to Bagaduce.* Chicago: H. Regnery, 1963.

Warren-Adams Letters: Being Chiefly a Correspondence among John Adams, Samuel Adams, and James Warren . . . 1743–1814. 2 vols. Boston: Massachusetts Historical Society, 1917–25.

Wheeler, George A., ed., *History of Castine, Penobscot, and Brooksville, Maine.* Bangor, Me.: Burr and Robinson, 1875.

Williamson, Joseph. "The Conduct of Paul Revere in the Penobscot Expedition." *Collections of the Maine Historical Society,* ser. 2, 3:379–92.

———. "Sir John Moore at Castine during the Revolution." *Collections of the Maine Historical Society,* ser. 2, 2:403–9.

Williamson, William D. *History of the State of Maine.* 2 vols. Hollowell, Me.: Glazier, Masters, 1832.

Willson, David Harris. *A History of England.* New York: Holt, Rinehart and Winston, 1967.

Index

About the Author

Commander George E. Buker, USN, retired from active duty in 1963. After earning his B.A. (magna cum laude) from Jacksonville University and his M.A. and Ph.D. from the University of Florida, he was professor of history at Jacksonville until his retirement in 1987. Presently, as professor emeritus, he enjoys scholarly research, writing, and traveling. He has published articles in a variety of publications including *American National Biography, American Neptune, Florida Historical Quarterly, North & South,* and *The Oxford Companion to American Military History.* He has also published numerous books on the history of Florida, including *Swamp Sailors in the Second Seminole War,* and *Blockaders, Refugees, & Contrabands: Civil War on Florida's Gulf Coast, 1861–1865.*